DATASC   COPY 1.

DSOLV080
COPY 1
D1

Structure, Logic, and Program Design

Structure, Logic, and Program Design

Alan Cohen
Computer Consultant, London, UK

JOHN WILEY & SONS
Chichester . New York . Brisbane . Toronto . Singapore

Library of Congress Cataloging in Publication Data:

Cohen, Alan.
 Structure, logic, and program design.

 Bibliography: p.
 Includes indexes.
 1. Electronic digital computers—Programming.
I. Title.
QA76.6.C623 1984   001.64   83-10207
ISBN 0 471 16400 3

British Library Cataloguing in Publication Data:

Cohen, Alan
 Structure, logic, and program design.
 1. Computer programs
 I. Title
 001.64′2   QA76.6

 ISBN 0 471 16400 3

Printed in Great Britain by Galliard (Printers) Ltd, Great Yarmouth

Contents

viii

Acknowledgements

In 1966 I started to work as a computer programmer in commercial data processing, and immediately became interested in the problems of program design. This interest was encouraged by employers and colleagues alike, and particularly by the Hoskyns Group based in London. After starting to work as an independent consultant (1971) I mixed teaching with consultancy and project development, and more recently real-time with commercial systems. Inevitably, I have learned from clients and colleagues, as I hope they have learned from me. This book is an acknowledgement and testimonial to all. I must mention the technical influence of Michael Jackson, with whom I worked at the Hoskyns Group and on a few brief occasions thereafter, the unfailing encouragement of John Bately over much the same period, and the marketing skills of Derek Johnson, who unselfishly promoted a successful series of training courses on my behalf. These courses both ensured my early survival as an independent consultant and produced much of the foundation material for this book. I must also thank Brian Bending, Telford Britton, Allan Fraser, Tony Lennard, John Marsh, Phil Pinder, Geoff Quentin, and Grahame Stehle for direct help and suggestions on the manuscript, Jill Schlaepfer for the cover design and Margaret Fowell, Jennifer Iles, and Pamela York for patient and thoughtful secretarial help. Most important, though, were the help of my wife Jeannie, who read the complete manuscript as a work of literature, and the special inspiration of my dear friend George Frankl who made it all possible. Final responsibility for the material, including any errors or omissions, rests with me. In order to simplify the text, specific references to related material are confined to Chapter 9; a brief and highly selective Bibliography giving some of the main sources is included at the end.

Preface

My purpose is to solve a problem in program design which has been seriously neglected. The problem concerns the design of program logic, and especially of the high-level, or control, logic. The solution is a general methodology which goes further than the commonly advocated and popular data structure approach (which takes too narrow a perspective for my purposes), and contrasts with the more traditional modular, or functional, techniques (to the extent that these are not concerned with logic at all). These terms are, of course, fully explained in the text, where familiarity with them is not assumed.

We take it as axiomatic that events of interest to a program always happen in a well-defined order; this order is often complex, sometimes very complex, but invariably falls into a pattern, called a structure, which can be defined and documented using the diagrammatic techniques described. Our theme is that the structure diagrams so produced can be used to drive the detailed organization and implementation of program logic. The result is a well-structured program whose internal logic is easy to follow, and which can be easily understood. We call this structured programming. The detailed methodology can be seen as a natural extension of that offered by the data structure approach; we shall maintain, however, that the concept of a data structure is only one case of the more general ordering concept described above, and that while it may be especially significant for batch-mode commercial, and other data-oriented, programs, we shall find it inapplicable, and sometimes misleading, when designing others. In particular for on-line, scientific, and real-time applications a much wider and freer interpretation is required.

Where structured programming is primarily motivated by a desire to improve the design and documentation of program logic, modular, or functional, techniques are concerned solely with the choice of, and interfaces between, program subroutines. The modular approach is, however, fully consistent with that advocated in this book. Indeed, I think that the two should live side-by-side, and that selection of one at the expense of the other (as if one were right and the other wrong) would be mistaken. Broadly, and with the risk of oversimplification, the approach described in this book is most suited to the design of high-level or control logic; this logic effectively controls the order in which the modules identified by the functional approach are invoked. In practice, these modules contain a description of the program functions, and in a real sense describe what the application is all about. The same techniques may also be applied to the design of their internal logic, but since this tends to be simpler (if sometimes more voluminous), there is perhaps rather less benefit to be obtained. Further, it is my belief that many of the interface problems (referred to briefly in Chapter 9) identified when using functional techniques would disappear if the control logic were correctly designed in the first place—hence the emphasis placed in this book on control logic design.

The design principles are illustrated using a range of examples, starting with the simplest and proceeding gradually to the more complex. Since the examples form an integral part of the book, the answers are always included with the main text, together with a note of the lessons learned. Each example given helps to consolidate the experience already gained, and to develop the concepts required. It is not essential to work through all the examples formally, but the reader should at least make himself familiar with the central points being made, if only because later sections may assume this knowledge. In particular, both text and examples reach their climax in Chapter 8, which brings together all the material developed earlier. Even so, the reader may break off at any point, and still apply the principles developed thus far with benefit to his own examples, whether these are drawn from the same or other application environments.

The main technical material and all the examples are contained in the first eight chapters. The final, ninth, chapter provides a brief historical and technical context, and covers some associated concepts and techniques outside the mainstream of the book. Each chapter is divided into sections; all cross-references to textual material, except those in the Index, refer to section (and not page) numbers. Each chapter is also supported by diagrams which are numbered consecutively within each chapter. Some of the examples recur from time to time, either within the same chapter or in different chapters; they are always referenced using the section numbers in which they occur. The notation used to describe logic is defined in the text, and is largely machine- and language-independent; it assumes no specialized knowledge of any design technique or programming language, though some familiarity with general programming concepts will be a help. An Appendix includes some notes on its implementation in commonly used programming languages and a summary of the COBOL-style language conventions used to describe other (non-logic) processing requirements.

To repeat: the book is primarily concerned with the design and documentation of program logic, especially of the high-level, or control, logic. Of course, it is true that programs will exist which require little, if any, control logic, and others in which the logic may be difficult to design. Further, there is a trend today towards program generators which can sometimes solve on the user's behalf some of the problems we set out to discuss. But this apart, there is a vast majority of programs for which serious logic design problems exist; failure to solve them now can only result in testing difficulties and/or maintenance headaches later. It is these problems we address.

   While we shall concentrate on design, we shall not fail to respect the needs of implementation. In fact we shall find that the facilities usually provided for implementation do not always match the needs of design, at least in commonly used programming languages. One manifestation of this is that our designs are GOTO-less (in the sense described in Sections 1.2, 3.1, 6.9, and 9.1), but sometimes require explicit GOTO's to implement them. Since the use of GOTO is controversial, this makes good material for polemics, in which we indulge from time to time. I hope that the polemics do not intrude on the book's central serious purpose. In any event, the reader is cautioned that any opinions expressed are always, or course, only a personal view. And with that, I leave you to read and judge for yourself. Whatever your disposition (to agree with me or not), I trust that you will find the material stimulating, useful, and enjoyable.

ALAN COHEN
London, 1983

Chapter 1
Nested Structures and Nested Logic

Program design, as we shall understand the term, is concerned to identify program functions and to ensure that the functions identified are executed in the correct order. Techniques which show how to identify the functions are the province of the so-called 'modular' or 'functional' approach; techniques to determine the order in which these functions are executed are the province of structured programming, and form the subject matter of this book. We shall find the two are largely complementary and fully consistent. A brief description of the principles governing the functional approach, and its synthesis with structured programming, is included in Chapter 9.

We start our development by introducing concepts and techniques to describe the order in which events of interest to a program happen. The main tool used for this purpose is the structure diagram. Later sections show how to exploit the diagrams produced, particularly to design logic to analyse event sequences detected. This logic then ensures that processing functions are executed in the correct order, particularly those processing functions which depend on a knowledge of the order in which events occur.

1.1 Structure Diagrams

Suppose that:

A, B represent events of type A, B respectively
X represents an ordered group, or set, of such events.

There are three types of group X of interest to us:

1. *Sequence.* There are two events in X; the first is of type A and the second of type B.
2. *Selection.* There is just one event in X, and this is either of type A or of type B.
3. *Iteration.* There are many events in X, all of the same type (A, say).

1

These are the simplest types of order; more complex ones will be introduced later. The concepts can be illustrated diagrammatically using the structure diagram notation given in Figure 1.1, where the term 'structure' is used to describe the pattern exhibited by the order in which events occur within X. In this diagram the special symbol C (an abbreviation for 'condition') represents any condition, or test, which may be evaluated to:

distinguish the possible events in a selection; or
determine the end of an iteration.

In practice, of course, the abstract names X, A, B would represent some unit meaningful in the context of a particular application, while the test C is frequently clear from the context, or not material to the discussion (and may then be omitted). Our first practical example occurs in Section 1.5.

We shall think of the upper box (X) as naming the ordered group of events represented by the lower box or boxes (A, B) which can themselves be thought of as the group members. The possible members of a selection are frequently referred to as 'cases'. The lines joining upper and lower boxes represent group membership; each symbol on these lines (space, '∘', and '*') shows the type of

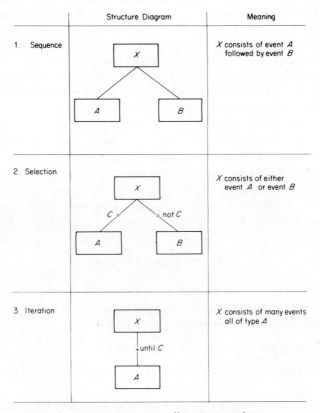

Figure 1.1   Structure diagram notation

order which exists among the group members and so represents a relationship between the group (X) and its members (A, B). The size of a box has no significance. The following points amplify the orders described:

1. The asterisk symbol ('*') is used here to mean 'many—an integral number of, including the possibility of none'. It will be refined further from time to time.
2. An iteration does not differentiate between its members.
3. There is no restriction on the number of members A, B, ... of a sequence, or cases A, B, ... in a selection; Figure 1.2 gives an example of the latter, in which the tests $C1, C2, \ldots$ are used to distinguish the various cases.

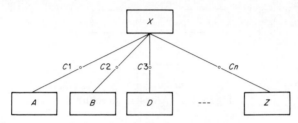

Figure 1.2   A many-way selection

Apart possibly from the choice and positioning of the symbols, these conventions are well established and commonly accepted, at least among users of the 'data structure' approach to program design. This term is explained further in Section 2.1. Other equivalent diagrammatic conventions are also found, but the concepts expressed are usually the same. If now we allow that A, B can themselves be used to represent ordered groups of other events, then we can think of events, and ordered groups of events (such as sequences, selections, and iterations) as building blocks from which we can build arbitrarily large diagrams. Any structure built in this way is said to be 'nested'. Figure 1.3 shows one such diagram; in this case A, E, G, H represent the events, while X, B, D, F represent significant groups of events. The precise tests applied to distinguish E, F and determine the end of the D's have been omitted. We prove below that the following would be an ordered event sequence consistent with the diagram:

$$A, G, H, E, E, G, H, G, H, E$$

Each pair (G, H) is equivalent to F. So the event sequence given is equivalent to:

$$A, F, E, E, F, F, E$$

Each E or F is a D, so the sequence is equivalent to:

$$A, D, D, D, D, D, D$$

This is equivalent to:

$$A, B$$

and this in turn is equivalent to X. Hence the original sequence is consistent with

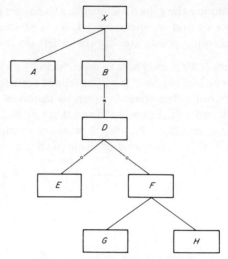

Figure 1.3   A nested structure

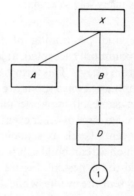

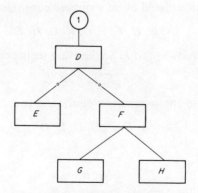

Figure 1.4   Using a connector

the diagram. In contrast, the following event sequences are not consistent with the diagram:

$$G, H, E, \text{etc.}$$

$$A, H, G, \text{etc.}$$

In this sense the diagram defines a set of rules; any event sequence then does, or does not, conform to the rules.

If a diagram is too large, it can be split into a series of smaller diagrams using a 'connector' convention. Thus Figure 1.3 may be equally represented by the two diagrams of Figure 1.4; the connector could be omitted if no ambiguity then arises. Apart from some annotation we shall find no further need to extend the diagrammatic conventions described until we come to the special problems described in Chapter 3.

We shall, of course, give many illustrations, starting with the simplest cases and gradually covering the more complex. These will be drawn from a wide range of applications, including batch, on-line, scientific, and real-time (such as process control) applications. We shall also stop from time to time to compare the results with those obtained using alternative techniques. But first we show how to exploit the structure diagram to analyse ordered event sequences.

1.2   Schematic Logic

The conventions given in Figure 1.5 provide a formal translation from structure diagram to schematic logic. We shall think of schematic logic as a machine- and language-independent subset of a programming language, whose purpose is to define logic groups and subroutines subject to the same building block conventions as structure diagrams. Any piece of logic built from the building blocks is said to be 'nested'.

	Schematic Logic

1. Sequence	X SEQ
	  DO A
	  DO B
	X ENDS

2. Selection	X IF C
	  DO A
	X ELSE
	  DO B
	X ENDS

3. Iteration	X LOOP until C DO A X ENDS

Figure 1.5   Schematic logic conventions

6

Because the rules are formalized we can think of them as a 'mapping', and summarize the mapping rules as follows:

1. The symbol (space, '∘', or '*') between the upper and lower boxes of the structure diagram tells us what kind of order is implied and so which keyword (SEQ, IF, or LOOP) to use.
2. The end of a sequence, selection, or iteration is always marked by the same keyword 'ENDS'.
3. Each keyword, including ELSE, is given a label (X) taken from the upper box; in particular the end of a logic group is always given the same label as the start.
4. Each of the lower boxes on the structure diagram becomes the subject of 'DO'; this represents a language-independent subroutine call but it may also be replaced directly by the equivalent code.

All labels and keywords (including 'DO') are written in capital letters. Apart from this we shall use upper and lower case in the normal way.

Like structure diagrams, any expression of schematic logic can be annotated (as in Figure 1.5) to show the condition which is evaluated to distinguish A, B (selection) or determine the end of the A's (iteration). While the principles are widely accepted, the detailed conventions used are not so widely agreed. The following is a sample of the many variations found:

1. Instead of IF...ELSE... use SELECT...OR...; or CASE...ENTRY...; or SELECT...WHEN...; or IF...WHEN...
2. Instead of LOOP use DOWHILE or ITER
3. Amend the ENDS to show the type of group ended—ENDSEQ, ENDIF, ENDLOOP, etc.
4. Omit all labels (the logic is then usually called 'pseudo-code' or 'structured English').

The differences are largely cosmetic. Finally, since the '*' symbol is defined to mean 'many including the possibility of none', the LOOP is so constructed that it allows the possibility of zero iterations; some presentations allow a second type of LOOP, which guarantees at least one iteration; in our view this is unnecessary and undesirable.

The schematic logic equivalent to Figure 1.2 would be written:

```
X   IF C1
       DO A
X   ELSE C2
       DO B
X   ELSE C3
       DO D
       ⋮
X   ELSE Cn
       DO Z
X   ENDS
```

This is often referred to as a CASE-type statement; as presented, the logic does not assume that the various cases are exclusive and exhaustive.

Schematic logic can be presented in either of two ways. This is illustrated using the structure presented in Figure 1.3, for which we assume that conditions C1, C2 can be suitably defined (for the loop and selection groups respectively). First, we give the 'in-line' code:

```
X   SEQ
    DO A
    B      LOOP until C1
           D      IF C2
                  DO E
           D      ELSE
                  F      SEQ
                         DO G
                         DO H
                  F      ENDS
           D      ENDS
    B      ENDS
X   ENDS
```

This is the general style used by block-structured languages such as PL/I; the indentation is optional. Next, the 'out-of-line' code:

```
X   SEQ
    DO A
    DO B
X   ENDS

B   LOOP until C1
    DO D
B   ENDS

D   IF C2
    DO E
D   ELSE
    DO F
D   ENDS

F   SEQ
    DO G
    DO H
F   ENDS
```

This is the style used by COBOL. Opinion differs as to the merits of each, and I have no wish to enter this particular debate here. For my purpose, in-line code with indentation is probably clearer, but that is not to be taken as a general recommendation.

8

Structure diagrams and schematic logic are equivalent. We shall usually prefer to use structure diagrams to express logic because we shall find that they are easier to relate to the problem being solved. Gradually we shall learn to read the diagram as if it were code, but we shall also occasionally present schematic logic, since this is closer to a more familiar programming language. We shall also take advantage of the relative informality of pseudo-code when the labels used in structure diagrams and schematic logic can be omitted without loss of meaning or clarity. As an installation standard, schematic logic should be replaced by the equivalent code written in the programming language used. Some guidelines for a language like COBOL are given in the Appendix; structure diagrams, schematic logic, and any implementation which avoids the use of explicit branch instructions (referred to generically as GOTO's) are said to be 'GOTO-less'.

1.3   Some Points on Notation

This section covers some general points on the notation used:

1. The use of shorthand
2. The interpretation of symbols used
3. Some consequences of the conventions used
4. Some examples of mistakes commonly made.

1.3.1 The use of shorthand

The diagram given in Figure 1.6 is a convenient abbreviation of, or shorthand for, Figure 1.3. The diagram does not seem to be open to ambiguity and misinterpretation; it has the advantage of brevity and occurs frequently in practice. However, the shorthand version does not identify, or give a name to, the

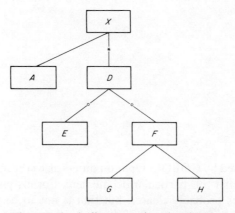

Figure 1.6   A diagram using shorthand

group originally called 'B'; since such a name is demanded by the labelling conventions of schematic logic, we can refer to the 'missing' box as either:

1. XBODY, on the grounds that the D's form the body or bulk of X, but with the disadvantage that only one label of this kind can be formed from X; or
2. {D}, using the mathematical convention for the name of the set whose members are all D's, but with the disadvantage that no programming language allows labels of this kind.

We shall opt for the second while recognizing that the alternative might be a more practical proposition as an installation standard. Diagrams (1) and (2) of

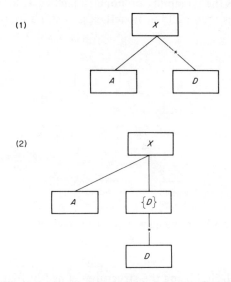

Figure 1.7   Removing shorthand from a diagram

Figure 1.7 are then equivalent; given a suitable condition C both are equivalent to the schematic logic:

```
X   SEQ
    DO A
    {D}     LOOP until C
            DO D
    {D}     ENDS
X   ENDS
```

Note that in practice the symbols X, A, D will be replaced by something meaningful and there might then be a more natural name for the box omitted.

1.3.2 The interpretation of symbols used

First the '∗' symbol. We have chosen to use '∗' to mean 'many including the possibility of none'; we should note in addition that:

1. On some occasions the precise number of iterations is known before starting the loop, on others not. The same symbol, and the same loop construction, is used in both cases.
2. For some loops it is possible to predict that there will be at least one iteration. As in 1 above, we shall continue to use the same symbol and the same loop construction.
3. No inference can be drawn from the structure diagram alone about the order in which the members of an iteration occur.
4. Since '∗' includes the possibility of 'none', a particular loop may iterate zero times; the loop is then null but nonetheless is still a loop.

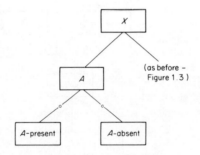

Figure 1.8   A diagram showing 'A' present or absent

Next the '∘' symbol. Still using the structure defined in Figure 1.3, we may on occasions want to express the idea that 'A' may be present or absent, as illustrated in Figure 1.8. In practice I have found that many students try to use '∗' to achieve the same effect, as in Figure 1.9. This is, however, misleading and bad practice; in general '∗' should not be used to mean '0 or 1', since it can easily cause confusion, and in any event does not distinguish the case 'A-absent'.

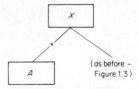

Figure 1.9.   An incorrect version of Figure 1.8

1.3.3 Some consequences of the conventions used

The labelling conventions used for schematic logic mean that the labels define boundaries which never cross; in the example given the labels and the boundaries they define are:

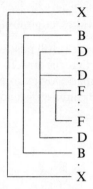

This property explains why the term 'nested' is used to describe the logic groups defined.

Equally, it will always be true that:

1. Terminal boxes in the structure diagram (e.g. boxes A, E, G, H in Figure 1.3) become the subject of the schematic logic 'DO' statement.
2. Non-terminal boxes in the structure diagram (e.g. boxes X, B, D, and F in Figure 1.3) become the labels of the equivalent schematic logic, and effectively control the order in which the terminal boxes are executed.

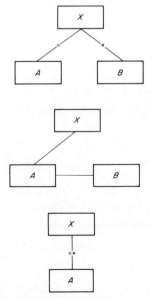

Figure 1.10   Examples of the misuse of structure diagram notation

12

Ideally the labels used in the schematic logic should be the same as the names given to boxes in the structure diagram; this makes the mapping from one to the other more visible. These points can provide a useful cross-check on the validity of code written.

1.3.4 Some examples of mistakes commonly made

Even though the rules are precise, it is still possible to misuse them. For practice, the reader is invited to confirm that the structure diagrams of Figure 1.10, and the following examples of schematic logic, do not conform to the conventions given; each illustrates a mistake commonly made. The reasons are given below.

```
1.  X   IF C1
        DO A
        Y       IF C2
                DO B
    X   ELSE
        DO C
    X   ENDS
        Y       ELSE
                DO D
        Y       ENDS

2.  X   LOOP until C
        DO A
        GOTO Y
        DO B
    X   ENDS
    Y   Etc.

3.  X   SEQ
        DO A
        {X}     LOOP until C
                DO D
        {X}     ENDS
    X   ENDS
```

The following notes refer to the structure diagrams of Figure 1.10:

(1) The 'o' and '*' symbols should not appear at the same level.
(2) Horizontal lines are not used to join boxes.
(3) The symbol 'o*' is undefined.

The following notes refer to the examples of schematic logic given above:

(1) The labels are not nested.
(2) The GOTO statement is not used in schematic logic.
(3) The label {X} should read {D}.

1.4 Flowcharts

Flowcharts, as their name implies, chart the flow, where 'flow' is here understood to represent the logic flow. The special symbols used are summarized in Figure 1.11. These symbols are subject to the following conventions:

1. *Connectors.* The connector usually contains an identifier used to locate another connector containing the same identifier on the same or another flowchart, and provides a means to split one large flowchart into two or more smaller ones. The special connectors ⓢ and ⓔ represent the start and end points respectively; it is assumed that there is only one of each, whereas all other connectors appear twice. (All other connectors will be given numeric identifiers.)
2. *Tests.* The result of a test is usually true or false, represented by the symbols ' $\sqrt{}$ ' and ' $\times$ ' respectively, as illustrated in diagram (1) of Figure 1.12. The symbol 'C' is used, as before, to describe the condition evaluated. If this admits of three results, then the alternative style shown in diagram (2) of Figure 1.12 is usually used. Whenever there is no risk of ambiguity the $\diamond$ symbol may be omitted. (It is always omitted in the main text of this book.)
3. *Module.* The module symbol represents a single-entry single-exit piece of code. It may, but does not have to, be implemented as a subroutine. Where the amount of code is small, and there is no risk of ambiguity, the symbol may be omitted.
4. *Flow of control.* The flow of control is assumed to be along the lines joining the other symbols—top to bottom and left to right. If the flow is otherwise, then either:
   the flow lines are given a direction indicator ↑ or ←; or
   a connector is used.
   This property explains the term 'flowchart' as a means to chart the flow.

It is always the symbols and their relative disposition which is significant. The scale used is of no significance; nor are there any other restrictions on the number or direction of flow lines, or the number of connectors used.

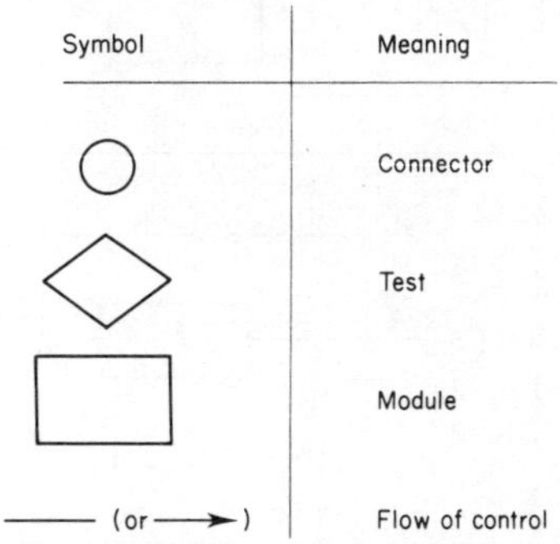

Symbol	Meaning
◯	Connector
◇	Test
▭	Module
—— (or ——▶)	Flow of control

Figure 1.11 Flowchart symbols

14

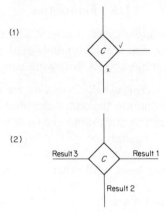

Figure 1.12 Showing tests and results on a flowchart

Each group, or building block, defined in Figures 1.1 and 1.5 has a flowchart equivalent. These are given in Figure 1.13 and obey the same building block conventions as structure diagrams and schematic logic; any flowchart constructed in this way is said to be 'nested'. An example is given in Figure 1.14 which shows the flowchart equivalent of Figure 1.3; the symbols C1, C2 represent the tests omitted in Figure 1.3 but used in the schematic logic

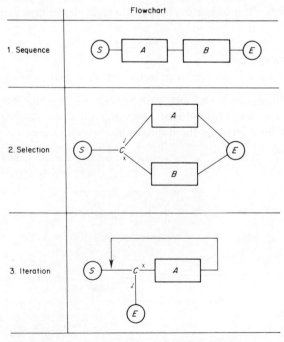

Figure 1.13 Flowchart building blocks

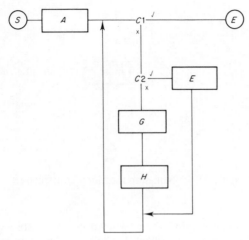

Figure 1.14 Flowchart equivalent of Figure 1.3

equivalent in Section 1.2. A comparison of Figures 1.3 and 1.14 shows that flowcharts make explicit the logic which structure diagrams and schematic logic leave implicit.

The flowcharts show clearly how:

1. Each building block has one entry and one exit (and is consequently said to be 'closed with respect to the logic flow'). This property imposes a strict discipline on the construction of program logic.
2. Loops are always constructed with the test for the end of the loop placed physically at the start of the loop. (This is a consequence of our decision to define '*' as 'many including the possibility of none'.)

Since the logic implied by a structure diagram could be made explicit using a flowchart, flowcharts could, in theory, be used instead. However, it is my belief that once the conventions are understood, structure diagrams are easier to create, provide a better picture of the design used, and are easier to follow. Furthermore, structure diagrams attempt to impose a discipline on the detailed organization of logic, which is difficult to obtain using flowcharts. Indeed, the very attraction of flowcharts is precisely the freedom they allow; but this freedom is easy to abuse, and experience suggests it can all-too-easily lead to 'spaghetti' code (of the kind described in Section 9.1). We shall, therefore, prefer the disciplines of structure diagrams, while acknowledging that flowcharts can achieve the same results if used with care.

The point may be further illustrated using a simple loop. We have adopted the standard defined in flowchart terms in Figure 1.13. As it happens, this is the same standard as that adopted by most high-level languages (Fortran IV being the notable exception). But flowchart techniques make it all too easy to construct a loop with the test placed physically at the end of the loop, as in Figure 1.15. Thus

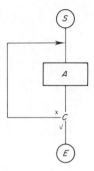

Figure 1.15   Non-standard loop construction

the use of flowcharts may tempt the unwary user not to observe standards even when those standards might be helpful; consequently, our opinion is that the freedom which flowcharts provide makes them unsuitable as a design and documentation tool.

In the last resort these are matters of judgement, and I would be the first to admit that structure diagrams can also be misused. Ultimately we must be judged by the quality of the designs we create. Since the important thing is to solve problems, let us not delay too long debating the notation used.

Figure 1.16 shows two other flowcharts which are not nested. From this point on we shall develop our design techniques using structure diagrams and schematic logic alone, stopping only occasionally to present a flowchart equivalent, or to take advantage of the freedom which flowcharts provide to help formulate a new logic pattern.

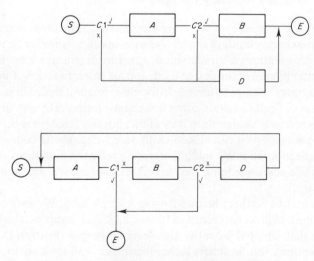

Figure 1.16   Examples of non-nested flowcharts

1.5   Illustration—A Nested Structure and the Equivalent Schematic Logic

This example is designed to illustrate the use of structure diagrams and schematic logic, and to evaluate the results obtained. Its flavour is 'commercial' but the principles should be equally clear to anyone not familiar with this type of application. The example will recur from time to time until completed in Chapter 3. In Section 1.6 we compare the results with those obtained using a more functional approach.

The data to be processed by a conventional validation program is batched onto a serial input file. There are three possible batch types; each batch starts with a batch heading record, and this may be followed by any number of records in the batch, including none. The records which can occur in each batch, and the restrictions which govern their sequence within the batch, are shown in the following table:

Batch Type	Batch Heading Record	Permissible Record Types	Sequence Conditions
1	B1	R1, R2	Occur alternately in pairs (R1, R2)
2	B2	R3, R4	None
3	B3	R5	Not applicable

On any file processed there may be any number of batches, and these may occur in any order. This completes the specification; the question is: how can we take advantage of the information given to design the program logic?

We shall at this stage attempt only to describe the order in which records are input on the assumption that no errors of any kind occur; we shall return to this example in Chapter 3, and then add in extra logic to detect and recover from record sequence errors (such as R1 not followed by R2). With this in mind, the correct file structure is shown in Figure 1.17. This shows clearly how the specification, and hence the structure diagram, is effectively a set of rules which describe the order in which batches, and records within batches, may be input. Thus, within batch type 1, records input in the order

$$R1 \quad R2 \quad R1 \quad R2 \quad R1 \quad R2$$

would be valid, while records input in the order

$$R1 \quad R1 \quad R1 \quad R2 \quad R2 \quad R2$$

would be invalid. The precise method used to provide the information required to evaluate the loop-terminating conditions will be covered when we return to this example in Sections 1.7 and 1.8, and again in Section 3.2.1.

18

The following are some of the errors commonly made by students presented with this example:

1. A structure which implies one batch only.
2. A structure which implies that all batches of type 1 precede those of type 2, and that these precede those of type 3.
3. The use of undefined symbols (such as '∗∘').
4. A structure which allows records of type R3 or R4 to occur after a header of type B1.

These points show that it is easy to misunderstand a specification, however carefully it is worded. In contrast to English narrative, structure diagrams are absolutely precise—that is, of course, their great advantage. The schematic logic equivalent to the structure diagram of Figure 1.17 follows:

```
FILE   LOOP until End-of-file
         BATCH   IF Batch Type 1
                 TYPE1   SEQ
                 DO B1
                 {PAIR}   LOOP until End-of-batch
                          PAIR   SEQ
                                 DO R1
                                 DO R2
                          PAIR   ENDS
                 {PAIR}   ENDS
                 TYPE1   ENDS
         BATCH   ELSE Batch Type 2
                 TYPE2   SEQ
                 DO B2
                 {RECORD}   LOOP until End-of-batch
                            RECORD   IF Record Type R3
                                     DO R3
                            RECORD   ELSE Record Type R4
                                     DO R4
                            RECORD   ENDS
                 {RECORD}   ENDS
                 TYPE2   ENDS
         BATCH   ELSE Batch Type 3
                 TYPE3   SEQ
                 DO B3
                 {R5}   LOOP until End-of-batch
                        DO R5
                 {R5}   ENDS
                 TYPE3   ENDS
         BATCH   ENDS
FILE   ENDS
```

As noted, this logic assumes the data is valid.

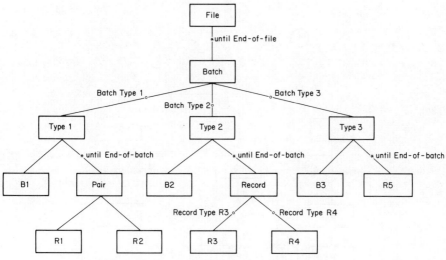

Figure 1.17 Illustration of a nested structure

If you prefer out-of-line code, the schematic logic would look like the following:

```
FILE     LOOP until End-of-file
         DO BATCH
FILE     ENDS

BATCH    IF Batch Type 1
         DO TYPE1
BATCH    ELSE Batch Type 2
         DO TYPE2
BATCH    ELSE Batch Type 3
         DO TYPE3
BATCH    ENDS

TYPE1    SEQ
         DO B1
         DO {PAIR}
TYPE1    ENDS
```

and so on.

An attractive feature of this approach is that compiler directives could be used (if available) to start each level on a new page. In case you have any doubts about how the logic works, an equivalent flowchart is given in Figure 1.18.

Finally, note that both structure diagram and schematic logic are GOTO-less in the sense described in Section 1.2. The implementation may or may not contain GOTO's; the reader can use the guidelines given in the Appendix to check that if all loops and selections are hand-coded the number of GOTO's implied is 14 (two for each loop, two for a two-way selection, and four for a three-way selection).

20

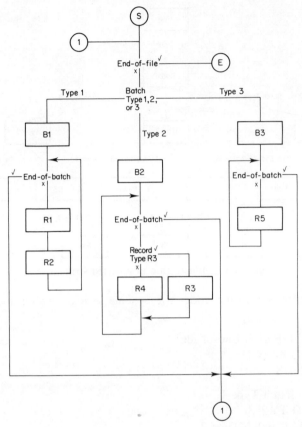

Figure 1.18   The flowchart equivalent of Figure 1.17

1.6   The Structured and Functional Approaches—Contrasting and Complementary

The analysis of Section 1.5 started with a structure diagram and proceeded to derive schematic logic. We shall think of the result as a framework which consists of logic (that is sequences, selections, and iterations) together with subroutine calls (for that is what the DO statement is intended to represent), and we shall also speak of the dependent subroutines as processing functions 'allocated' within the logic defined. Further processing functions (that is, processing functions not yet considered) may always be allocated at a later stage; this might include, for example, additional subroutines to execute input/output operations, perform 'end-of-batch' processing, and so on. All this is typical of structured programming. We shall have more to say on it shortly.

Whereas structured programming is motivated by its desire to design the logic, the functional approach to program design is motivated by its concern to identify the functions executed. A function may be anything from an individual activity to the complete program, and should have a natural meaning in terms of the application concerned. Each function so identified is thought of as a module, and each module (except the program as a whole) is usually, but not necessarily, implemented as a subroutine. Each subroutine then performs a subset of the total processing; the advantages are that the modular units can be separately and independently developed and tested, that one module may be changed without affecting others, and that the program can be integrated from the modules so created. The results are usually portrayed in a diagram such as that given in Figure 1.19; if you are not familiar with this 'module hierarchy' notation you need note only that Figure 1.19 is read as follows: 'Module A contains within it calls to subroutines B and C, while subroutine B contains within it calls to subroutines D and E.' The structure diagram and module hierarchy diagram notations are similar and must not be confused.

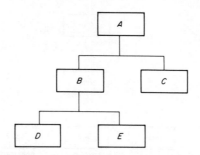

Figure 1.19   A module hierarchy diagram

The question of how to choose such modules for a given program, and how to design their interfaces, is generally outside the scope of this book, but is taken up briefly in Chapter 9. For this particular program, there is no difficulty; at least as a first step, the natural thing to do is to define one module to process each record type. Other functions, such as those noted above, can be added later. On this basis a suitable design is given in Figure 1.20. Now examine the box marked 'Program'; this contains within it calls to subroutines 'B1', 'R1', and so on. But the intention is that statements like 'DO B1', 'DO R1' in schematic logic represent language-independent calls to subroutines to process records of type B1, R1 respectively. The 'structured' program, therefore, makes the same subroutine calls as the 'modular' program. But in addition, the structured

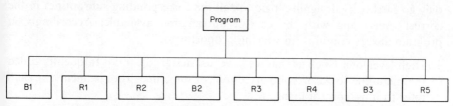

Figure 1.20   Module hierarchy corresponding to Figure 1.17

program provides logic which determines when, and in what order, to make the subroutine calls. (This is the schematic logic presented in Section 1.5; those lines with labels represent the logic and those lines without labels represent the subroutine calls.) Structured programming goes further, therefore, than the functional approach; in this case the structured techniques have designed the logic internal to the box called 'Program' in Figure 1.20. More generally, we may assert that the same subroutines can be used whichever approach is adopted, but structured programming provides additionally a method for designing the logic internal to the topmost module.

For completeness, the module hierarchy diagram corresponding to the out-of-line schematic logic is given in Figure 1.21; the high-level logic is now split between several high-level modules. Figures 1.20 and 1.21 are the extreme cases; in practice a compromise between the two would be likely.

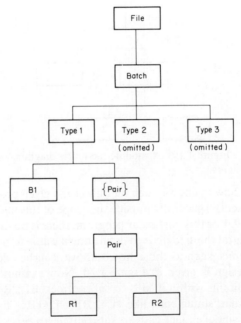

Figure 1.21   Alternative module hierarchy

This is a very important result. Structured programs are always modular, but they go further by designing logic to call the corresponding subroutines in the correct order, and with the correct information available. Accordingly, a program always contains (in varying proportions):

1. High-level logic (such as that we have just designed); this is frequently called the 'main-line' logic, or 'control section', or sometimes 'root segment'; we shall refer to it as 'control logic'.
2. Subroutines called to execute processing functions (such as 'B1', 'R1', etc.).

In my view, these two parts of a program each merit their own distinct design approach. Generalizing, we can say that the first is characterized by the complexity of its logic with relatively simple processing functions allocated; at present these are restricted to subroutine calls to provide links with 2 above but will later be extended, particularly to include input/output. The second is characterized by the volume of processing described but the relatively straightforward logic required; although we have not specified the subroutines used in detail, it is not difficult to see that they tend to be concerned with a description of the application (or, in this example, business) rules of the system being implemented. In principle the design of logic internal to the dependent subroutines is in no way different to the design of the control logic which calls them; but in practice the logic is often significantly less complex (even if more voluminous). Unless the record's internal structure, or the processing required, is complex, there is less need for specialized techniques and rather less benefit from their use.

Structured programming as defined in this book concentrates on the design of control logic, while the functional techniques tend to concentrate on the identification of program functions; the two could, and should, live happily side-by-side. In this type of example structure diagrams are, accordingly, drawn from file level to record level and provide a natural interface with those subroutines which describe application processing. Of course, there may sometimes be debate as to what constitutes a record, but that is another matter. Further comment on the detailed design of record processing subroutines is outside the scope of this book.

1.7 The Read-ahead Principle

A structure diagram describes the order in which events of interest to a program occur. It assumes, therefore, that events have names, or identifiers, associated with them, and that there is a mechanism for moving on from one event described to the next. Inevitably the implementation of such a mechanism depends on the nature of the events themselves, but in general we shall refer to it as a 'Read' instruction. Since the program is expected to analyse the results of Read instructions executed, each event identifier must contain at least sufficient information to enable the logic to interpret the event detected. Normally each event will also have other information associated with it, but extreme cases also exist where there is no explicit identifier (e.g. the identifier is implied by the event's physical position relative to other events), and where the event consists of its identifier only.

Our design approach is to highlight the significant events first, then describe the order in which those events take place, then deduce the control logic required to analyse the event sequence detected; we shall now develop a simple algorithm to locate suitable points at which to allocate the Read within the framework so defined. This algorithm is known as the read-ahead principle. It is important to emphasize that the role of the read-ahead principle is only to show how to allocate the Read instruction as necessary inside a framework already designed.

The reader is first asked to note that later work will allow us to introduce new structural concepts, and to vary the interpretation of loop-terminating conditions and of the Read instruction itself; the concept of read-ahead (as a means to allocate the Read) will remain the same, but the results may look different, as might be expected, in contrasting application environments. We may then be able to resolve some of the confusion felt by those programmers who find the concept of read-ahead misleading when applied to on-line and real-time systems (such as those described in Chapters 5 and 8 respectively). A more straightforward example to caution the unwary against too literal an interpretation of the read-ahead principle is given in Section 1.9.

In order to develop the details, we continue to use the example given in Section 1.5 for which we have already designed the logic. Noting that the events described are records on a serial file, 'Read' must be taken to mean 'read next record from the serial input file'. More accurately, we shall interpret it as a logical Read, implemented as a call to a subroutine. This subroutine always returns to the instruction following the call in the normal way; the result of a call is the next record (if there is one), or a dummy record (if there is not one). The dummy record is a convention indicating that a hardware End-of-file has been detected and is usually implemented by using 'high values' as the record identifier. This is a standard commercial programming technique and is equivalent to the creation of a file trailer record.

The logic given in Section 1.5 contains both iterations and selections, and all the tests implied can only be evaluated by inspecting the results of Read instructions executed. Now, the loop through the batches comes to an end on detecting End-of-file, while each batch comes to an end on detecting either the start of the next batch or End-of-file. It follows that:

1. An initial Read must appear before beginning the loop through the batches. This is required so that when we come to the schematic statement:

   FILE   LOOP until End-of-file

   we shall be in a position to evaluate the test implied. A consequence is that the logic will still work if there are no batches on the file.
2. For Batch Type 1 a further Read must appear after the statement DO B1 and before beginning the loop through the pairs. This is required so that when we come to the schematic statement:

   {PAIR}   LOOP until End-of-batch

   we shall again be in a position to evaluate the test implied. A consequence is that the logic will still work if there are no pairs for a particular batch.
3. Further Reads are required in Batch Type 1 after both the schematic statements:

   DO R1
   and
   DO R2.

In particular, the Read after 'DO R2' ensures that when the logic returns to the beginning of the loop it can evaluate whether or not we have now come to the end of the batch.

Similar considerations apply to the other two batch types.

This is sufficient to demonstrate that multiple Reads are necessary, and that for the example used these are allocated according to the following pattern:

1. The first Read is allocated at the beginning (effectively as part of the file Open instruction).
2. Further Reads must be allocated immediately after completion of processing of the previous record.

This algorithm is known as the 'read-ahead principle'. It is attractive and important because the Read is the most significant processing function to be allocated, and because the results contrast with those obtained using the traditional 'single-read' approach (described in Section 1.10). In another sense, of course, the read-ahead principle is trivial—you have to read to get started, and once you have finished with the previous record you have to read again to find out what to do next. The point is, however, that the tests required to evaluate the results of Reads are first built into the structure diagram. So we start by designing the logic, and the Reads then slot naturally into place, and once allocated there is no need to add in any further logic. As formulated above, the read-ahead principle, together with nested logic, provides a very natural way to design a wide range of programs, particularly those which are concerned with analysing serial files.

1.8   Further Points on Notation

The Read may be displayed on the structure diagram or within the schematic logic. On a structure diagram the Read is shown by the symbol ⓡ. (We distinguish this from a connector by making the convention that connectors always contain a number, while a Read contains the letter 'R'. The Read symbol will be refined further from time to time.) Continuing with the logic of Figure 1.17, the first Read is shown on the diagram as if there were a sequence: 'Read, and then continue as per the diagram'. Figure 1.22 is, therefore, interpreted as 'Read, then loop until End-of-file'. The remaining Reads are usually attached to the bottom right-hand corner of a box. Thus the diagram shown in Figure 1.23 signifies 'DO Record, then Read'. The logic given in Figure 1.17 could now be updated to show all the Reads, as in Figure 1.24.

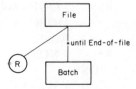

Figure 1.22   Allocating the initial Read instruction

Because the choice of a Read instruction is inextricably bound up with the identification of events, and the logic to analyse ordered event sequences, we shall treat the Read as part of the schematic logic, so distinguishing it from other processing functions allocated. The schematic logic equivalent to Figure 1.24 is now:

```
        Read
FILE    LOOP until End-of-file
        BATCH   IF Batch Type 1
                TYPE1   SEQ
                        DO B1
                        Read
                        {PAIR}      LOOP until End-of-batch
                                    PAIR    SEQ
                                            DO R1
                                            Read
                                            DO R2
                                            Read
                                    PAIR    ENDS
                        {PAIR}  ENDS
                TYPE1   ENDS
        BATCH   ELSE Batch Type 2
                TYPE2   SEQ
                        DO B2
                        Read
                        {RECORD}    LOOP until End-of-batch
                                    RECORD    IF Record Type R3
                                              DO R3
                                              Read
                                    RECORD    ELSE Record Type R4
                                              DO R4
                                              Read
                                    RECORD    ENDS
                        {RECORD}  ENDS
                TYPE2   ENDS
        BATCH   ELSE Batch Type 3
                TYPE3   SEQ
                        DO B3
                        Read
                        {R5}    LOOP until End-of-batch
                                DO R5
                                Read
                        {R5}    ENDS
                TYPE3   ENDS
        BATCH   ENDS
FILE    ENDS
```

Figure 1.23   Allocating other Read instructions

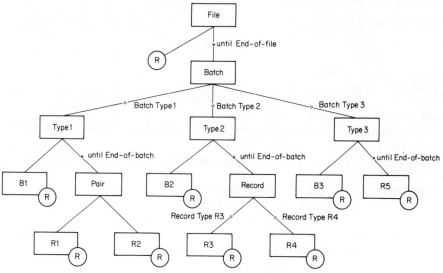

Figure 1.24   Figure 1.17 updated to show the Read instructions allocated

The initial Read could be integrated into the schematic logic framework by forming an additional sequence (Read, then loop until End-of-file); the significance of this will be covered in Section 2.2. At this stage the building blocks (sequences, selections, iterations) are formed only from ordered event sequences, and the Read is a (particularly significant) processing function allocated within the framework defined.

It is now clear how the Reads provide the information required to evaluate all the tests shown on the structure diagram and in the schematic logic. Indeed, now that the pattern is established we shall tend not to annotate the diagram with these conditions, unless such annotation makes a positive contribution to our understanding; if the conditions are omitted from the diagram they will usually be included in schematic logic, or described in the text.

If you prefer full out-of-line code the schematic logic would look like the following:

```
          Read
FILE      LOOP until End-of-file
          DO BATCH
FILE      ENDS

BATCH     IF Batch Type 1
          DO TYPE1
```

28

```
BATCH   ELSE Batch Type 2
        DO TYPE2
BATCH   ELSE Batch Type 3
        DO TYPE3
BATCH   ENDS

TYPE1   SEQ
        DO B1
        Read
        DO {PAIR}
TYPE1   ENDS
```

and so on.

The addition of Read instructions to the equivalent flowchart presents no problems, and is left as an exercise.

The number of Reads could be acceptably reduced by one if we replace:

```
{RECORD}   LOOP until End-of-batch
           RECORD   IF Record Type R3
                    DO R3
                    Read
           RECORD   ELSE Record Type R4
                    DO R4
                    Read
           RECORD   ENDS
{RECORD}   ENDS
```

by:

```
{RECORD}   LOOP until End-of-batch
           RECORD   IF Record Type R3
                    DO R3
           RECORD   ELSE Record Type R4
                    DO R4
           RECORD   ENDS
           Read
{RECORD}   ENDS
```

An amended structure diagram is given in Figure 1.25.

An immediate consequence of the read-ahead principle is that a simple loop to read through the records on a serial file would be written:

```
        Read
FILE    LOOP until End-of-file
        DO Record
        Read
FILE    ENDS
```

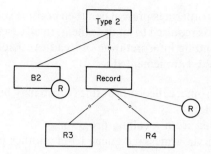

Figure 1.25   An adjustment to reduce the number of Read instructions

This may be re-expressed as:

          Initialize
FILE   LOOP until End-of-file
          DO Record
          Increment
FILE   ENDS

The general pattern:

1. Initialize
2. Test for End-of-loop
3. Execute content of loop
4. Increment
5. Unconditional branch back to 2

now forms a standard method for the construction of all loops, at least until the additional concepts and techniques of Chapter 3 are available.

1.9   Examples of Read

In general, 'Read' may be thought of as any mechanism required to move the logic on from one event of interest to the program to the next, and to provide information to evaluate the event so detected. The following are a few instances of the term 'event':

   records on a serial file
   entries in a table, list, or index
   segments in a data base
   keywords, or fields, in a syntax

In on-line and real-time systems we might extend this list to include:

   operator commands entered
   hardware interrupts detected
   intermediate results produced by cooperating processes

30

We shall find that the orderings present can then become very complex, and that some careful thought is required to analyse them. In all cases, however, there will always be a corresponding interpretation of Read. Anticipating later work, the result of a Read may be implemented as:

1. A reply returned from a called subroutine (which may be replaced directly by the equivalent code).
2. A parameter passed from a calling program.
3. A message passed via a message queue from another process.

Case 1 above was used in Section 1.7.

In both cases 1 and 2 the implementation may use facilities provided by intermediate software running under the control of an operating system, such as:

conventional data management systems
transaction processing (tp) monitors
purpose-built data base access software
blocking/deblocking routines
sort utilities

In case 3 above, the implementation would normally use facilities provided directly by a real-time operating system. In each case the software may be user-written or manufacturer-supplied.

The order in which events are detected as a result of Reads executed is always described using a structure diagram. The Reads provide the information required to evaluate conditions associated with selections and iterations, and so to analyse the event sequence detected. In each case the Read is allocated according to the read-ahead principle, although, as noted, this will require more interpretation later, especially in Chapters 5 to 8. The following example is included here to show that even the simplest program may need careful thought to avoid confusion.

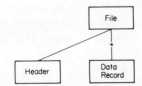

Figure 1.26   A file structure

Data input at a device (such as a card reader, or magnetic tape unit) consists of records; the first record is a 'Header' record and this is followed by 'Data' records. The Header contains a count of the number of Data records following. Assuming that no errors of any kind can arise, the structure is as shown in Figure 1.26. Now, since the number of Data records is taken from the Header, the loop is

controlled by a count and the schematic logic, including all Reads and loop
control, must be:

```
FILE   SEQ
       Read (Header)
       DO Header
       Set limit (N) of number of Data records
       Move 1 to I
       {DATA}  LOOP until I > N
               Read (Data record)
               DO Data-record
               Add 1 to I
       {DATA}  ENDS
FILE   ENDS
```

The interpretation of the COBOL-style instructions such as 'Move 1 to I' should
be clear from the context. It would be fatal to interpret the read-ahead principle
as implying the following logic:

```
FILE   SEQ
       Read (Header)
       DO Header
       Set limit (N) of number of Data records
       Move 1 to I
       Read (Data record)
       {DATA}  LOOP until I > N
               DO Data-record
               Add 1 to I
               Read (Data record)
       {DATA}  ENDS
FILE   ENDS
```

since the result of 'Read' after N data records is undefined. The lesson is to
remember that the term 'Read' as in 'read-ahead principle' is the means for
providing:

1. a mechanism for moving on from one event to the next; and
2. the information required to analyse the event sequence (that is, to evaluate
   any tests implied by the structure diagram and schematic logic).

In the example just given these two tasks are split between the Read (which
reads a record) and the count (which controls the loop); a little extra thought is
required to allocate both functions correctly. Interpretation of this kind will
occur from time to time as experience shows the need to allow different meanings
for Read in new and unfamiliar contexts, and to introduce new concepts to
describe event sequences. All this is, of course, the major task of program design.
Indeed in many ways this book is all about identifying a suitable meaning for
Read, and providing methods for analysing the results of Read instructions
executed.

32

1.10 The Single-read Approach

We have now arrived at an important stage in the development of our techniques. The programming style described contrasts with traditional programming practice; the two can be summarized as follows:

1. The use of multiple Read statements, as described in Sections 1.7 to 1.9. (Remember that Read means a logical Read—often implemented as a call to a subroutine which contains the physical Read statement.) Following the principles outlined so far, we design the logic (based upon the structure) and *then* allocate the Reads. A consequence is the need for multiple Reads.
2. The use of a single Read statement. Traditional programming practice is often based on the use of a single Read statement. This Read is often said to 'drive' the logic in the sense that after the Read there inevitably follows a succession of tests to evaluate the result; the processing so selected is then always followed by a return to the common Read instruction.

If the use of structured techniques leads to multiple Reads, then it follows that the logic of a program based on a single Read cannot be structured in our sense even if it could, in practice, often be implemented without the use of GOTO's. We have, therefore, a decision to take. The new techniques imply multiple Reads; the traditional approach demands a single Read. Which is better? There is no absolute answer—both approaches are possible. And ultimately it is for the reader to judge; I can only say that in my view the structured approach gives a much clearer presentation of the logic and its relationship to the problem being solved. And that to my mind is the important point.

Figure 1.27 shows in flowchart terms how the logic of Figure 1.17 might be

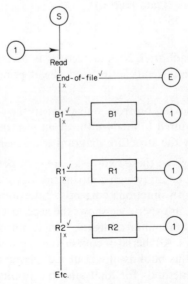

Figure 1.27   The single-read approach

reorganized if just one Read instruction were used. (I recognize that this is to some extent a caricature, but I am only trying to draw out a contrast in styles.) There is no exact way to express this logic using structure diagrams; it is really based upon the structure diagram shown in Figure 1.28 except that even this would strictly require two Reads. It might be acceptable if the sole purpose of the program were to read through the file, distinguish the record types, and process accordingly. But it does not express the relative sequencing of records found, and

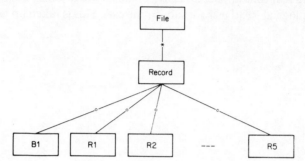

Figure 1.28   A structure diagram corresponding to Figure 1.27

(anticipating Chapter 2 a little) would not provide a satisfactory framework in which to allocate those processing functions which depend on a knowledge of the order in which records occur (such as those processing functions executed at the start and end of significant record groups). There is no doubt that the logic *could* be made to work; the question is only which design is the clearer, and more accurately describes the order in which the records occur. On this criterion there cannot be much doubt that the solutions given are better. In passing, we must acknowledge that the structure of a file does depend on the use to which it is put. Further reflections on this point are included in Section 3.9.

We could also take the opportunity to clear up a point about efficiency. The use of a single Read instruction is often held to be more efficient, on the grounds that nine Read instructions means nine subroutine calls. But it is not difficult to see that there are hidden inefficiencies in the use of a single Read. Suppose, for example, we have just processed R1; the structured solution makes no tests on the result of the Read after R1, since if there are no errors this is guaranteed to be R2. On the other hand, the unstructured solution makes four tests before it is ready to process R2. (I know this could be reduced but that is not the point.) The structured program visibly makes only those tests which are necessary; the unstructured program does not. This argument becomes even more significant once the logic is enhanced to handle record sequence errors. In general one can say:

1. A structured program is so clear that any potential source of inefficiency can easily be seen.
2. An unstructured program is often so obscure that any potential source of inefficiency is frequently well disguised.

Without doubt it is better to write clear programs. In either case there must be an identical number of Reads actually executed.

On reflection, at least in commercial programs, the use of a single Read may have arisen from a need (real or imagined) to replace each Read statement in a program by all the detailed data management software required to effect the input transfer implied. The use of subroutines means that we are free to have one physical Read, and as many logical Reads as we like. Other considerations apply in on-line and real-time application environments where it may not be possible to implement a logical Read using a subroutine call. This is taken up later, starting in Chapter 5.

Chapter 2
Applications for Nested Logic

The most common application for nested logic is to the analysis of serial files. These occur most frequently in batch-mode commercial systems, from which the examples used in this chapter are drawn. The principles developed are nonetheless fundamental and familiarity with them will be assumed in later chapters where the examples become more varied and complex.

In each case the structure is derived from an examination of the data used. A simple generalization suggests that structure is always inherent in the data used, and has led to the term 'data structure approach'. I would like to emphasize that data structures, as used in this chapter, are a special case of the more general ordering concept described in Chapter 1. It is, therefore, important to remember that it is not always only data which has a structure. The best one can say is that programs execute functions in an order; an inspection of data structures may (as in this chapter) help to determine the order required, but equally (as in later chapters) it may not. In those cases where the concept of data structure does not help we shall have to look elsewhere for a suitable structure on which to base the logic.

2.1   Data Structures

2.1.1 Serial sorted files

Consider first a conventional Customer Master File on which there is just one record per customer. The content of a record is illustrated in Figure 2.1. In this diagram:

each customer is identified by an Account Number and allocated to an Account Region; together these fields are said to constitute a record key

further information relating to the customer identified is omitted, but is referred to collectively as the record details

36

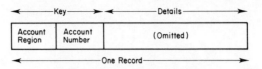

Figure 2.1   The content of one record

In this, as in all the examples used, there is no significance in the application chosen to illustrate the principles described; any other similar file would serve equally well. If the records on the file are sorted into ascending key sequence (as is usual), that is Account Number within Account Region, then a typical key sequence for a file containing just 12 records would be as tabulated below.

Record Number	Account Region	Account Number
1	1	2
2	1	4
3	1	26
4	1	38
5	1	57
6	2	1
7	2	4
8	2	12
9	2	94
10	3	7
11	3	72
12	3	94

This simple description is sufficient to demonstrate that serial files are often deliberately organized so that the records on them occur in a precise and predictable order. We may assume that the order in which records, and groups of records, appear is convenient for processing (e.g. the program must analyse the file into regions in order to produce Region Summary Reports). In that case, by following the principles of Chapter 1, we may reasonably expect to design control logic by first describing the order in which the records occur.

The file structure is given as Figure 2.2, in which, as is now our habit, the loop-terminating conditions have been omitted. We note that:

1. The key is used to sort records on the file into an order, which is then reflected in the structure diagram.
2. The term 'Region' is used both to identify a field within the sort key, and to identify a group of records on the file. This can cause confusion, but there is no convenient way to avoid it.

A program based on this structure will process each region in turn, and within

Figure 2.2   The structure of a customer master file

each region each customer. The precise identity of each region/customer is not of interest to the control logic.

Not all serial sorted files are as simple as this. The following are two possible variations:

1. For each customer there is now one header record and several detail records; as is customary, the header record of one customer precedes the corresponding detail records.
2. For each customer, each detail is either of Type 1 or of Type 2.

These variations are described in Figure 2.3 which is now typical of a wide range of similar files.

2.1.2 Indexed files and data bases

The great attraction of serial files is that the records must be accessed in the same order as they appear on the storage device. We might say that the logical view

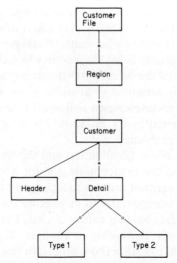

Figure 2.3   A more complex file structure

(that is, as seen by the program) and physical view (that is, as seen by the storage device) necessarily coincide. In recent years a great deal of effort has gone into the provision of alternative access paths for a given set of records; the result is the provision of indexed files and data bases. So far as we are concerned the implications are simple, but should be noted.

Suppose then that we take the file defined in Figure 2.2 and provide this file with an index. Suppose further that the index is organized to allow the following file access operations:

1. Retrieve record for a specified customer.
2. Retrieve next record (where 'next' means 'next record in ascending key sequence').

Such a file is sometimes known as indexed sequential. Since records can now be read randomly, it becomes possible to access a subset of all the customers and, indeed, to access some customers twice. The file structure then only becomes meaningful when considered in conjunction with some form of reference list, which may itself be another file, and which tells us *which* customers are of interest and in what order; such a reference list is always accessed serially. The file index then enables us to access those records required, and these need not occur on the list in the same order as they are physically stored on the device; in contrast to serial files which do not have an index, we can now distinguish the logical file structure (as seen by the program) and the physical file structure (as seen by the device). The latter is of interest when designing the files and their indexes, and would be used to design the software required to realize the access paths required by application programs. No detailed examples of this kind are given here.

Data bases take this idea further. Apart from providing different types of access to records held on the same file, the data base may provide direct access paths between records previously held on separate files, and implement different types of file. The opportunity is usually also taken to eliminate duplication of data across systems, but that is another matter. Lists provide further examples of data structures where the data is held in a form which can provide access paths convenient to the program; the access paths frequently involve the use of built-in pointers, and are usually arranged so as to avoid the need to traverse the list serially. The physical structure chosen will usually be one which provides the logical access paths required by the program, and which also minimizes search times and maintenance problems.

For a full description of the possibilities, and the facilities made available in typical implementations, the reader must consult a specialist text. We shall continue to assert that events of interest to a program happen in a well-defined order; it does not particularly matter to us whether the events are records on a serial file, segments in a data base, or entries in a list. The program must know, or be able to discover, the order in which events happen; likewise the data structures must provide access paths to realize those orders. In this sense system design and program design go hand-in-hand. Henceforth, we shall refer to data structures, always taking a logical view, independently of the physical storage techniques used. Some examples of the new possibilities created by data bases are included in Chapter 5.

2.2   Program Structures

In most programs there is more than one data structure present though these are not usually independent. We now show how to take advantage of relationships which may exist between them, in order to develop the concept of a program structure. As an illustration we start with what is almost the simplest possible commercial program. The specification is, therefore, outrageously simple, but do not be put off by that—it is the principles which are important, and we are quite definitely concerned to walk before we run. The more complex examples given later simply vary the types of structure present and expand on the relationships between them.

Consider then a simple batch-mode program which edits a serial customer file input to produce an edited file and a control file output. The input file is sorted into ascending key sequence, and each file is held on tape, as illustrated in Figure 2.4. (This 'input/output' diagram, or 'system flow diagram' is a special

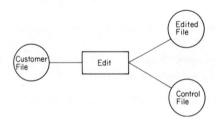

Figure 2.4   A file edit program

case of a flowchart, in which the central box represents the program and the peripheral boxes represent files or devices. It will be used from time to time to help describe the function of a program. Special symbols are used to represent different device types; their interpretation should always be clear from the context.) The input file consists of customers; for each customer there is one header followed by several details; each detail shows an amount outstanding against the corresponding customer's account. The file is processed serially to produce two output files; the Edited File is identical to the input file except that summary records are inserted, one for each customer, and one for the complete file. Each customer summary shows a total amount outstanding; likewise for the file summary record. The Control File contains a copy of each summary record created, but nothing else.

This completes the specification. The three data structures present are given in Figure 2.5, but need a little supplementary interpretation. First, in diagram 1 of

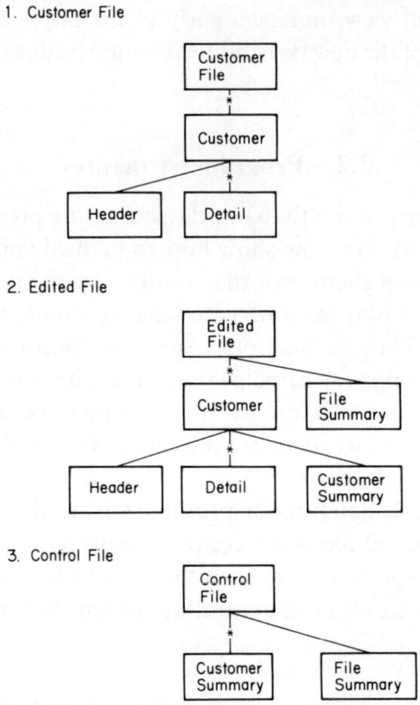

40

1. Customer File

Customer File

Customer

Header   Detail

2. Edited File

Edited File

Customer   File Summary

Header   Detail   Customer Summary

3. Control File

Control File

Customer Summary   File Summary

Figure 2.5   The data structures present

Figure 2.5 the upper '∗' symbol means (as is normal) many customers including the possibility of none; we note in addition that:

we shall find out how many customers there are when we come to read the file; and
the customers occur in a specific order (ascending key sequence).

With this in mind, the upper '∗' in diagram 2 of Figure 2.5 means:

many customers including the possibility of none;
as many as there are on the input file; and
in the same order.

Likewise, in diagram 3 of Figure 2.5 the '∗' means:

many customer summary records including the possibility of none;
one per customer on the input file; and
in the same order.

Diagram 3 of Figure 2.5 may, therefore, be rewritten as in Figure 2.6, provided the '∗' is taken to mean:

many customers including the possibility of none;
as many as there are on the input file; and
in the same order.

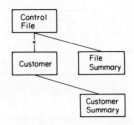

Figure 2.6   Alternative data structure for the control file

Contrary to appearances (possibly), this is not pedantry: the exact meaning and implications of the '*' symbol are not always apparent from an inspection of the diagrams alone. If necessary, the diagram can always be annotated to make it more explicit. The attraction of Figure 2.6 is that it exhibits greater structural commonality with diagrams 1 and 2 of Figure 2.5. Now consider the following reasoning:

1. A data structure diagram describes the order in which data elements (in this case, records) and groups of data elements (in this case, all records for a customer) appear (in this case, on a serial file), in so far as this order is of interest to the program.
2. We can expect the data elements, and groups of data elements, on the various files to appear in an order which has significance in terms of the processing required. That is why data structure is important for this type of program.
3. Since structure diagrams represent an ordering, we can use them to represent any ordering so long as the order can be described using the concepts of sequences, selections, and iterations; in particular we can use structure diagrams to describe the order in which data elements, and groups of data elements, are processed.
4. In order to generalize, we can think of the data structure in Figure 2.7 as leading to the need for processing functions:

   Start-of-X (which will include at least initializing the loop)
   A (which will include all details directly concerned with A)
   End-of-X (which will include summarizing the loop—though this is sometimes null).

In order to complete processing of X, these are executed in the order described in Figure 2.8.

Figure 2.7   A simple data structure

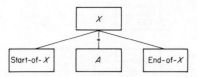

Figure 2.8   The processing functions executed

5. If two (or more) files in a program exhibit a common data structure, then one diagram will suffice to describe the order in which processing functions are executed by the program, provided that this diagram takes full account of the needs of each of the separate data structures present.

These points, together with the correspondence noted between the separate data structures, lead to the structure diagram given in Figure 2.9. We can now distinguish between:

1. A structure diagram which describes the order in which data elements appear on a file (as in Figure 2.5).
2. A structure diagram which describes the order in which processing elements are executed (as in Figure 2.9).

These are often referred to as 'data' and 'program' structures respectively. More generally, a program structure shows the order in which processing functions are executed, and this must necessarily take account of the needs of all the separate data structures present. The relationship between data structures and program structures may then not be as simple as that just given, and examples are included later.

Using convenient abbreviations of the names attached to the boxes in Figure 2.9, the equivalent schematic logic is:

```
PGM   SEQ
      DO Start-of-program
      {CUS}   LOOP until End-of-file
              CUS     SEQ
                      DO Start-of-customer
                      {DET}   LOOP until End-of-customer
                              DO Detail
                      {DET}   ENDS
                      DO End-of-customer
              CUS     ENDS
      {CUS}   ENDS
      DO End-of-program
PGM   ENDS
```

Interpretation and implementation of the loop-terminating conditions are covered in Section 2.4.

In this framework the sequence (SEQ) construct does not affect the logic flow. If it were omitted we would cease to think of the 'Start-of-' and 'End-of-' processing functions as an integral part of the framework; instead, we would

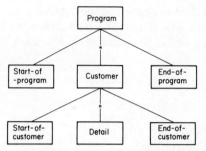

Figure 2.9 The program structure formed from the data structures of Figure 2.5

think of them as allocated within the reduced framework which consists of two nested loops only. The corresponding structure diagram is given in Figure 2.10. The distinction is, perhaps, a fine one but this style is sometimes useful in complex examples in which there is not such a clear distinction between events (in this case, records) and processing functions. A common application is to exhibit the Read instruction (but no other processing functions) on the diagram, as in Section 1.8; we shall use it again informally later.

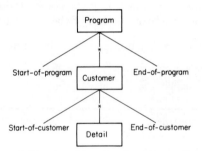

Figure 2.10 An abbreviated structure diagram

2.3 Processing Functions

The program structure controls the order in which processing functions are executed. The processing functions identified so far are generalized to subroutines called:

Start-of-program
Start-of-customer
Detail
End-of-customer
End-of-program

These may of course be implemented as in-line code, and must include at least the following:

1. All input/output, especially Reads and Writes
2. All loop controls (if not covered in 1 above)
3. Any counts or controls accumulated
4. Any other processing necessary (calculations made, etc.).

We now want a method to determine the detailed content of each subroutine. We start by making a list of detailed instructions to be executed. For this program the following would be adequate (it depends a bit on how much detail you want to include):

1. Open files
2. Close files
3. Read input file
4. Write record to Edited file
5. Write record to Control file
6. Initialize Customer total
7. Accumulate Customer total
8. Initialize File total
9. Accumulate File total

As in Section 1.9, we shall continue to use this informal COBOL-style expression when listing or allocating detailed instructions. The interpretation of each should be clear from the context. If, and when, new technical terms are introduced, these will be explained and defined first.

Using the numbering convention implied above, these instructions can be allocated to the subroutines listed in one of the following ways:

1. *On the structure diagram.* We tabulate the subroutines and cross-refer to the list given.

   Either:

Subroutine	Content
Start-of-program	1, 8, 3
Start-of-customer	4, 6, 3
Etc.	

   or:

Subroutine	Content
Start-of-program	Open files
	Initialize File total
	Read input file
Start-of-customer	Write record to Edited file
	Initialize Customer total
	Read input file
Etc.	

We then annotate the structure diagram as in Figure 2.11.

2. *In the schematic logic.* We take the schematic logic given in Section 2.2 and expand the processing functions required. This gives:

Either:

```
PGM   SEQ
      1, 8, 3
      {CUS}   LOOP until End-of-file
              CUS   SEQ
                    4, 6, 3
                    Etc.
```

or:

```
PGM   SEQ
      Open files
      Initialize File total
      Read input file
      {CUS}   LOOP until End-of-file
              CUS   SEQ
                    Write record to Edited file
                    Initialize Customer total
                    Read input file
                    Etc.
```

The choice is largely a matter of style; this in spite of evidence that for some programmers the choice seems to be a matter of life or death.

The complete schematic logic is:

```
PGM   SEQ
      Open files
      Initialize File total
      Read input file
      {CUS}   LOOP until End-of-file
              CUS   SEQ
                    Write record to Edited file
                    Initialize Customer total
                    Read input file
                    {DET}   LOOP until End-of-customer
                            Accumulate Customer total
                            Write record to Edited file
                            Read input file
                    {DET}   ENDS
                    Accumulate File total
                    Write record to Edited file
                    Write record to Control file
              CUS   ENDS
      {CUS}   ENDS
      Write record to Edited file
      Write record to Control file
      Close files
PGM   ENDS
```

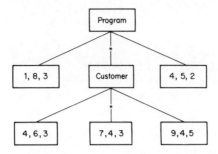

Figure 2.11   Allocating processing functions on the structure diagram

For this program, then, three Read statements are required. You can check that the logic works by simulating its execution using a particular record sequence such as:

H1   (Header, first customer)
D11   (First detail, first customer)
D12   (Etc.)
H2
D21
D22
H3
End-of-file

This establishes a general method; its objective is to design structure diagrams from which we can derive schematic logic. We think of the result as a framework in which the logic controls the order in which processing functions are executed. The processing functions may be expressed as generalized subroutines (such as 'Start-of-program') or expressed directly (such as 'Open files', 'Read input file'). The reader should confirm that the same subroutines could have been identified using a more functional approach, and check the distinction drawn in Section 1.6 between the high-level control logic and any other logic which may appear within the modules identified (of which there is none in the example just completed). All this will, of course, be thoroughly reinforced by later examples. Further observations on the implementation of the designs produced are included in Section 2.4.4.

2.4   A Typical Print Program

This is the first program we have considered so far which is recognizably realistic. A program summarizes the content of a serial input file, producing two printed reports and two serial output files as shown in Figure 2.12. The input file is sorted

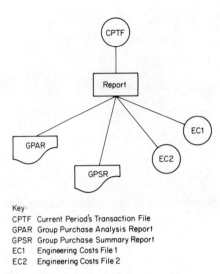

Key:
CPTF Current Period's Transaction File
GPAR Group Purchase Analysis Report
GPSR Group Purchase Summary Report
EC1   Engineering Costs File 1
EC2   Engineering Costs File 2

Figure 2.12   A print program

on the following key:

Group
Department
Section
Charge Account
Invoice Number
Transaction Type

(Remember that no special significance is attached to the illustrative names used for either key fields or file names.) Several records can exist with the same key, while the last record on the input file has a special key value (higher than all other records) and contains control totals.

The two reports produced are called Group Purchase Analysis Report (GPAR) and Group Purchase Summary Report (GPSR); for the Group Purchase Analysis Report one detail line is printed per input record, and one total line for each charge account; for the Group Purchase Summary Report one section total line is printed for each section, and one department total line for each department. A sketch layout for the GPAR is shown in Figure 2.13, while that for GPSR would be similar. For both reports, a new page is required each time the group changes, and the current group name is always printed at the top of each page. The group names used are omitted.

Finally, each input record which belongs to any department numbered 410 is written to the file called Engineering Costs 1 (EC1); likewise, each record which belongs to any Department numbered 298 is written to the file called Engineering Costs 2 (EC2).

48

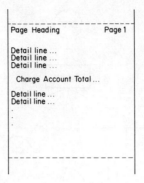

```
Page  Heading                Page 1

Detail line ...
Detail line ...
Detail line ...

    Charge  Account  Total ...

Detail line ...
Detail line ...
    .
    .
```

Figure 2.13   Sketch layout of the Group Purchase Analysis Report

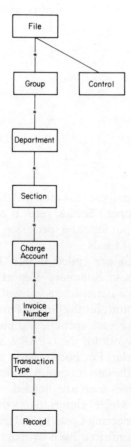

Figure 2.14   Input file data structure

This completes the specification; following the ideas developed in Sections 2.2 and 2.3, the design is completed below in the following steps:

1. Identify the data structures present
2. Form a program structure
3. Allocate the processing functions

The schematic logic is omitted, since it follows the pattern already established in Section 2.3. A design review is held in Section 2.4.4.

2.4.1 Design step 1: Identify the data structures present

2.4.1.1 Input file

The structure of the input file is shown at Figure 2.14; this follows from:

1. An inspection of the sort key
2. The presence of records with duplicate key values
3. The presence of a file control record.

This is typical of all serial files. In general, your first clue to a data structure is the sort key, but you must also be prepared to look around for the presence of header and trailer records, and duplicate key values. Note that it would be wrong to omit the 'Record' box in Figure 2.14 since that would allow only 'many different transaction types'.

2.4.1.2 Printed reports

Taking GPAR as typical, the printed reports are laid out as illustrated in Figure 2.15. In this diagram the dotted lines represent page boundaries, while:

1. the brackets on the left-hand side represent the groupings of print lines into charge accounts (remember: one total line per charge account)
2. the brackets on the right-hand side represent the grouping of print lines into pages.

The charge account and page boundaries, as shown by the brackets, overlap. This means it is not possible to produce one diagram (at least, a useful diagram) which fully takes account of both charge accounts and pages. Figure 2.16 is tempting but wrong; a typical page does not consist of many charge accounts (page 2, for example, consists of part of one charge account and part of another). For similar reasons the diagram in Figure 2.17 is not good enough either. All other diagrams either suffer from the same problem or do not adequately describe the ordering present.

This lack of correspondence between pages on the one hand and charge accounts on the other is known as a 'structure clash': we cannot satisfactorily accommodate both the concept of 'Page' and the concept of 'Charge Account' on the same structure diagram. We shall consider structure clashes generally in

50

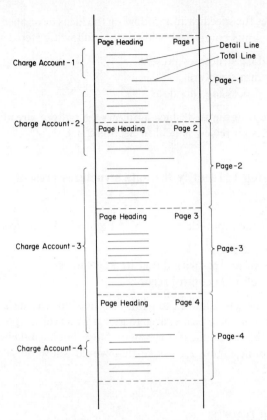

Figure 2.15　Charge account and page boundaries

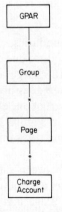

Figure 2.16　An incorrect data structure diagram

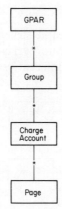

Figure 2.17   A second incorrect data structure diagram

Chapter 7, and this clash in particular in Section 7.3.1; for the moment we have no alternative but to content ourselves with the structure given in Figure 2.18. As a consequence we shall (in Section 2.4.3) treat the logic of page overflow as an exception not displayed on the structure diagram.

The structure of GPSR follows a similar pattern. The following additional points should also be noted:

1. Figure 2.18 (and likewise for the corresponding diagram for GPSR) has been drawn by considering the report in isolation from the rest of the program. Its relationship with other data structures present is not considered until the program structure stage.
2. The group level has been inserted since change of group is significant for the report:

    the page headings are changed
    a new page is started

We shall also return to this point (in Section 7.3.3).

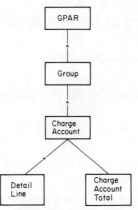

Figure 2.18   A logical structure for the printed report

2.4.1.3 Other serial output files

The two serial output files have simple structures; that for EC1 is described in Figure 2.19. In this diagram the group level is inserted to show that departments numbered 410 may occur within different groups.

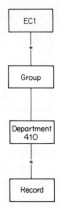

Figure 2.19   Serial output file data structure

2.4.2 Design step 2: Form a program structure

The levels on the various files used display much the same kind of correspondence as we found in Section 2.2. That is (for example), the groups on GPAR are the same groups as those on Current Period's Transaction File (CPTF) and in the same order, and so on. However, two new points arise:

1. The invoice number and transaction type levels do not appear on any output file. In constructing a program structure we can either

   leave these levels in, on the grounds that they may be required (possibly for program maintenance) at a later stage;
   leave these levels out, on the grounds that they are not used and could easily be put in at a later stage.

   We shall take the second view.
2. The program needs to

   treat all departments equally (for the purpose of producing the printed reports); and
   treat particular departments differently (for the purpose of producing the two serial output files).

   This is not possible without compromising the neat hierarchical nature of the program structure. We must either:

   differentiate the departments at department level; or
   reintroduce the concept of Department at record level.

This particular problem arises from the fact that we have here two logical programs combined into one; the requirements of one (to produce the reports) are, strictly speaking, inconsistent with the requirements of the other (to produce the two serial output files), but not enough to create a major design problem. We have to compromise. This is a common feature of programming. If, for good reasons, one program is required instead of two, then the best that we programmers can do is to accommodate the compromises necessary carefully but deliberately into our design. We shall choose to reintroduce the concept of 'Department' at record level. The reader can check that if the different departments were distinguished at department level, it would then be necessary to repeat the lower-level loops (section, charge account, and record) for each department distinguished.

These design decisions are typical of those which arise in practice. The resultant program structure is given as Figure 2.20. The loop-terminating conditions may be expressed as 'until End-of-file', 'until End-of-group', ..., 'until End-of-charge-account', and their implementation is explored in Section 2.4.4.

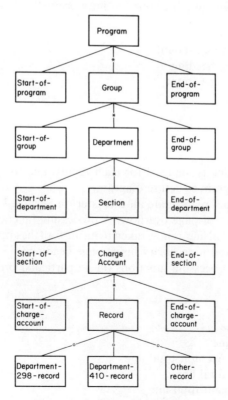

Figure 2.20   Program structure

2.4.3 Design step 3: Allocate the processing functions

As noted above, the concept of 'Page', and hence the logic of page overflow, cannot be accommodated on the structure diagram. We shall, therefore, imagine the existence of a subroutine whose function it is to print a line and, if necessary, to insert page headings. We define a processing function 'Print' to mean 'call a subroutine to print a line and insert page headings when appropriate'. To achieve this:

the printed reports are opened at Start-of-program and closed at End-of-program

the subroutine maintains a count of lines printed on a page, and of pages printed in the report

the field which contains a count of the lines printed is initialized to some artificially high value (at compile time, or at Start-of-program), in order to force the subroutine to print page headings the first time it is called

the field which contains a count of the pages printed is initialized to zero

The print subroutine now need contain only the following pseudo-code (in which the data names used are self-explanatory and the condition 'End-of-page' is evaluated by examining the count of lines printed):

```
IF      End-of-page
        Increment Page-count
        Print Page-heading
        Initialize Line-count
ELSE
ENDS
Print Line
Increment Line-count
```

One such subroutine is required for each report, and its internal logic is not shown on the program structure diagram.

As noted, we shall re-evaluate all this later (in Section 7.3.1) to give the full 'structured' account of page overflow. A processing function expressed as, for example, 'Print Detail line' is now taken to mean 'Call the appropriate subroutine to print the line, and if necessary insert page headings'.

The full list of processing functions (in no particular order) is:

1. Open files
2. Close files
3. Read input file
4. Print Detail line
5. Print Charge Account total line
6. Print Section total line
7. Print Department total line
8. Write record to serial output file EC1

9. Write record to serial output file EC2
10. Initialize Charge Account total
11. Accumulate Charge Account total
12. Initialize Section total
13. Accumulate Section total
14. Initialize Department total
15. Accumulate Department total
16. Change the page headings (GPAR and GPSR) and start printing on a new page

These can now be allocated as follows:

Routine	Functions
Start-of-program	1, 3
Start-of-group	16
Start-of-department	14
Start-of-section	12
Start-of-charge-account	10
Department-298-record	11, 4, 9, 3
Department-410-record	11, 4, 8, 3
Other-record	11, 4, 3
End-of-charge-account	13, 5
End-of-section	15, 6
End-of-department	7
End-of-group	None
End-of-program	2

Those processing functions common to the three record-level routines could alternatively be allocated to a common routine. We note also that there is no need in this program to read beyond the control record (since this marks a software End-of-file), unless a further check is required to make sure that there are no other records on the file.

This completes the design steps listed above; in the following review some points of implementation are raised.

2.4.4 A design review

In this section we think about:

1. The termination of control levels.
2. Some assumptions made.
3. Design documentation.

2.4.4.1 *The termination of control levels*

In this kind of program, termination of any high level means automatic termination of all lower levels. To illustrate this, and the flow of control implied, take the following record sequence:

Record Number	Group	Department	Section	Charge Account
1	1	297	24	56
2	1	297	24	57
3	1	297	24	57
4	1	298	24	57
5	1	298	24	58

This is consistent with Figure 2.14. Now suppose we are processing record number 3. Then we are sitting (in the program structure diagram) in the record-level box marked 'Other-record'. On reading the next record (record number 4):

1. It *is* now End-of-charge-account-57 and End-of-section-24 (because it is End-of-department-297). Consequently we execute in turn:

   End-of-charge-account
   End-of-section
   End-of-department

2. It is *not* End-of-group, so we begin a new department, within that a new section, and within that a new charge account; in all we execute in turn:

   Start-of-department
   Start-of-section
   Start-of-charge-account

First time through, we execute all the 'Start-of-' boxes from highest level to lowest level; at End-of-file we execute all the 'End-of-' boxes from lowest level to highest level.

For the record sequence given, we would execute the processing functions in the order:

Start-of-program
Start-of-group   (Group 1)
Start-of-department   (Department 297)
Start-of-section   (Section 24)
Start-of-charge-account (Charge Account 56)
Other-record   (Record 1, Department 297)
End-of-charge-account   (Charge Account 56)
Start-of-charge-account (Charge Account 57)
Other-record   (Record 2, Department 297)

Other-record	(Record 3, Department 297)
End-of-charge-account	(Charge Account 57 in Department 297)
End-of-section	(Section 24 in Department 297)
End-of-department	(Department 297)
Start-of-department	(Department 298)
Start-of-section	(Section 24 in Department 298)

And so on.

2.4.4.2 Some assumptions made

The program is built on the assumption that records on the file occur in the correct sequence. If this assumption turns out to be untrue, the function of the program is undefined. This contrasts with, say, validation programs where detection of, and recovery from, errors form an integral part of the program, and for which suitable recovery actions must be defined so that the program can continue. It is very important to be clear about any assumptions of this kind which are built into the diagram. In general we may distinguish:

1. *Error-free processing.* In the present context this means processing a file which is in-sequence and in which no errors of any kind occur.
2. *Error conditions from which the program recovers and continues.* There are no such conditions in this program; if there were, then the additional logic for error recovery would form part of the 'normal' processing and be built into the diagram. This is one of the central topics covered in the next chapter.
3. *Error conditions from which the program cannot continue.* An example in this program would be an out-of-sequence record, for which the action required is undefined (normally the program would abort). Detection of such abnormal conditions should be confined to the Read subroutine, which then protects the main program structure from those conditions which violate the assumptions on which it is built. The Read subroutine may also carry out any other work, such as record reformatting, which is best kept out of the main program structure.

2.4.4.3 Design documentation

Finally, without wanting to take too many short cuts, you may feel that formal and mandatory observance of all the design steps, together with supporting documentation, is sometimes long-winded and unnecessary. I would agree. For our purpose it will be sufficient to adopt a pragmatic approach. We shall start to think of a structure diagram as a piece of logic, and make it just sufficiently detailed to cover the logic required; in particular it is frequently not necessary to be so formal about program structures, especially where (as in later chapters) a program is dominated by just one structure, or the program is built from two or more separate structures. It is, however, usually advantageous to allocate all the major input/output functions and identify all the loop-terminating conditions.

Further, the more we learn to think of a structure diagram as logic, the less we need (as in the example just designed) always to present schematic logic. In any case, we should aim to anticipate the program structure from a knowledge of the type of program under consideration. To this end, the reader should think of the designs presented as 'models', to be followed when next confronted with an instance of the same program type. The more the models are understood and agreed, the more can be taken for granted, at least between parties familiar with the models. I accept that as an installation standard all this would probably be much too vague, but I am more concerned with principles than with implementation standards. I would suggest that you try to develop a feel for the documentation required as we go along; this will depend on your familiarity with the concepts, and with the complexity of the program. In general, the guideline is: 'produce as much documentation as is necessary for *someone else* to understand how the logic is arranged—and no more'.

2.5   Multiple Input Files—File Matching

File-matching problems are characterized by the presence of two or more input files. We shall consider the simplest case first:

1. There are two input files (called X, Y).
2. Both X and Y are serial files and have the simple structures illustrated in Figure 2.21. In particular there is only one record for each customer on X, and likewise on Y. Both files are sorted into customer number order.

The following illustrates a typical record sequence:

Customer Number	Record present for this customer on:	
	X	Y
1	✓	✓
2	✓	✓
3	✓	
4	✓	✓
5		✓
6	✓	
7	✓	
8		✓
9	✓	✓

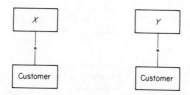

Figure 2.21   Two input file data structures

In other words, customers numbered 1, 2, 3, 4, 6, 7, and 9 are present on X; customers numbered 1, 2, 4, 5, 8, and 9 are present on Y.

Since the customers present on X are not necessarily the same as those present on Y, the '*' symbol has a slightly different meaning in each of the diagrams used:

1. On file X, '*' means all customers identified on file X.
2. On file Y, '*' means all customers identified on file Y.

The difference in the range of customers denoted by the '*' on the separate files is the distinguishing feature of this type of program, and suggests a slight revision to the structure diagrams, as in Figure 2.22. Special processing is usually required for the three cases:

a customer is present on X but not on Y
a customer is present on both X and Y
a customer is present on Y but not on X

illustrated above by customers numbered 3, 4, 5 respectively.

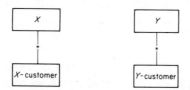

Figure 2.22   Revised data structures for X and Y

This completes our description of file-matching programs. We now set out to analyse the program logic using structured programming principles. To this end we imagine that another file exists on which all customers identified by X and all customers identified by Y are present, and that this file is also sorted into customer number order. Since such a file does not really exist, we shall refer to it as a 'logical' or 'notional' file, and call it 'XY'. For each customer on the logical file XY, we imagine that a 'logical record' is present constructed from the corresponding 'real' records on X, Y. We shall refer to these logical records as being of type 'X', '$X + Y$' and 'Y' respectively. The structure of the logical file XY is given in Figure 2.23. In this diagram the '*' is taken to mean 'all customers on X together with all customers on Y in customer number order'. We rely on the name

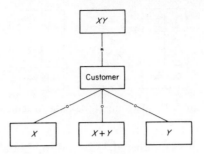

Figure 2.23   A logical file structure

XY to exhibit the relationship between this diagram and the two separate diagrams *X, Y.* We can now work out how to allocate Read instructions. In the illustrative sequence given, suppose we are pointing at customer number 5 on file *XY*; referring to Figure 2.23:

file *Y* is pointing at customer number 5, while file *X* must be pointing at customer 6 (since it is this which proves the absence of customer number 5 on *X*)

the logical record for customer number 5 is of type '*Y*', since customer number 5 does not exist on *X*

it follows that after processing customer number 5, we want to read file *Y* only (since any read of file *X* would access customer 7 before customer number 6 has been processed)

A similar argument can be applied to the other cases, represented by customers numbered 3 and 4. The result is that Read statements (*x*), (*Y*) (to read files *X, Y* respectively) can be allocated within the structure diagram for *XY* as illustrated in Figure 2.24. This is, of course, precisely the type of reasoning which led us to the read-ahead principle. The distinguishing feature of this example is that we have two input files, and must, therefore, read ahead on both *X* and *Y* in the same diagram.

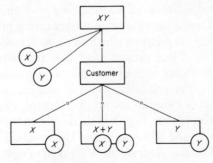

Figure 2.24   Allocating read instructions

Taking Figure 2.24 as our example, we note the following points:

1. The loop terminates on detecting End-of-file on *both* X and Y.
2. The selection is evaluated by comparing the current key values on X and Y.
3. It is the Read instructions which provide the information required to evaluate the tests implied by points 1 and 2 above.

This general approach is known as the 'simple collating' technique and is suitable for a wide range of programs. The simple collated diagram *XY* (Figure 2.24) can be thought of as both data structure and program structure:

insofar as it describes the structure of the logical file *XY*, it is a (logical) data structure
insofar as it describes the relationship between separate files (*X*, *Y*) used in the program, it is a program structure.

In either case, it represents an ordering of logical records on the logical file *XY*. The distinction between data structure and program structure is not so clear-cut as we may have thought. In fact, we do not need to insist on it at all, so long as the ordering described is clear.

A formal program structure would also take account of any output file created, and would insert all 'Start-of-' and 'End-of-' boxes. The latter point is easily accommodated. On the former, suppose that all records on X and Y are written forward to a new output file. Then that file has a structure identical to *XY*, and a formal program structure, taking account of all the files present, could be constructed in the normal way. Similar considerations apply to the presence of any output file created by a file-matching program, so long as the range of customers present on it is a subset of those on *XY*; Example 4 in the next section illustrates the kind of changes required when this is not the case.

2.6   Examples of Simple Collating

1. Multiple records for one customer on X

The revised diagram for file *X* is left as an exercise; the new simple collated structure is illustrated in Figure 2.25. Note the use of the box marked '*X + Y*' to establish that the customer is present on both *X* and *Y*, and that consequently each of the transactions present on *X* matches the same customer on *Y*.

2. Matching at two levels

Consider the following cumulative extensions to Example 1 above. In each case, the changes necessary are described, but production of a new diagram is left as an exercise to the reader. First, suppose there is a region level on both *X* and *Y*; if there is a need to detect Start-of- and End-of-region, but no need to detect mismatched regions, then the only change required in the collated diagram is to insert a region level. Second, suppose there is now a need to detect mismatched regions; then the three-way branch must be repeated at both region and customer level. Third, suppose there is a region header on file *Y*; then a logical region

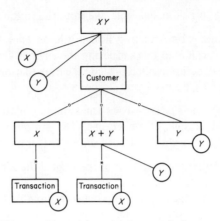

Figure 2.25   File matching with multiple records for one customer

header must be introduced on the collated diagram for those regions which exist on *Y*. This is now as complex a case as you will find for a two-way match.

3. Three-file match

There are now three serial files, each of which follows the pattern of Figure 2.22. The collated structure is illustrated in Figure 2.26. (In this case the Read instructions are attached to each box in the form of a list; this is only done to save space, and has no other significance.)

4. More matching—an extra case

Suppose that you are asked to amend the diagram in Figure 2.26 so that the program now produces a report listing all key values which are possible customer numbers, but for which no customer exists on any of the three files. A possible

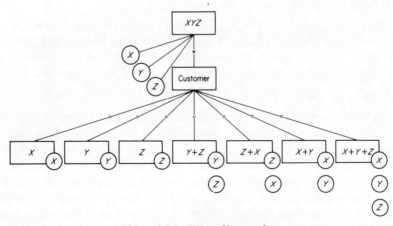

Figure 2.26   Three-file match

customer number is (say) any number in the range 1 to 999. As an example, given the typical sequence tabulated below, then the program required produces the list 3, 7, 11, 15.

Customer Number	Record present for this customer on:		
	X	Y	Z
1	√		
2		√	
3			
4	√		
5		√	√
6	√	√	
7			
8		√	
9	√	√	√
10	√		
11			
12		√	
13		√	
14	√		
15			
16	√	√	√

In Figure 2.26 the '*' symbol in the collated diagram was used to mean 'many customers—all those which exist on at least one of X, Y, Z, and in customer number order'. In the variation given we are asked to consider all possible customers, whether they exist on one or more of X, Y, Z, or not. With this in

64

mind we have to introduce an eighth possibility—namely that a possible customer is identified but that no records exist for this customer on any of the three files. The collated structure must now be amended:

1. The loop is controlled by a count which starts at the lowest possible customer number (1, say) and proceeds through to the highest possible customer number (999, say).
2. The count determines which customer is processed next. The files X, Y, Z are now read to determine only which files exhibit a record for the current customer number, and the results of these reads are used to determine which case of the 8-way selection to use.

The simple collated diagram can be amended as in Figure 2.27; this now shows all Read and loop control functions allocated.

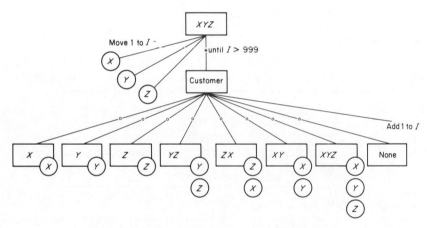

Figure 2.27   An extension to the three-file match

2.7   Transaction-driven and Pseudo-direct Access Techniques

The following are two new designs, with a few comments on each; both use the same two basic files described in Figure 2.22.

1. Transaction-driven

With this approach we choose one file (X, say) as the driver. We then process each X-customer in turn; given a particular customer on X, we scan through Y until we find a customer on Y (if there is one) which matches the current customer on X. Because X would usually be a transaction file, with Y a master file, we call this the transaction-driven approach; but the same technique may also be used with the master file as driver.

For example, suppose we are given the following record sequence (this is possibly an extreme case to make the point):

Customer Number	Record present for this customer on:	
	X	Y
1		✓
2		✓
3	✓	✓
4		✓
5		✓
6		✓
7	✓	
8		✓
9		✓
10		✓
11	✓	✓
12		✓
13		✓
14		✓

We set out to process each X-customer in turn; but to process a particular customer from X, say customer number 3, we have first to 'wind Y on' through customers numbered 1 and 2 until we find the match. It is as if the records on Y 'map on to' the next customer number on X which is greater than or equal to the current customer number on Y. The record sequence given makes it clear that there may be some Y's for which there is no corresponding X (those numbered 12, 13, 14 in the record sequence above). The logic of this program is described in Figure 2.28.

The design can now easily be amended, for example:

1. There are multiple transactions on file X for each customer
2. As 1 above, but the program is driven by file Y.

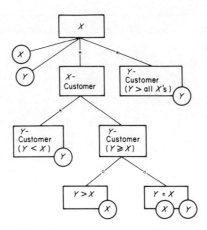

Figure 2.28 Transaction-driven file matching

Finally, note that this approach is not recommended if there are more than two files present.

2. Pseudo-direct access

If one of the two files specified in Figure 2.22 (*Y*, say) is indexed and accessed directly, then the file-matching logic would be as specified in Figure 2.29 where 'Get *Y*' represents a direct-access read, the result of which is *Y*-present or *Y*-absent (that is, excluding the possibility of error conditions).

Now suppose that the number of customers accessed on *Y* during different executions of the program is variable, possibly so variable that on some occasions it would be more efficient to access *Y* sequentially. It may still be desirable (for some application-dependent reasons) for *X* to think of *Y* as a direct-access file; in that case we should want a new design in which we replace 'Get *Y*' by a new read instruction, such that we are able to access *Y* sequentially and still provide for *X* the same interface as that provided by 'Get *Y*'. This is known as the 'pseudo-direct access' technique. It requires the construction of a subroutine which reads

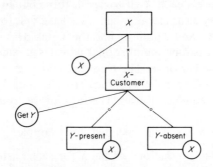

Figure 2.29 Direct-access file matching

Y sequentially but provides for X the same interface as a direct-access read. Implementation of this subroutine requires the use of logic inversion, and is, therefore, left here as a 'loose end' to be 'tied off' in Section 7.6.

Neither of these techniques is as flexible as the basic simple collating technique, but each can be useful. They do, however, illustrate how a given problem (that is, file matching) can frequently be looked at in more than one way. In the last analysis the important point is not the design you choose, but that having chosen a design you must make that design available to a third party (to aid maintenance, etc.). It is then your job, and requires your skill, to make your design understandable to someone else.

2.8 Optimization and Structure

We conclude this chapter with a brief exercise designed to demonstrate the effects of optimization. First, we draw a flowchart of the logic implied by the basic structure diagram for simple collating. This is given in Figure 2.30. Next, we amend this logic (in flowchart form) to try and optimize it; we reduce the number of reads on X to one, and likewise for Y, and test for End-of-file only after we have first detected matching keys (that is, when both files have key values equal to

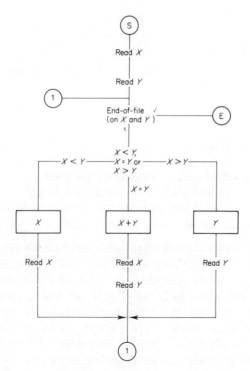

Figure 2.30   Flowchart of logic for simple collating

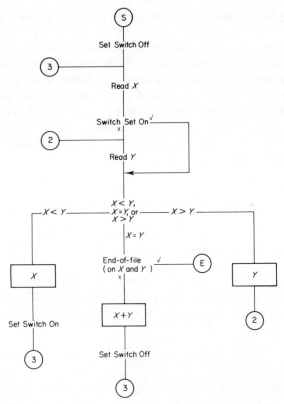

Figure 2.31 Optimized flowchart showing loss of structure

'high-values'). The result is the logic given in Figure 2.31. We make the following observations:

1. The finished (optimized) version no longer exhibits the structure of the problem.
2. The logic is no longer built from closed logic units.
3. One effect of the optimization is the need for a switch.
4. It is now much more difficult to amend the optimized version to take account of the design variations discussed in Section 2.6.

We think of these as disadvantages and consequently prefer the logic of Figure 2.30 and, even better, the same logic but expressed as a structure diagram (Figure 2.24). (If you have any doubts, try to amend the optimized flowchart to implement all the variations in Section 2.6; if you find this more difficult than using the structure diagrams, then my point is made.) I do not wish to minimize the importance of optimization; I just want to emphasize the structural price sometimes paid. We shall give examples later where the MONITOR concept (introduced in the next chapter) can be used as an optimization tool while still preserving structural integrity.

Chapter 3
The Concept of a Logic Monitor

3.1 A Pause for Stocktaking

This is about as far as we can usefully take the concept of nested logic, including the read-ahead principle. We have left three loose ends:

1. How to detect and recover from record sequence errors in validation programs (Section 1.5)
2. How to handle the logic of page overflow in print programs (Section 2.4)
3. How to implement pseudo-direct access techniques in file match programs (Section 2.7)

Any other significant programs we chose to design at this stage would be subject to similar limitations.

Here is a summary of the major points to emerge so far:

Control logic is concerned to analyse the order in which events of interest to the program happen; this order can be described using structure diagrams which are then used to 'drive' the design of the control logic required. The designs produced are still fully modular in the conventional sense.

Orders can be described using concepts of nested sequences, selections, and iterations; program logic is accordingly built around three corresponding logic units, or building blocks; these building blocks are single-entry, single-exit, and a consequence of their use is the need for the 'read-ahead' principle.

Thus far, structure diagrams have been used mainly to describe an ordering of data elements (usually records), or groups of data elements, which go to make up a file; this has given rise to the term 'data structure approach'. More generally, there is nothing to stop us applying the same concepts to anything which exhibits an order, so long as the order can be described using nested sequences, selections, and iterations.

A variety of applications has pointed to the need for flexibility when

69

interpreting the meaning of the '*' symbol, and of the Read instruction, in particular contexts.

Although there is nothing to stop us using the techniques presented at a more detailed design level, the greatest benefits are to be found in the design of high-level control logic. Accordingly our analysis has usually proceeded from file level to record level.

All of these points should be apparent from the text. Here are a few more points which are implied, but not so immediately evident:

For each building block (sequence, selection, or iteration) there is a guarantee implied that once started it will reach its normal end. (This follows from the fact that the building blocks are single-entry, single-exit.) The logic units are said to be 'complete' and 'closed with respect to the logic flow'.

For a selection group, there will always be an associated test which can be evaluated at the start of the group; whatever the result of this evaluation, control will always eventually reach the common end point.

For an iteration group, there will always be an associated test which can be evaluated at the start of the group; the group will continue to iterate until the condition implied is true; furthermore, there is no way out of an iteration other than via the test which begins the group.

Apart from the loose ends noted, these restrictions have presented no problems for us so far—largely because we have chosen programs which conform neatly to the patterns described. From now on we could take either of the two following paths:

1. Relying on the structure theorem (referred to in Section 9.1 and described in the Appendix), postulate that *all* logic in *all* programs should always be built from nested logic alone, possibly with minor extensions. For some purposes this may be a satisfactory approach, and it is certainly one frequently advocated. A price paid (as explained in the Appendix) is the introduction of switches.
2. Continue to refine the concept of structure, introducing new logic building blocks as and when new structural features are identified in the programs we have to write. A disadvantage is that any new building blocks defined might not be so readily assimilated, or so easily implemented in existing languages.

For some purposes the first approach is justified. Broadly speaking, application processing, that is to say detailed manipulation of data to express business rules or application algorithms, can often be written using nested logic alone; this is also true of the more complex high-level control logic, provided that the programs are kept small and simple. But as soon as additional complexities arise (of the kind described below), then the introduction of new concepts becomes a necessity if we are to preserve structural clarity and integrity. Because we are interested in providing general techniques of wide application, and particularly techniques suited to the analysis of complex problems, we shall pursue the second approach. The reader may want to stop from time to time to compare the approach we advocate with the results which would be achieved using nested logic alone.

As always in this book we preface our discussion with examples. None of the examples used would cause any overwhelming practical headaches, but each is symptomatic of a fundamental restriction in the concepts presented so far. Together, they point the way to a new technique. For reasons yet to be given, this technique is known as the logic monitor, and is similar to the more familiar so-called 'backtracking'. It is also worth pointing out that, in contrast to nested logic, the implementation of the logic monitor requires the explicit use of GOTO in commonly used high-level languages.

3.2   Some Problems Unresolved

Here, then, are three brief examples; the common problem they raise is summarized in Section 3.2.4.

3.2.1 Record sequence errors

We return to the example of Section 1.5 (developed further in Sections 1.7 and 1.8) and consider the additional logic required to detect and recover from record sequence errors for Batch Type 1. For convenience, the basic structure diagram together with the Reads is reproduced as Figure 3.1; remember that since this is part of a larger diagram (Figure 1.24) the B1 record has already been read by the time this logic is executed.

If we are guaranteed that there are no record-sequence errors, then the following are all true:

1. The loop through the pairs terminates on detecting a new Batch Header or End-of-file. This is the definition of 'End-of-batch' used in the schematic logic (Section 1.8).
2. The Read after B1 is guaranteed to find either a Batch Header, or an R1, or End-of-file. The same is true of the Read after R2.
3. The Read after R1 is guaranteed to find an R2.

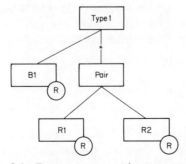

Figure 3.1   Data structure without error checking

Now suppose that we have started Batch Type 1 and that record sequence errors can occur. We are concerned with the logic required to interpret a record sequence of the following kind:

B1   R1   R2   R1   R1   R3   R7   ...   B2   ...

Further detailed errors which could arise when validating in-sequence records are outside the scope of this discussion.

We ask first how End-of-batch is now detected. For the record sequence given some possibilities are:

1. No change; that is, terminate the batch on finding B2.
2. Terminate the batch after the first sequence error detected, on the grounds that the batch is now presumably invalid.
3. Terminate the batch after finding R3 on the grounds that this record belongs to Batch Type 2, and that therefore there is a missing B2.
4. Terminate the batch after finding R7—an unrecognizable record type—on the grounds that something serious must be going on.

Each of these has some plausibility; the point is that a decision has to be taken; not taking it is the cause of many a programming debacle. My own inclination would be to implement possibility 1 (that is, terminate on finding a new Batch Header or End-of-file) on the grounds that the headers are provided precisely to demarcate the batches, and that in this type of program, record sequence errors within a batch are expected, however regrettable. Indeed, it is the very purpose of the program to detect and recover from such errors. However, it makes no fundamental difference to the general argument if you want to take a different view.

With this in mind we can now inspect Figure 3.1 again. In theory, each Read can now detect a record of any type whatsoever; if detection of the errors is to be done as part of this logic (and not, for example, within the Read itself), then evidently some extra logic is required. In particular, we must now monitor (in the sense of inspect) the results of each Read to see whether the results are valid or not. The diagram covers only the valid results. For the invalid results two additional checks will suffice, one before R1 and one before R2. These checks are represented by the upward arrow in Figure 3.2. This symbol is taken to mean: 'stop and check whether what the diagram says should happen next does indeed happen'; it does not yet explain what to do if the check fails. The lowest level of the diagram is, therefore, read left-to-right as:

Check if next record is R1
DO R1
Check if next record is R2
DO R2

If either of the checks shown fails then we have an error; in particular if the second check (the one just before R2) detects End-of-batch, then we have to terminate the sequence (R1, R2). But the concepts of nested logic insist that the

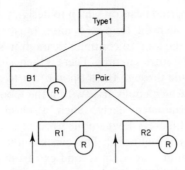

Figure 3.2 Identifying the points at which errors can arise

sequence (R1, R2) is closed. There is no way to terminate it after R1, at least not without resorting to some device, such as a switch, which enables us to bypass R2. This is not a serious practical difficulty; the point is that we can now distinguish two levels for the logic:

1. Assuming no record sequence errors, the logic of Figure 3.1 applies unconditionally; in particular, the Read after R1 is guaranteed to find an R2 and the sequence (R1, R2) is closed with respect to the logic flow
2. If we cannot assume the absence of record sequence errors, we can only say that most of the time (we hope) the logic of Figure 3.1 will continue to apply. But we must continually watch out for errors; if errors do arise further logic may be required and the sequence (R1, R2) may no longer be closed.

This suggests that we leave the underlying logic (Figure 3.1) alone, on the grounds that this tells us something useful (namely, what happens if there are no errors), and add something extra to deal with the errors. Exactly what form the extra logic should take will be decided after looking briefly at two more examples.

3.2.2 Table look-up

The next example concerns table look-up. Suppose we have a table of entries held in main memory. Each entry in the table is identified by a key value; a program is required to inspect all entries in the table in order to find out whether there is an entry in the table with some pre-specified key value. The search terminates when a matching entry is found, or failing that, when all entries have been inspected.

The data structure for the table is elementary (Figure 3.3). But the trouble is

Figure 3.3 Data structure for table look-up

74

that it provides only a partial basis on which to design the logic of the program. For the condition on which the loop terminates must surely be 'until End-of-table', since this allows the loop to continue through to its normal end, and the program to inspect all the entries in turn. There is then a need to add further logic to monitor progress made through the loop in order to detect those conditions (namely, Entry-found) which could arise within the loop, and which mean that the loop must be terminated early. Such a check might be expressed diagrammatically as in Figure 3.4, where the upward arrow symbol is subject to the same conventions as in Figure 3.2. This check cannot be implemented using nested logic, since it would generate a second exit from the loop, and the loop would no longer be single-entry, single-exit.

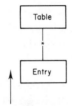

Figure 3.4   Identifying Entry-found

The techniques commonly used in practice to solve this problem all suffer from some disadvantage. For example, suppose that when a matching entry is found we set a flag and alter the loop's termination condition to 'until End-of-table or Flag-set'. Even though such an approach can apparently be implemented using nested logic alone, there are at least two disadvantages we can identify:

1. After terminating the loop, the logic is no longer pointing at the entry which gave rise to the match (at least, not if our standard method for controlling loops is employed); instead, it is pointing at the next entry.
2. If different processing is required depending on the result of the search (Entry-found or Entry-not-found), then further logic must be introduced to test the flag to see how the loop ended, and this logic is not portrayed on the structure diagram.

This flag is, incidentally, a good illustration of an undesirable switch:

'A switch (or flag) is something you set in one part of the program (in this case inside the loop, on detecting a matching entry) to remind you that when you get to another part of the program (after the loop has ended) you must do something (whatever is done on Entry-found) which you did not do when you should have done it (i.e. on detecting Entry-found).'

I do not want to make too much of this, but I repeat the point: generally, when you know what is the case, get on and do whatever you have to do, and do not set switches to remind you to do it later. Of course, we have to be careful not to confuse undesirable switches and flags with other legitimate uses of memory. In general structured programming has no use for switches (though you may want to quote this back at me when we consider logic inversion in Chapter 6). Instead, we try to arrange program logic so that at any point we know what is true because otherwise we would not be there—in particular, we do not have to test switches or flags to find out what is, or is not, the case. The price to be paid for eliminating undesirable switches is the introduction of further GOTO's. We shall shortly relate these GOTO's to a structural feature we have so far been careful to avoid.

As in Example 3.2.1, there is no insuperable practical difficulty here, and it is quite an easy matter to devise a program which will work. Nor does it make any difference if we choose to terminate the loop on the condition 'until Entry-found', since we shall then need to monitor progress through the loop to detect 'End-of-table'; if End-of-table arises before a matching entry is found the loop is, again, no longer closed. The point is to see the limitations and restrictions implied by a strict interpretation of the rules of nested logic as defined in Chapter 1. If we are to avoid the kinds of disadvantages of solutions such as that just described, then evidently something new is required.

3.2.3 Printed report

The third example concerns a simple printed report. The layout of the report is illustrated in Figure 3.5; each page is given the usual page headings and page number while the content of a page is printed 'three up, 56 lines to a page'. Now

Figure 3.5   Layout of a printed report

assume that whatever the reports represent, they correspond one-for-one to records on a serial input file; then the structure of the report, together with the Read instruction allocated, is given in Figure 3.6. We note that the two '*' symbols mean 'until End-of-file' and 'until End-of-page'. The structure of a line could be expressed differently as an iteration of three entries, but this does not materially affect the discussion.

It should be immediately evident that the program logic, as described by the diagram, is incomplete, since no account is taken of the fact that End-of-file might occur in the middle of a page. In fact, any of the three Reads at line level could detect End-of-file and whatever else happens this must surely terminate the current line, and the current page. Additional logic is therefore required at line level to monitor the result of each of the three Read instructions. The additional

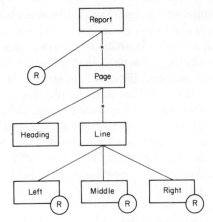

Figure 3.6   Data structure for the printed report

tests are shown using the upward arrow notation in Figure 3.7. (The final upward arrow could be omitted if End-of-file is taken to imply End-of-page; for reasons given later we shall prefer to include the extra check.)

Evidently the nested logic building blocks provide no way of terminating either the current line, or the current page. In fact, this example shows the need to terminate at least two levels at End-of-file; it compounds the problems already discussed in Sections 3.2.1 and 3.2.2, and is, therefore, not discussed further.

3.2.4 Incomplete structures

Each of these three examples is a victim of the same problem. Remember: a structure diagram contains a guarantee at the beginning to get through to the end; in other words, nothing can happen in the middle of a sequence, selection, or

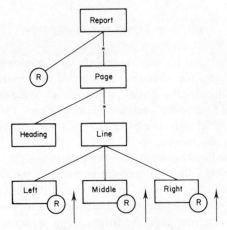

Figure 3.7   Detecting End-of-file

iteration that affects your decision at its beginning to go through to its end. This is what it means for a building block to be complete, and closed with respect to the logic flow. Yet here we have three examples where there is plainly no such guarantee available. The most we can say is that *under certain conditions* the building blocks will be closed with respect to the logic flow; in each case we are in no position at the beginning to say whether or not these conditions will remain true during the building block's execution; in each case if the conditions do not remain true we are forced to terminate execution of the respective building blocks, and they are then no longer closed.

In detail, for each example:

1. *Example 3.2.1.* If there are no errors, the pair sequence is closed; but at the beginning of a pair we are in no position to predict whether or not errors are going to arise; for some errors early termination of a pair is essential, and the pair is no longer a closed sequence.
2. *Example 3.2.2.* If a matching entry is not found, the loop through the entries is closed; but at the beginning of the loop we are in no position to predict whether or not a matching entry is going to be found; if a matching entry is found, early termination of the loop is required, and the loop is no longer closed.
3. *Example 3.2.3.* If End-of-file does not arise in the middle of a page, the page is closed; but at the beginning of a page we are in no position to predict whether or not End-of-file is going to arise; if it does arise, early termination of a page is essential, and the page is no longer a closed unit.

Henceforth we shall have to distinguish carefully those conditions under which completeness can be guaranteed, and those conditions under which it cannot be guaranteed. Note that the existing structure diagram notation simply cannot cope with both sets of conditions. Figures 3.8 to 3.10 are all structure diagrams based on the examples given which use the notation correctly, but which cannot be implemented because either:

1. The condition implied by the 'o' symbol cannot be evaluated at the point shown; or
2. The test for the end of the loop implied by the '*' symbol cannot be evaluated at the point shown.

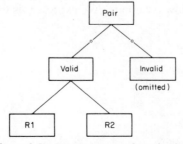

Figure 3.8   Incorrect use of a selection

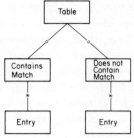

Figure 3.9   A second incorrect use of a selection

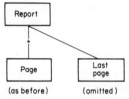

Figure 3.10   Incorrect use of an iteration

In future any structure diagram must be examined to ensure that a suitable condition can be attached to each '○' and '*' symbol. If not, this is a sure sign that a building block exists which is not necessarily closed. We must then identify both the building block, and the conditions (if any) under which it may be incomplete. Any additional logic to deal with incompleteness must be covered by a new logic construct which we shall now define.

3.3   MONITOR: A New Schematic Construct

Let X represent a nested logic building block (sequence, selection or iteration) well-defined according to the rules presented in Chapter 1, except for the following: there is a condition C such that C cannot be evaluated before X starts but can be evaluated inside X; if C becomes true inside X then X must terminate, but otherwise X goes through to its normal end. We now introduce a new building block which allows us to monitor (in the ordinary sense of the word) progress within X; if C becomes true then X terminates, otherwise X continues to its normal end; built into the logic is the ability to distinguish directly the two ways in which X can now terminate. We express this first in schematic logic:

```
M   MONITOR C
X   SEQ, IF or LOOP
    ⋮
    QUIT M IF C
    ⋮
X   ENDS
M   ADMIT
    ⋮
M   ENDS
```

In this logic:

1. The MONITOR statement announces that there follows a piece of nested logic (X), and that if C becomes true within X then X terminates early.
2. The QUIT statement shows the point inside X at which C can be evaluated. By definition, if C is true X terminates, and it is not possible to evaluate C without first starting X.
3. The ADMIT statement controls the early termination of X; thus, if X terminates early, control is transferred to the ADMIT.

Although X is usually replaced by a meaningful name, we shall usually reserve the label M to identify any monitor present. We shall often think of the QUIT as an 'escape' from the building block monitored.

Remember now that the idea of schematic logic is to provide a logic framework, and that between any two lines of schematic logic processing functions can be allocated. Evidently the ADMIT provides a point at which to carry out any processing required if X does not complete; it is implied therefore that if X does complete, we do not execute the ADMIT. Processing functions may, therefore, be allocated as follows:

```
M    MONITOR C
X    SEQ, IF or LOOP
     ⋮
     QUIT M IF C
     ⋮
X    ENDS
     Normal-end-of-X-processing
M    ADMIT
     Early-termination-of-X-processing
M    ENDS
```

Whether the ADMIT is executed or not, control always reaches 'M ENDS' as illustrated in Figure 3.11. This shows clearly how the QUIT means that X is no longer closed with respect to the logic flow. But even though X is no longer closed, M is closed.

Some essential features of the new construct are:

1. Without the use of a switch the logic now provides the ability to distinguish the two ways X terminates.
2. Although X is no longer closed with respect to the logic flow, M is closed with respect to the logic flow.
3. MONITOR is very like IF, where evaluation of the associated condition C is deferred. This is confirmed by comparing the logic flows implied by the two constructs as illustrated in Figures 3.11 and 3.12.

The implementation of MONITOR follows immediately from the logic flow illustrated in Figure 3.11; details are included in the Appendix. We note that explicit GOTO's will be required in most high-level languages, and that out-of-line code can be conveniently used for M but not for X.

80

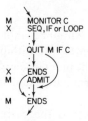

Figure 3.11   The logic flow within the MONITOR group

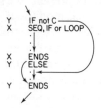

Figure 3.12   The logic flow within a selection

One of the great attractions of nested logic is the discipline imposed, particularly the fact that the logic building blocks are single-entry, single-exit, and that the ideas can be implemented in many languages without the explicit use of GOTO. We can see now that this is acceptable provided we choose problems for which the structures present are guaranteed to be complete. Some programming problems introduce structures which are not complete and for these we need the additional power provided by MONITOR. This power can easily be misused, and some programmers may object to it, since, they feel, it reintroduces the need for explicit GOTO's. It needs, therefore, to be emphasized that:

1. Distinguishing between an underlying structure which may be usefully described by nested logic, and those additional conditions for which MONITOR is required, is a major task of software design. My purpose is to describe the principles involved, provide a notation to express the results, and give examples; it is up to you to use the ideas correctly.
2. Although the QUIT is a GOTO by another name, it is a controlled GOTO; for the only place to GOTO is the associated ADMIT, and the only way to reach the ADMIT is via a QUIT. Correctly used, therefore, it does not produce 'spaghetti' code.
3. If the solution proposed is felt to be unattractive, the use of more switches is always an alternative, but in my opinion these tend to make matters worse, not better, at least on the more complex problems. The doubtful reader may want to keep checking this assertion for himself.
4. The solution proposed has the advantage that it continues to show how program logic is related to problem structure, and aids project development

by providing proper design documentation suitable for discussion and amendment before implementation starts.

So: use MONITOR when the problem demands it, and not otherwise. There are plenty of examples in this book to help develop your judgement. In spite of possible objections, including those given above, there is a wide acceptance of the need for an 'escape' construct of this kind. And since the logic is still highly disciplined we shall continue to think of it as GOTO-less in spirit, even if not strictly according to the definition used in Section 1.2.

In the next section we continue to develop this new construct. A structure diagram notation for MONITOR will then be given in Section 3.5, after which it can be used to drive the organization of program logic exactly as before.

3.4 Some Properties of MONITOR

This section continues to refer to the definition of MONITOR used in Section 3.3. The following are a few additional points designed to build the new construct up into something really useful.

1. Multi-level escapes

Since there are no restrictions on the position of QUIT inside X, the QUIT might be within one building block which is itself within X. And this could apply to any level. It is then possible for the QUIT to escape not just one level but any number of levels.

For example, if Z is a building block within X, we could have:

```
M   MONITOR C
X   SEQ, IF or LOOP
    ⋮
    Z     SEQ, IF or LOOP
          ⋮
          QUIT M IF C
          ⋮
    Z     ENDS
    ⋮
X   ENDS
M   ADMIT
    ⋮
M   ENDS
```

The QUIT transfers control outside both Z and X.

2. Multiple QUITs and ADMITs

By analogy with the multiple ELSE clauses of the selection group, we shall allow

82

multiple QUITs and multiple ADMITs within one MONITOR group:

```
M    MONITOR C1, C2 ...
X    SEQ, IF or LOOP
     ⋮
     QUIT M IF C1
     ⋮
     QUIT M IF C2
     ⋮
     (Other QUITs)
     ⋮
X    ENDS
M    ADMIT C1
     ⋮
M    ADMIT C2
     ⋮
     (Other ADMITs)
     ⋮
M    ENDS
```

The rule is: start executing X; either complete the execution of X, in which case bypass the ADMITs, or escape from X, in which case execute the appropriate ADMIT; after executing one ADMIT do not execute any other ADMIT. The flow of control is illustrated in Figure 3.13. Since schematic logic is relatively informal, the conditions (C1, C2, etc.) are used to show which QUIT ties up with which ADMIT. (A different approach would be required if one were to formalize schematic logic into a compilable language.)

From this description we could think of 'IF' as a special case of MONITOR in which:

1. C1, C2, ... can all be evaluated before X starts
2. X is executed if the condition not (C1 or C2 or ...) is true.

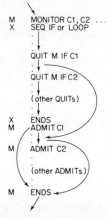

Figure 3.13   Figure 3.11 amended to show the effect of multiple ADMITs

3. Building blocks

MONITOR is a new logic building block. We can, therefore, have one MONITOR nested within another. Ultimately, the only restriction is that all the labels should remain nested. This is, incidentally, the reason why the QUIT does not have a label. (Since the purpose of QUIT is precisely to enable us to go across the normal block boundaries, the QUITs are not nested with respect to the remaining lines of schematic logic.) An outer MONITOR may then imply that an inner MONITOR is not closed, as for example:

```
M1   MONITOR C1
X1   SEQ, IF or LOOP
     :
     M2   MONITOR C2
     X2   SEQ, IF or LOOP
          :
          QUIT M1 IF C1
          :
          QUIT M2 IF C2
          :
     X2   ENDS
     M2   ADMIT C2
          :
     M2   ENDS
          :
X1   ENDS
M1   ADMIT C1
     :
M1   ENDS
```

So the strict rule is that one MONITOR may override another; and consequently MONITOR is a closed logic group unless another MONITOR indicates otherwise.

The following additional points should be noted:

1. If there is no need to distinguish the various ways in which X ends then the following 'default' notation may be useful:

```
X   SEQ, IF or LOOP
    :
    QUIT X IF C
    :
X   ENDS
```

Here the QUIT simply transfers control to 'X ENDS'. On occasions you may even be able to use an unconditional QUIT:

```
X   SEQ, IF or LOOP
    :
    QUIT X
    :
X   ENDS
```

2. Where multiple QUITs and ADMITs are used, we have presented one ADMIT per QUIT; if the processing required in one ADMIT is the same as that in another, it may be useful to allow one ADMIT to serve two or more QUITs. This would be written:

M   MONITOR C1, C2, C3 ...
X   SEQ, IF or LOOP
    ⋮
    QUIT M IF C1
    ⋮
    QUIT M IF C2
    ⋮
    QUIT M IF C3
    ⋮
X   ENDS
M   ADMIT C1 or C3
    ⋮
M   ADMIT C2
    ⋮
M   ENDS

It is not usually necessary to provide for further code-sharing within the ADMITs.

3. On occasions it may be convenient to include some intelligence (in the form of additional logic) within an ADMIT, though this will usually be of a simple nature. An example occurs in Section 4.1.

3.5   A Structure Diagram for MONITOR

We have introduced and described the logic monitor using concepts of schematic logic. This is possibly easier to grasp since it is closer to a programming language, but there is no essential reason for it; we now turn to the provision of an equivalent structure diagram, using Example 3.2.3 as an illustration. We shall apply the notation to other examples later.

Structure diagrams, as defined in Chapter 1, provide a good notation for describing nested structures (usually, so far, data structures), provided that those structures are complete; they are concise, readily assimilated, and concentrate attention on the essential features. There is no point, therefore, in trying to apply this same notation to the description of incomplete building blocks—it was not designed for that purpose.

Instead we shall retain structure diagrams, exactly as described so far, but emphasize that the building blocks they describe are assumed to be complete. The diagrams are now enhanced as follows to accommodate the presence of incompleteness. First we examine all the building blocks displayed to see if any may be incomplete, and mark the point, or points, at which incompleteness may be detected by using the upward arrow notation (exactly as illustrated in

Figure 3.7). Now think of these as the QUITs of the equivalent schematic logic. Next, determine the building block which each such condition is deemed to terminate. The rules are:

if a building block may be incomplete, it must be subject to a MONITOR; but if there is no need to distinguish the various ways in which it can terminate, then the MONITOR can be placed at a higher level
any building block for which different processing is required depending on whether or not it terminated early, must itself be subject to a MONITOR

As a check, remember that if a building block is always complete, it must not be subject to a MONITOR.

Next, for any building block subject to MONITOR, surround the corresponding building block on the structure diagram with square brackets: [ ]; thus, if End-of-file in the middle of a page is deemed to terminate the current page, the square brackets [ ] surround the box called 'Page', as in Figure 3.14.

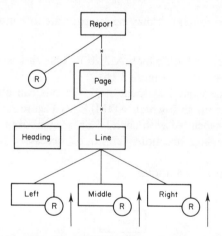

Figure 3.14   Showing MONITOR on a structure diagram

The square brackets [ ] representing the MONITOR always surround one box only; apart possibly from removing any shorthand in order to make extra room for the square brackets, the rest of the structure diagram remains quite unaltered. The positioning of the symbols between boxes should make it clear which building blocks are inside, and which outside, the MONITOR.

Finally, for each MONITOR, decide how many ADMITs are required. As a first step, it is usually best to allow one ADMIT for each QUIT; if later analysis shows that the same processing is required in two or more ADMITs then these can later be condensed into one. Each ADMIT is represented by a further set of square brackets placed at the same level as, and to the right of, the building block MONITORed. For Example 3.2.3 only one ADMIT is required; this is illustrated in Figure 3.15.

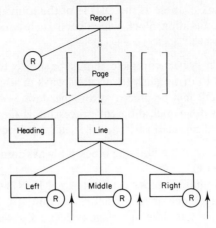

Figure 3.15   Showing ADMIT on a structure diagram

Depending on the context, it may be appropriate to annotate the diagram to show, for example:

1. which QUIT ties up with which ADMIT. This can be done with a simple connector convention (as Figure 3.16)
2. the conditions associated with each QUIT; this can also be used to show which QUIT ties up with which ADMIT (as Figure 3.17)
3. the conditions associated with each '∘' or '*' symbol (as Figure 3.18)
4. any other processing functions felt to be necessary (as, for example, in Figure 3.19)
5. any combination of 1–4 above.

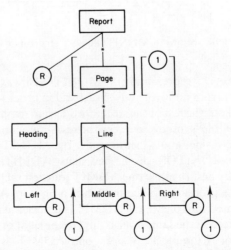

Figure 3.16   Controlling the escapes with connectors

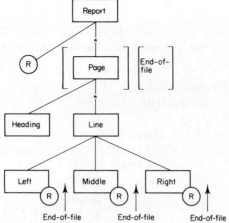

Figure 3.17   Showing the escape conditions

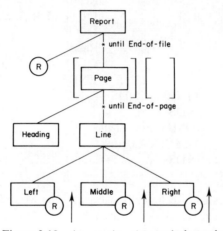

Figure 3.18   Annotating the symbols used

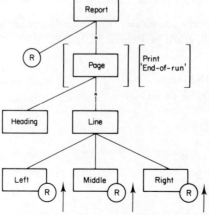

Figure 3.19   Showing additional processing functions

The MONITOR is not usually labelled on the structure diagram. For completeness, here is the schematic logic corresponding to Figure 3.19:

```
            Read
REPORT   LOOP until End-of-file
         M          MONITOR End-of-file
         PAGE   SEQ
                DO Heading
                {LINE}   LOOP until End-of-page
                            LINE    SEQ
                                    DO Left
                                    Read
                                    QUIT M IF End-of-file
                                    DO Middle
                                    Read
                                    QUIT M IF End-of-file
                                    DO Right
                                    Read
                                    QUIT M IF End-of-filc
                            LINE    ENDS
                {LINE}   ENDS
         PAGE   ENDS
         M          ADMIT End-of-file
                    Print 'End-of-run'
         M          ENDS
REPORT   ENDS
```

There is, of course, no technical reason why the MONITOR should not be placed at line level, or at file level, though in the first case some consequent changes would then be necessary so that the inner loop unwinds correctly at End-of-file.

The following are two extreme cases to consolidate the conventions:

1. *Allocation of processing functions*. The following schematic logic is equivalent to the structure diagram of Figure 3.20:

```
Y   SEQ
    M          MONITOR ...
    X          SEQ, IF or LOOP
                  ⋮
    X          ENDS
               DO A
    M          ADMIT
               DO B
    M          ENDS
    DO C
Y   ENDS
```

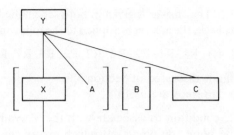

Figure 3.20   A complex diagram with processing functions allocated

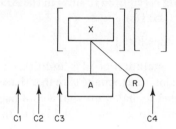

Figure 3.21   A diagram with multiple QUITs

2. *Multiple QUITs*. Since there is no restriction on the number of QUITs, we could in theory produce a complex diagram as in Figure 3.21; in this case the QUITs are read naturally from left to right:

M   MONITOR C1, C2, C3, C4
X   SEQ
    QUIT M IF C1
    QUIT M IF C2
    QUIT M IF C3
    DO A
    Read
    QUIT M IF C4
X   ENDS
M   ADMIT
M   ENDS

As the examples used become more complex, so we shall make greater use of these types of diagrams.

3.6   Problem Resolved—Record Sequence Errors

We return to the example discussed in Section 3.2.1 to determine the additional logic required to detect and recover from record sequence errors in Batch Type 1. The discussion assumes familiarity with the points made in Section 3.2.1 and the content of Figure 3.2. The answer is given in both schematic logic and structure diagram form. As a check, the answer is applied to the following record sequence:

B1, R1, R2, R1, R1, R1, R2, R2, R2, R1, R3, R7, R1, B3, etc.

An alternative design is discussed in Section 3.9.
The following design steps are useful:

1. Define a suitable condition to associate with the '*' symbol.
2. Now identify the point, or points, at which errors can arise. (These will become the QUITs.)
3. Choose a suitable level for the MONITOR to control the escapes.
4. Decide what processing is required (if any) in the ADMIT(s) associated with the MONITOR and QUIT(s).

Following the design steps listed:

1. The most suitable interpretation of '*' is 'until Batch Header or End-of-file'.
2. Two QUITs are sufficient, one to make sure that the sequence (R1, R2) begins with an R1, and the other to make sure that it continues with an R2. Note that it is perfectly permissible to use more QUITs but these two are all that are strictly necessary.
3. Each QUIT defined must relate to a MONITOR, and may relate to the same MONITOR. For this exercise only one MONITOR is necessary, although there is nothing technically wrong in using more than one. Further, the MONITOR must be placed at a level which does not necessarily entail End-of-batch. It follows that the MONITOR cannot be outside the loop (for each QUIT would then terminate the loop, which is effectively going to End-of-batch, while not all sequence errors imply End-of-batch); the MONITOR must, therefore, be inside the loop, which leaves the pair (R1, R2) as the only group to be monitored.

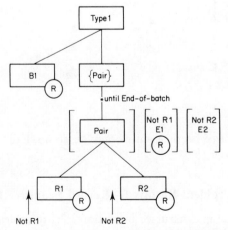

Figure 3.22   Figure 3.1 amended to show the logic to detect and recover from record sequence errors

4. Since there are two QUITs, we start off with two ADMITs, one for each QUIT. Each ADMIT represents an error; let E1 be the error produced if the first member of a pair is not R1, and E2 be the error produced if the second member of a pair is not R2. On detecting E1, the logic knows that the record pointed at is not a Batch Header, End-of-file, or R1; it is, therefore, useless, and the read-ahead principle tells us to Read the next record. On detecting E2, the logic only knows that the record pointed at is itself not the R2 to go with the previous R1; this record may still turn out to be useful (it could be End-of-batch, for example) and so no read-ahead is required.

We now have the complete logic as illustrated in Figure 3.22; this is equivalent to the following schematic logic:

```
TYPE1   SEQ
        DO B1
        Read
        {PAIR}  LOOP until End-of-batch
                M       MONITOR Record sequence errors
                PAIR    SEQ
                        QUIT M IF not R1
                        DO R1
                        Read
                        QUIT M IF not R2
                        DO R2
                        Read
                PAIR    ENDS
                M       ADMIT not R1
                        DO E1
                        Read
                M       ADMIT not R2
                        DO E2
                M       ENDS
        {PAIR}  ENDS
TYPE1   ENDS
```

The record sequence specified produces the following errors:

$$E2, \quad E2, \quad E1, \quad E1, \quad E2, \quad E1, \quad E1, \quad E2$$

The following are two errors commonly made when designing this logic:

1. If the Read after 'DO E1' is omitted, then the logic gets into a loop (when processing the second of the three consecutive R2's in the sequence given)
2. If an extra Read is inserted after 'DO E2' then the logic produces fewer error messages but misses End-of-batch (by eventually overwriting the B3 before it has a chance to terminate the loop)

If you are still puzzled, then here is the full record sequence again, annotated to show the pairs detected and the error messages produced:

B1
R1
R2   First pair
R1

      Missing R2 (E2)
R1

      Missing R2 (E2)
R1
R2   Second pair
R2   Not R1 (E1)
R2   Not R1 (E1)
R1

      Missing R2 (E2)
R3   Not R1 (E1)
R7   Not R1 (E1)
R1

      Missing R2 (E2)
B3
etc.

The errors may be interpreted as:

1. E1 means 'the sequence (R1, R2) did not get started, so begin again from the next record'
2. E2 means 'the sequence (R1, R2) got started but did not complete, so report the R1 found as an incomplete pair and begin again from whatever caused the error'.

For completeness, here are a few notes on the detection and recovery from errors in the other two batch types.

Batch Type 3 has such a simple structure that the logic of Figure 3.23 would suffice. Thus, even with errors, the structure is still nested. If you feel that errors

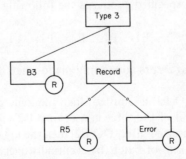

Figure 3.23   Record sequence errors in Batch Type 3 (without MONITOR)

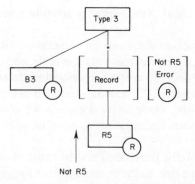

Figure 3.24   Record sequence errors in Batch Type 3 (with MONITOR)

should be detected using MONITOR, you may prefer the logic of Figure 3.24. I leave it to you to prove that these are equivalent. Similar considerations apply to Batch Type 2. The logic required to detect a missing batch header at Start-of-file can be treated in a variety of ways and raises no new points of principle. This now covers all possible record sequence errors.

3.7   Problem Resolved—Table Look-up

This is a slight extension of the problem considered in Section 3.2.2. We are given a table whose structure is as described in Figure 3.25. Each entry in the table consists of an entry-key (which identifies the entry) and an entry-value (which contains some associated information). We are also given a parameter which consists of a parameter-key and a parameter-reply. We shall now design a program to search the table; if an entry is found whose entry-key is equal to the parameter-key, the corresponding entry-value must be moved to parameter-reply and the search terminated; otherwise, if no matching entry-key is found, an

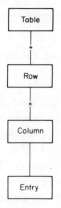

Figure 3.25   Data structure for a two-dimensional table

error subroutine is executed. The answer is given in schematic logic, and as a structure diagram.

First, recall that structure diagrams are generally written from file level to record level; in this case the counterpart of file is table, and of record is entry. And just as we have usually found no need to describe the internal structure of record, so there is no need to describe the internal structure of entry. Even so, no harm would be done by showing entry as (say) a sequence of entry-key followed by entry-value, or even by showing entry-key as equal to, or not equal to, parameter-key.

Next, the two '*' symbols: provision must be made to examine all rows in the table and all columns in a row, so the outer and inner loops terminate on 'End-of-table' and 'End-of-row' respectively. If a matching entry is found, both loops terminate early, and the only way to do this is with MONITOR. The MONITOR must be placed outside the outer loop (since if it were inside the loop then any QUIT associated with the MONITOR would not terminate the loop). Since there is only one QUIT, we need only one ADMIT. All this is described in Figure 3.26 which also shows the two main processing functions allocated on the diagram. The equivalent schematic logic (with standard loop control functions also allocated) is:

```
              Move 1 to I
M             MONITOR Entry-found
TABLE   LOOP until End-of-table
              Move 1 to J
       ROW    LOOP until End-of-row
                    COLUMN    SEQ
                              QUIT M IF Entry-key (I, J) = Parameter-key
                    COLUMN    ENDS
                    Add 1 to J
       ROW    ENDS
              Add 1 to I
TABLE   ENDS
              DO Error
M             ADMIT
              Move Entry-value (I, J) to Parameter-reply
M             ENDS
```

Very many table searches are of this kind. The differences usually concern the detailed mechanism to move on from one entry to the next, and to detect the end of each loop. In the example given, a simple indexing scheme is implied; but a variety of other options is available to the systems designer, usually based on the use of pointers of one kind or another. Thus, lots of tables might have the same structure; the only difference between one instance and the next concerns the type of pointer used, and hence the detailed mechanism for controlling the loop.

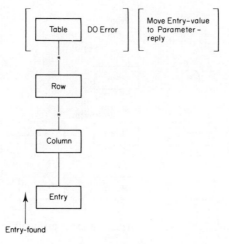

Figure 3.26   The logic to detect Entry-found, with processing functions allocated

3.8   Problem Resolved—Printed Report

This is a variation on the example used in Section 3.2.3. We are given a printed report whose structure is as illustrated in Figures 3.5 and 3.6 and asked to amend the logic to print the following page footings:

Page Footing	When Printed
F1	For the last page if it is not complete
F2	For the last page if it is complete
F3	For all pages except the last page

We shall also prove that under no circumstances will a page be printed which contains page headings and no detail lines. (This exercise is not as easy as it looks!)

As a first step, we should amend the basic structure diagram to show F3 printed for all 'normal' pages (that is, all pages except the last). Next, note that the two loops terminate on 'End-of-file' and on 'End-of-page' respectively. These points are illustrated in Figure 3.27.

There is no difficulty in seeing that if End-of-file occurs after printing Left or Middle, then the final page is incomplete and F1 must be printed. This leads us to Figure 3.28 (the expanded version of the diagram being used to give more room). The only problem remaining is End-of-file occurring after printing Right. Here we have to distinguish:

1. End-of-file at the end of a line but in the middle of a page; from
2. End-of-file at the end of a line and at the end of a page.

96

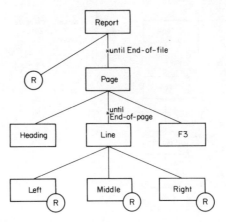

Figure 3.27   Revised structure for a printed report

This could be done by putting two QUITs to check the result of the Read after printing Right. It is better to notice that if no QUIT is placed at this point, then in case 2 above the loop through the lines will unwind, whereas in case 1 it will not. We can, therefore, distinguish the two cases by placing one QUIT before Left (this detects case 1) and another QUIT before F3 (this detects case 2). This leads us to Figure 3.29. The equivalent schematic logic is left to the reader.

Finally, if page headings are printed then we can deduce that it is not End-of-file. (This follows from the fact that the test for the end of the loop through the

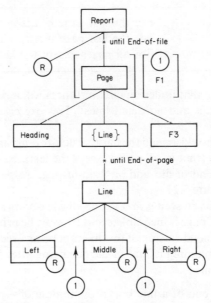

Figure 3.28   The addition of some logic to detect End-of-file

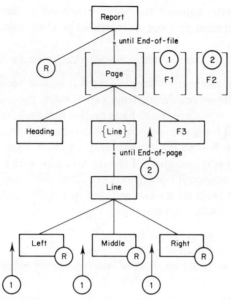

Figure 3.29   The complete logic with all processing functions allocated

pages is placed at the beginning of the loop). If it is not End-of-file then at least the Left of the first line must be printed. Hence there is no chance that a page will be printed which consists of page headings and no detail lines.

The main lessons from this exercise are:

1. The loop through the lines on a page terminates on End-of-page. If End-of-file occurs in the middle of a page, then this is simply End-of-file in the middle of a page. This contrasts with many examples (such as that in Section 2.4) where end of a high level is taken as end of all lower levels.
2. The QUITs may turn up in surprising places; in this case it is by no means obvious to place a QUIT before Left; equally it is not obvious to place a QUIT before F3.
3. It is certainly possible to produce alternative solutions, either by allocating different conditions to the loops, or by placing the QUITs differently. The solution given seems to me to be the best.

This type of logic is typical of a wide range of examples, such as multipage invoices or statements in accounts applications.

3.9   Further Reflections on the Role of Structured Programming

We return (for positively the last time) to the example first introduced in Section 1.5 and last considered in Section 3.6, and ask:

1. Is the logic given in Section 3.6 the best, or only, way to handle the errors, and can we judge between the alternatives?

98

2. Does this example support the views expressed in Section 1.6 about the separate, complementary roles of structured programming and the functional techniques?
3. What would be the consequences of not using structured programming?

We start with an alternative design. Given the same basic problem, we now detect and recover from record sequence errors using the following philosophy: first look for an R1; having found it, hang on to it and look for an R2 to go with it; having found an R2 repeat the process until eventually End-of-batch is detected.

The phrase 'look for an R1' means 'loop until an R1 is found rejecting all records up to the next R1 as errors'. Likewise when looking for an R2. A monitor is still required because no R1 or R2 may be found. With this in mind the logic to detect and recover from errors is illustrated in Figure 3.30, in which the error messages have the following meanings:

E1 means 'R1 not found after B1 or R2'
E2 means 'R2 not found after R1'
E3 means 'we have an R1 but End-of-batch occurred before we found an R2 to go with it'.

The reader should check that, using the typical record sequence given in Section 3.6, the logic now detects a different R1 as belonging to the second pair, and that the error messages produced are:

E2, E2, E1, E1, E2, E2, E2, E3

These results contrast with those of Section 3.6.

I happen to think that the logic of Section 3.6 is the best way to design this

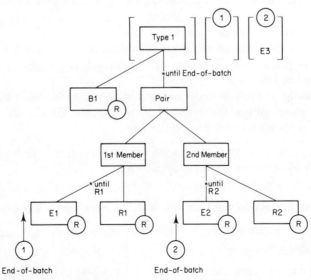

Figure 3.30   An alternative strategy to Figure 3.22 to detect record sequence errors

program (because it is the easiest to generalize), but we can now see that it is certainly not the only way. Indeed, further designs could be introduced by trying to process two records at a time, or even by treating End-of-batch as an escape from a loop which proceeds indefinitely. Perhaps there are yet more. But the real point is that there are frequently different ways of doing things. One could try to find criteria to show which is the 'best way', but it is sufficient to admit that in practice different people like to do things in different ways; and the most that can be asked of any programmer is: having chosen one design, do please produce some design documentation which clearly displays the design principles used, so that somebody else can, if necessary, find their way around your program. In the last resort, any judgement between the possible designs must be taken by a systems analyst, since it is he or she who is responsible for designing the user interface, and it is the user who will have to interpret the results.

We now turn to questions of modularity, and the separate roles of functional and structured techniques. As in Section 1.6, it remains true that all diagrams produced are fully modular ('DO R1' still means 'validate record of type R1'; 'DO E1' means 'execute error subroutine to produce report E1', and so on). We have simply used structured programming concepts to help design the logic internal to the topmost module. Indeed, we can corroborate the distinction drawn in Section 1.6 between the design and presentation of high-level control logic, and the design and presentation of application processing routines. Broadly, we confirm the view then expressed that:

1. High-level control logic is difficult to design and requires specialized techniques (namely, those with which this book is concerned). Comparatively little processing is carried out at this high level.
2. Apart from the high-level control logic, the rest of a program is concerned with the description of application processing, or business rules. While these might be voluminous, the logic required should be relatively straightforward.

All this remains true. In my opinion the need for high-level control logic arises as a consequence of decisions taken during systems design; the low-level modules normally contain a simple description of what the application is all about, and would be much the same however the system were implemented. In a commercial context we might expect to find that systems analysts would be most at home describing the application processing, or rules of business; programmers, on the other hand, are closer to the computer and should be more comfortable dealing with control logic (and the design of data structures to support it). Thus it seem to me that the two major roles in commercial systems definition are systems design (with its implications for control logic) and systems analysis (as the description of business rules); in other environments these roles are frequently played by one and the same person. The two tasks are contrasting and complementary; the former demands the use of new and purpose-built techniques, while the latter is generally well understood.

Finally, we may check the consequences of not using structured programming techniques for control logic design. Taking the extreme case, we could revert to the simple logic of Figure 1.27 (with its single-read approach) and take steps now to add in the extra logic to detect and recover from record sequence errors. For example, if this logic detects an R2, switches are now required to remember the context, and used to check for record sequence errors:

was the previous record an R1?
was the last batch header a B1?

We readily acknowledge that this logic can always be implemented retaining the single Read, frequently without the use of GOTO; but the logic is then no longer based upon the structure. I have also come across a widespread tendency to push control logic down into the application processing routines as if it formed part of the detailed record validation. It is my view that these routines should never be concerned with questions of context. In the solution presented in Section 3.6, we interpret 'DO R1' to mean 'execute subroutine R1 given that the current record is R1, and is in context'; it is simply bad practice (in my opinion) to interpret 'DO R1' as meaning 'execute subroutine R1 given that the current record is R1', and then expect this subroutine itself to check that the record is in context.

We are concerned in general to separate out the control logic, place it in a purpose-built top-level control routine, and provide new techniques for its design. These techniques may involve the use of a logic monitor. But for the reasons explained earlier we feel that the use of MONITOR is clearer and more expressive than the alternatives using switches. The subject is important since control logic design is frequently neglected in practice and can be the cause of major headaches if designed incorrectly. The next chapter extends the range of applications considered.

Chapter 4
Six Worked Examples

The examples used in Chapters 1 to 3 were drawn mainly from commercial systems. In each case the structure was elicited from an examination of the data used. At its simplest, the data used was organized into an order which was convenient for processing; program structure and data structure were then closely related. But, as we have already warned, there are other programs where the concept of data structure is hardly present at all. In these cases we shall need to look more widely to identify the structures required.

Accordingly, this chapter applies the principles of structured programming to six new examples. These illustrate further applications drawn from commercial data processing, but also system utilities and scientific applications. The intention is to show that the principles described in earlier chapters are universal; the designer's skill then comes in recognizing familiar patterns in new and unfamiliar contexts. You are encouraged, therefore, to study each example at least sufficiently to get the 'flavour'. The particular complexities of on-line systems are reserved until Chapter 5, and of real-time systems until Chapter 8.

All the examples in this chapter use the concepts of nested logic and logic monitor, often for different effects. In each case nested logic is used to analyse structures (that is, ordered event sequences) which are complete. We shall find that such structures can frequently only be identified by making certain simplifications; removing the simplifications then introduces the possibility of incompleteness—that is, early termination of an otherwise nested structure. The additional logic then required to analyse the full event sequence is described using the monitor. Together, nested logic and the logic monitor provide a unifying conceptual framework for program design; it is then for the reader to apply the concepts to his own examples. We shall find, too, that the examples introduced in this chapter extend the range of structures considered from 'static' data structures (which exist independently of the program which analyses them) to 'dynamic' structures (which are created during a program's execution, but have no tangible existence). Later chapters will serve both to consolidate and extend these points.

102

While extensive use is made of the logic monitor, I would like to repeat that each example could be written without MONITOR, but only by introducing switches and with a consequent loss of design and structural clarity. (This last point is, of course, a subjective judgement, but is a major justification for the design approach advocated.)

4.1 A Complex Batch-mode Validation Program

4.1.1 Error detection and recovery

We start with a more complex batch-mode validation program. The results can be applied to many programs concerned with error and invalidity conditions; one such application is given in Section 4.2.

A program is required to analyse data input. Under normal error-free conditions this will have the structure shown in Figure 4.1.1. We shall now design the additional logic required to detect and recover from all record sequence errors. (The answer given is expressed in both structure diagram and schematic logic notation.)

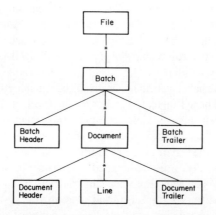

Figure 4.1.1   Structure of data input to a validation program

Assuming no record sequence errors, Figure 4.1.2 shows how the Read instruction is allocated, and the conditions attached to each '*'. Since records are guaranteed to occur in the correct sequence:

1. The condition 'until End-of-batch' can be implemented as 'until Batch Trailer'.
2. The condition 'until End-of-document' can be implemented as 'until Document Trailer'.
3. The result of each Read must be an in-sequence record.

We now allow the possibility of record sequence errors, so that each Read can, in theory, read a record of any type (including one whose type is unrecognizable).

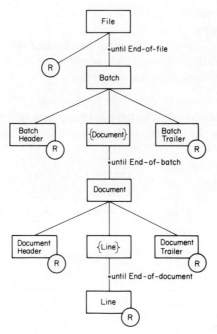

Figure 4.1.2   The Read instruction, and loop-terminating conditions

The following steps define a suitable design strategy, and summarize the design principles.

Step 1: Re-evaluate the conditions which terminate each level

We take advantage of the header and trailer records to define the following conditions:

1. Each level starts on finding the header record for that level, with the proviso that a lower level cannot start until all higher levels have been correctly started.
2. Each level terminates on finding either the trailer record which terminates that level, or any other record which belongs at a higher level.

As a consequence, we can implement:

'until End-of-batch' as 'until Batch Trailer, Batch Header, or End-of-file'
'until End-of-document' as 'until Document Trailer, Document Header, Batch Trailer, Batch Header, or End-of-file'.

Step 2: Identify the points at which errors can arise

By inspection, there are five possible errors:

1. No batch header
2. No document header

104

3. Document trailer missing
4. Batch trailer missing
5. After finding an in-sequence document header and before detecting End-of-document, a record is found which is not a batch header, batch trailer, document header, document trailer, or line.

Detection of these errors is illustrated in Figure 4.1.3. We refer below to the errors as E1 to E5 respectively. (We have assumed here that it is perfectly valid to have a batch with no documents, and a document with no lines. This point is covered again below.)

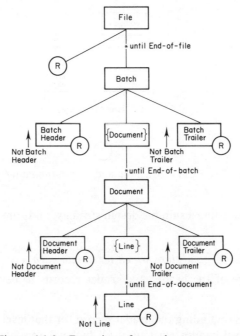

Figure 4.1.3   Detection of record sequence errors

Step 3: Add in extra logic for error recovery

The principles of Section 3.6 suggest that for each of the two sequences (batch level and document level), there are two errors which can arise. At batch level:

1. The sequence does not even get started (E1), in which case begin again from the next record.
2. The sequence starts but is incomplete (E4), in which case begin again from whatever caused the incompleteness.

Likewise at document level. Finally, an error at line level (E5) does not terminate the loop through the lines. Together with the points made in steps 1 and 2 above, this suggests the logic given in Figure 4.1.4. This diagram has been simplified by re-using the error numbers given in step 2 for the connectors and omitting any

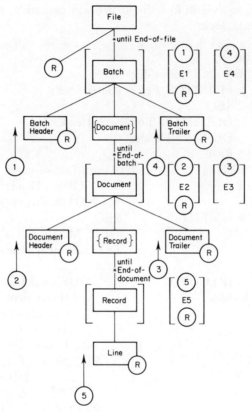

Figure 4.1.4   The complete logic to detect and recover from record sequence errors

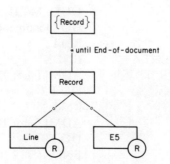

Figure 4.1.5   An alternative for detecting line-level errors

narrative describing the error; even so, it is still a perfectly clear and concise summary of what is, on any account, a complex piece of logic. The monitor at line level is, of course, equivalent to a simple two-way condition, as in Figure 4.1.5 and in the schematic logic:

```
              Read
FILE          LOOP until End-of-file
   M1            MONITOR Errors (Batch level)
   BATCH         SEQ
                 QUIT M1 IF not Batch Header
                 DO Batch Header
                 Read
      {DOCUMENT}          LOOP until End-of-batch (Batch Trailer,
                                        Batch Header or End-of-file)
          M2                  MONITOR Errors (Document level)
          DOCUMENT            SEQ
                              QUIT M2 IF not Document Header
                              DO Document Header
                              Read
              {RECORD}            LOOP until End-of-Document
                                        (Document Trailer,
                                        Document Header, Batch
                                        Trailer, Batch Header or
                                        End-of-file)
                                     RECORD   IF Line
                                              DO Line
                                              Read
                                     RECORD   ELSE
                                              DO E5
                                              Read
                                     RECORD   ENDS
              {RECORD}               ENDS
                              QUIT M2 IF not Document Trailer
                              DO Document Trailer
                              Read
          DOCUMENT            ENDS
          M2                  ADMIT not Document Header
                              DO E2
                              Read
          M2                  ADMIT not Document Trailer
                              DO E3
          M2                  ENDS
      {DOCUMENT}          ENDS
                 QUIT M1 IF not Batch Trailer
                 DO Batch Trailer
                 Read
```

```
BATCH          ENDS
M1             ADMIT not Batch Header
               DO E1
               Read
M1             ADMIT not Batch Trailer
               DO E4
M1             ENDS
FILE      ENDS
```

This is easily the most complex example we have used so far, so let us take this opportunity to remind ourselves of the essential points:

1. Great care must be taken over the conditions attached to each '*' symbol (and, although it does not apply in this case, over each '○' symbol). Once suitable conditions have been attached, it is possible to inspect the diagram, and locate precisely all the points at which errors can arise. Even though it might now be possible to arrange the logic for error recovery in different ways to achieve different effects, the logic given is, in my view, the most elegant and the most easy to generalize.
2. The design is fully modular. Thus, for example, the statement 'DO Document Header' means 'execute a subroutine to carry out all the detailed validation'; in our presentation this subroutine is only called when the control logic is absolutely confident that it has detected a document header, and that this record is in sequence. The detailed validation may itself detect other errors, and this may even have consequential effects for the control logic, but is outside the scope of our consideration.
3. The logic given will require the use of some GOTO's when implemented in most high-level languages. These could be eliminated, but only through the introduction of other complications such as switches; in my view it is better to accept the need for the explicit GOTO's.

4.1.2 Some specification changes, testing, and backtracking

4.1.2.1 Specification changes

We consider briefly the effect of three specification changes. The points made should answer some of the queries frequently raised by students of this example.

1. Insist on at least one document in a batch

We could either:

1. Amend the structure diagram at batch level to insist on at least one document; another sequence check (using MONITOR) is then required in case a batch is found with no documents;

or

2. Keep a count of documents found and treat the check to make sure that there is at least one document as part of the validation of the batch trailer. This check is then treated in the same way as any other detailed validation error.

Similar considerations would apply if the specification were to insist on at least one line in a document. My own preference would be for option 2.

2. Reduce the number of errors reported

This can be done by introducing intelligence into the ADMITs. We consider two cases:

1. No batch header; the following amendment will produce one error message and then loop until the main logic can restart:

   ```
   M1        ADMIT not Batch Header
             DO E1
   M1LOOP    LOOP until Batch Header or End-of-file
             Read
   M1LOOP    ENDS
   M1        ENDS
   ```

2. Missing batch trailer; it would be a simple matter to avoid printing an error by creating a batch trailer record inside the ADMIT. This might introduce new complications; any benefits can only be assessed in the context of the application concerned.

3. Add in further processing constraints

The logic distinguishes two ways in which a batch can terminate: with, or without, a batch trailer. Sometimes full interpretation of a batch, and the processing functions required, would also be affected by additional considerations such as:

were the batch header and batch trailer valid, and did any cross-checks (such as the accumulation of control totals) fail?
were there any other record sequence errors within the batch, or any significant record validation errors?

Further logic is necessary to express all of these conditions, and is best treated as part of the processing of a batch trailer. Further observations on this are made in Section 4.1.2.3.

4.1.2.2 Testing

To check that the logic works, we adopt the following abbreviations:

BH: Batch Header
DH: Document Header
L: Line
DT: Document Trailer
BT: Batch Trailer
X: Any other record (i.e. unrecognizable record type)

and use the (deliberately weird) record sequence below:

BH, DH, L, L, DT, DH, DT, BT, BH, BT, DH, BH, L, DH, L, DH, L, DT, DT, BH, L, BH, DH, BH, DT, DH, L, DH, L, BT, DH, BH, DH, L, X, L, X, End-of-file

Using the numbering convention given in Step 2 in Section 4.1.1 above, the errors detected are:

E1, E2, E3, E2, E4, E2, E4, E3, E4, E2, E3, E3, E1, E5, E5, E3, E4

The following shows where the errors are detected:

BH
DH
L
L
DT
DH
DT
BT
BH
BT
DH   Not Batch Header   (E1)
BH
L   Not Document Header   (E2)
DH
L
       Missing Document Trailer   (E3)
DH
L
DT
DT   Not Document Header   (E2)
       Missing Batch Trailer   (E4)
BH
L   Not Document Header   (E2)
       Missing Batch Trailer   (E4)
BH
DH
       Missing Document Trailer   (E3)
       Missing Batch Trailer   (E4)
BH
DT   Not Document Header   (E2)
DH
L
       Missing Document Trailer   (E3)
DH
L

110

```
        Missing Document Trailer   (E3)
BT
DH   Not Batch Header   (E1)
BH
DH
L
X    Unrecognizable record type   (E5)
L
X    Unrecognizable record type   (E5)
     Missing Document Trailer   (E3)
     Missing Batch Trailer        (E4)
End-of-file
```

4.1.2.3 Backtracking

Suppose now that processing of individual records depends on a knowledge of whether a batch is valid or not. For example, if a batch is valid each record in the batch updates a reference file, but not otherwise. Evidently, we do not know how to process individual records until we have reached End-of-batch. In such a case we have a choice; either:

update the reference file while processing the batch, accepting the risk that such processing may later have to be undone if the batch turns out to be invalid

or

defer any updates to the reference file until we have reached End-of-batch, and are then in a position to decide whether or not to carry out the updates

The first choice illustrates an idea commonly known as 'backtracking', as if at the end of a batch we may have to track back to its beginning and reinterpret work already done; the second choice is the one more commonly taken, and is based on the strategic considerations analysed below.

Whenever insufficient information is available to determine completely the processing required for each record, then we have no choice but to take defensive measures when processing a record in order to protect ourselves later. This usually involves the creation of a temporary intermediate file to hold the records in a batch, and the use of memory to keep a note of the results of processing thus far. The temporary file may be held in main memory or on disk; in either case it represents an additional data structure, created because the problem itself restricts the order in which processing functions can be executed.

For one batch the sequence of events is now strictly:

1. Start processing the batch.
2. As records are read, save them in the intermediate file, and remember any other data which may be required to interpret the records later.
3. At some point (such as End-of-batch) interpret the records saved (e.g. as valid or not) using the data remembered.

4. Then retrieve and process the intermediate file accordingly, possibly undoing some work already carried out.

Now the logic is always moving forwards processing one data structure to create another. I find this preferable to the concept of backtracking. Whether it is essential to show such intermediate data structures explicitly in the design process depends upon the complexity of the problem being analysed.

4.2   An Application to Syntax Analysis

This section assumes familiarity with the results of Section 4.1. Suppose that a program is required to analyse a stream of characters. The recognizable characters are, say:

$$/ \quad \% \quad -$$

and these take on a significance similar to the header and trailer records of the previous example according to the following table:

Old Record	New Character
Batch Header	/
Document Header	%
Line	-
Document Trailer	%
Batch Trailer	/

Then the order in which characters appear can be described by means of the structure diagram shown in Figure 4.2.1; an illustrative valid character string would be:

$$/\%--\%\%---\%\%\%/// \quad \text{etc.}$$

If characters must appear consecutively (that is, no space or other 'noise' characters are allowed), then we can define a subscript (I, say) to index the character string, and define a new Read instruction:

$$\text{Add 1 to } I$$

The logic to detect and recover from errors follows immediately from Figure 4.1.4; the result is given in Figure 4.2.2, in which the names attached to boxes should be self-explanatory. This ignores the presence (if any) of blocking, and assumes some suitable technique to detect End-of-file.

If 'noise' characters are allowed, then the only alteration required is to redefine Read as: 'loop until first non-noise character found'.

We could think of the character sequence described as defining a kind of

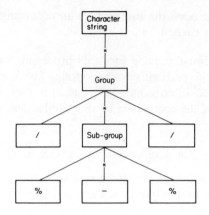

Figure 4.2.1   Structure of a character string

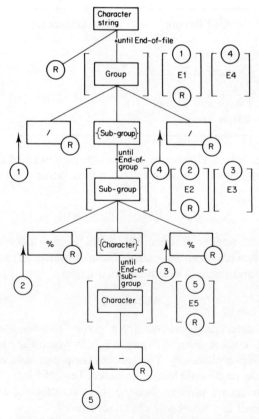

Figure 4.2.2   Analysis of the character string

syntax, albeit a primitive syntax. Let us now extend the syntax, using a simple job control language in which the statements used are as follows:

Statement	Function
Job Header	Defines the job to be done and provides job level parameters (accounting code, date, etc.)
Program	Names the program to be executed
File	Locates the units and files to be used
End	Terminates the job

We assume that these statements are input on some device, and that the job control stream can only be terminated by detecting an End statement. Suppose now that each statement constitutes a record, suitably identified, and that statements should appear in the order described by Figure 4.2.3; in this diagram

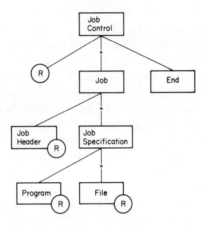

Figure 4.2.3   Job control statements

the result of executing a Read is the next job control statement. If now we allow the possibility of record (that is, job control statement) sequence errors, then the logic required to detect and recover from these errors can again be based on that given in Figure 4.1.4. The details are omitted; the errors detected would be:

1. No Job Header statement
2. No Program statement
3. After finding an in-sequence Program statement, and before detecting End-of-job-specification, a statement is found which is unrecognizable (that is, not a Job Header, Program, File, or End statement).

We note that as defined there is no possibility of a missing End statement.

Suppose further that each statement has itself got an internal structure, as given in Figure 4.2.4. If the keywords used were 'JOB', 'PROGRAM', 'FILE', and 'END', then a typical statement might be written:

$$PROGRAM = ABCD$$

We refer to the components of a statement (in this case 'PROGRAM', '=', 'ABCD') as fields; without yet considering how fields are recognized, the Read statement of Figure 4.2.3 could now be implemented as a call to a subroutine

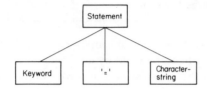

Figure 4.2.4   Internal structure of a job control statement

whose internal logic is defined in Figure 4.2.5, and in which the new Read instruction means 'Get next field'. The result of a call to this subroutine is now, as required, a job control statement identified as JOB, PROGRAM, FILE, END, or marked as unrecognizable; each statement is marked invalid if the remaining fields are incorrect (further definition of this term being omitted).

Figure 4.2.3 is, therefore, designed as if there existed a serial file on which each record were a job control statement, and suitably identified. Some records act as header and some as trailer records. Record sequence errors can be detected in the normal way. As it happens, the Read instruction is implemented as a call to a subroutine whose job it is to protect the calling program from the need to consider those additional rules which affect the recognition of statements. While Figure 4.2.5 implements one such (and a particularly crude) set of rules, some alternatives would be:

1. Alter Figure 4.2.5 so that it returns to the main program only after detecting a valid keyword (JOB, PROGRAM, FILE or END).
2. Alter Figure 4.2.5 so that when looking for a particular field (Keyword, '=', or string) it discards all others until the one sought is found, and then continues by looking for the next field.
3. Alter Figure 4.2.5 so that it allows a different internal structure for each of the possible keywords.

The detailed changes required in each case are omitted. The possibilities suggest that logic design and syntax definition are inseparable. It is not for us to choose between them since we are concerned only to show how to analyse the problem. The additional considerations which may arise from blocking and deblocking (including field recognition) are covered in Section 7.3.4.

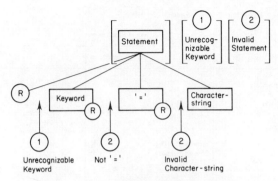

Figure 4.2.5   Validation of a statement

4.3   A Micro-based Screen Editor

4.3.1 The editing facilities available

This example illustrates how a simple underlying structure can be greatly complicated by the need for multiple loop-terminating conditions. These conditions are best analysed using the MONITOR concept.

A microcomputer is being used to control editing of data held on a cassette (or other serial device). The editing is done at a terminal (consisting of keyboard and VDU screen), and the updated information is written forward to a new cassette, as illustrated in Figure 4.3.1. Information is held on the cassette in fixed-length records, 12 records to a block. On the VDU, one line is sufficient to display the contents of one record, and up to 20 records can be displayed at any one time. The microcomputer's memory is large enough to hold up to 4 blocks (48 records) at a time. These points are illustrated by the 'snapshot' shown in Figure 4.3.2. The following editing operations are allowed on the VDU:

1. Add a line (before or after any line currently displayed)
2. Delete a line (any line currently displayed)
3. Scroll screen forward (1 line at a time)
4. Scroll screen backward (1 line at a time)

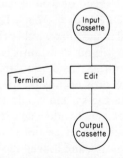

Figure 4.3.1   A screen editor program

116

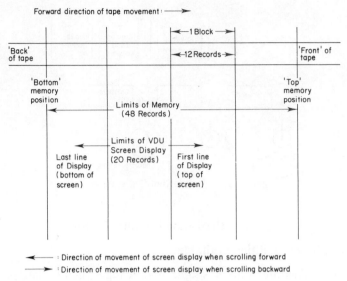

Figure 4.3.2   A snapshot of memory

The operations defined result in the following actions:

Operation	Action
Add	Add line to screen; move higher lines up and drop first line off screen
Delete	Delete line from screen; move up remaining lines and add new line from memory as last line on screen
Scroll forward	Drop first line off screen; move up remaining lines and add new line from memory as last line on screen
Scroll backward	Drop last line off screen; move down remaining lines and add new line from memory as first line on screen

Since neither cassette can be read or wound backwards, the last operation is necessarily restricted to those records currently held in memory.

In practice the records held in memory would probably be chained together to allow the operations required without constantly moving the records themselves; the detailed method used is omitted. In addition, the system would probably limit the screen display to those records occupying the bottom 36 of the possible 48 memory positions; otherwise the system would risk a sudden loss of records available to the user if the user were to add a new record and this happened to fill up memory. Assuming that suitable instructions (or subroutines) are available to read from and write to the cassette, and to read the keyboard, and that the size of memory available is sufficient for the workspace required, we shall now design a program to control the editing, defining suitable 'boundary conditions' (such as scrolling forward beyond the records currently held in memory), and the actions to be taken on detecting them.

4.3.2 Identifying boundary conditions

We can think of the VDU as providing a 'VDU window' on to the current contents of memory, and the memory as providing a 'memory window' on to the cassette. For each position of the memory window, a number of operations can be carried out on the VDU window until the memory window needs an adjustment. This is expressed in Figure 4.3.3, which shows how:

1. The outer loop is controlled by adjustments made to the memory window (by reading from the cassette).
2. The inner loop is controlled by adjustments made to the VDU window (by responding to a user request).

Now think of the operations on the VDU window as a loop which ends after any operation which requires an adjustment to the memory window; that is, the inner loop ends after any edit which:

1. reduces the number of lines in memory below a minimum (say, 24), or increases the number of lines in memory above a maximum; or
2. moves the window up to the limit of records available to the user (which, as noted, need not be all of those currently in memory); or
3. both 1 and 2 above, in which case we allow 2 to take precedence.

The following table lists for each operation suitable boundary conditions; if the execution of an operation results in the boundary condition noted then the memory window must be adjusted; the memory window is, therefore, always left

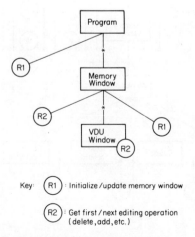

Figure 4.3.3   An initial program structure

118

in a position such that the next operation requested can be carried out; it assumes that End-of-file has not yet been reached on the cassette.

Operation	Boundary conditions	Adjustments to memory window
Add	1. Too many lines in memory	Write block
Delete	2. No line available to add to screen (last line on screen is last line in memory)	Write block, read block
	3. Too few lines in memory	Read block
Scroll forward	4. VDU window at limit of memory window (last line on screen is last line in memory)	Write block, read block
Scroll backward	5. VDU window at limit of memory window (first line on screen is first line in memory available to user)	None

After repositioning the memory window, the next Add, Delete, or Scroll forward operation requested by the user can always be carried out, but Scroll backward remains null under the conditions specified. The inner loop could, in theory, proceed indefinitely (and so the Read be brought into the loop), while the

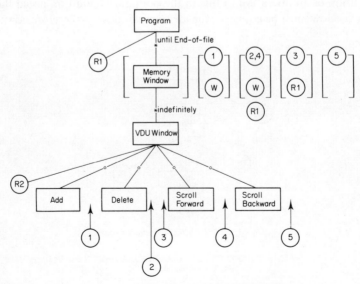

Figure 4.3.4   The basic logic to control editing

outer loop terminates on reaching End-of-file on the cassette. All this is expressed in Figure 4.3.4 in which the symbols used take the following meanings:

(1)–(5) Connectors, cross-referring to the conditions 1 to 5 respectively, as listed in the table above
(R1) Initialize/update memory window
(R2) Get first/next editing instruction from user
(W) Write block

As presented, the escape on condition 5 is not necessary, but is included for uniformity. The memory window could be suitably initialized by reading two (or three) blocks into the lower memory positions.

After End-of-file on the cassette has been reached, the actions change as follows:

Operation	Boundary conditions	Adjustments to memory window
Add	1. Too many lines in memory	Write block
Delete	2. No line available to add to screen (last line on screen is last line in memory)	None; when screen empties write blocks remaining in memory
	3. Too few lines in memory	None
Scroll forward	4. VDU window at limit of memory window (last line on screen is last line in memory)	None; when screen empties write blocks remaining in memory
Scroll backward	5. VDU window at limit of memory window (first line on screen is first line in memory available to user)	None

This additional logic is given in Figure 4.3.5. The symbols used are the same as before.

This example illustrates how a simple basic structure can become complex because of the manifold boundary conditions. The logic is easy to analyse provided you keep a clear head about the various ways a loop can terminate.

4.4 A Data Analysis Program

The next example describes a program written to analyse data collected during a series of experiments and is typical of a range of programs found in 'scientific' applications.

The 'raw' data is collected, using some form of automatic data recording

120

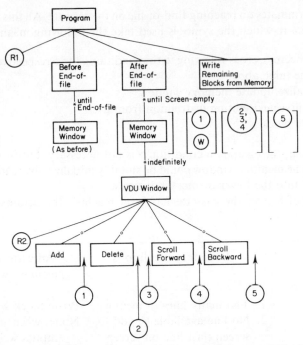

Figure 4.3.5   The special logic after reaching End-of-file

device, and is then edited to produce a 'clean' tape. The clean data is organized into files, blocks, records, and readings according to the following rules:

1. The first file on the tape occupies one block and contains a tape directory; subsequent files occupy several blocks. Each file is identified by a number (corresponding to its position on the tape), and contains data relating to one experiment. Each block is 256 bytes long.
2. The first block in each file is a file header. It provides file identity information, and shows how to interpret the readings which follow. Each subsequent block in a file is divided into records which may be 128, 64, or 32 bytes long. Each record includes a record number and one or more readings; the record numbers are consecutive ascending integers, while the readings within a record may be of different types (temperature, velocity, etc.).
3. A file header specifies the record size, and the record layout, for each record in the file. This covers the position of the record number and the type of each reading recorded in each byte. Thus, if the record number and each reading each occupy one byte, and a record is, say, 64 bytes long, then 64 bytes in the file header are used to show the contents of each corresponding byte in a record. The record number may occur anywhere.

The data editing procedures are responsible for ensuring the integrity of this tape. These are built into software containing rules to measure the feasibility of data collected, and to interpolate results where errors or omissions arise; the design of this software would be heavily application-dependent; for our purpose, it is enough to assume that as a result of data editing, all readings, records, and blocks are present, in the correct order, and valid.

The structure of the data tape is given in Figure 4.4.1; there is no very convenient way of showing diagrammatically how the record number and reading types are distributed in a record.

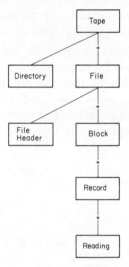

Figure 4.4.1   A file of experimental data

Suppose now that a program is required to analyse the data. Typically this might be so arranged that a user (that is, whoever wants to analyse the data) can enter his requirements (in the form of instructions, or parameters) via a terminal; after one analysis, the user may then terminate his activity, or enter further instructions. In the example given, the user might be able to specify:

1. The data used. This covers the:

    file number
    start/end record numbers

2. How the data is to be used for this analysis. This covers the:

    reading types to be selected
    interpretation mode (that is, whether the readings were recorded as absolute or calibrated values, function parameters, etc.)
    recording mode used to display the results of analysis (listing, tabulation, plot).

Usually the entry of parameters is subject to certain rules governing the order in which different types of analysis may be made, and the order in which individual parameters may be entered to specify the analysis required. The following would be an extreme case:

1. First time through, all parameters must be specified in a fixed order. If validation fails, all parameters must be re-entered in the correct order.
2. For the second and subsequent analyses the reader is invited to change any of the parameters in any order. A special 'ENTER' option is provided to indicate that all parameters have been entered and that processing should begin.
3. While entering parameters the user may at any stage request 'TERMINATE' or 'RESET'; the former terminates all processing while the latter resets all parameters to their values at the start of the analysis.

In practice the user facilities provided do not usually look so clear-cut. Sometimes this is because they are just complex; in others because they are 'ad hoc', or highly optimized. Whatever the detail, we shall refer to rules of this kind in Chapter 5 as controlling a 'conversation', and show there how to exploit them (in a different context) to control activity at a user terminal. Further detail is, therefore, omitted here except to note the basic program structure given in

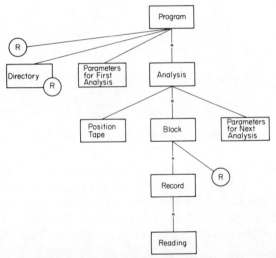

Figure 4.4.2   An initial program structure

Figure 4.4.2, where the parameters entered first time through become 'defaults' which may be overwritten for later analyses. In this diagram the Read instruction means 'Read a block'. Further Reads would be necessary to position the tape at the file requested by the user at the start of each analysis.

An interesting feature of the final design would be the use of three forms of loop control in the control logic:

1. The loop through the blocks is controlled by a 'Read block' instruction.
2. The loops through the records within a block, and through the readings within a record, are controlled by counts whose limits are determined by the header block.

3. The loops through parameters entered are controlled by operator commands (as described in Chapter 5).

As noted, we shall learn how to design conversations in detail in Chapter 5; we shall find that our design techniques can help define the facilities available to the user, and so document the results of systems design; the same documentation then provides the basis for the design of program logic. Further discussion of this example is, therefore, omitted.

4.5 An Approximation Algorithm

4.5.1 Problem description and notation

This is a program designed to apply the 'first-order approximation' technique to solve three simultaneous non-linear equations. If you do not have a head for algebra, please feel free to pass on; equally, however, I can recommend this example as showing how apparently complex mathematics can be made to look simple. It also illustrates how an algorithm can be thought of as a structure which is created dynamically during a program's execution, but which has no independent, or static, existence (for example, in the data used by the program).

Let X, Y, Z represent three variables. If you wish, think of these as Cartesian coordinates; in the example from which this is taken they actually represent physical quantities like 'roll' and 'pitch'. In any event X, Y and Z are not independent. In fact three functions $(F_1, F_2,$ and $F_3)$ are known to exist such that:

$$X = F_1(X, Y, Z)$$
$$Y = F_2(X, Y, Z)$$
$$Z = F_3(X, Y, Z)$$

Given any values of X, Y, Z, subroutines exist to evaluate each of these functions. A program is now required to solve them simultaneously; that is, to find one set of values for X, Y, Z which satisfies all three equations. Using the first-order approximation technique, the program is presented with initial values for X, Y, Z and then makes successive approximations to the final values required; the method used to make each approximation and the criteria used to determine whether or not more approximations are necessary are described below; the formal algorithm is given in Section 4.5.2. Any debate as to whether this is the 'best' algorithm to use would be too application-dependent to be included here.

We shall need some notation. Let:

1. u denote any one of X, Y, Z.
2. u_r denote the value of u after r approximations.
3. u^1 denote a final value for u.

If later (as described below) u^1 is used as an initial value, then the successive approximations are called:

$$u_1^1, u_2^1, \ldots, u_r^1$$

and the final value is called u^2. In general, u_r^p denotes the rth approximation to a final u^{p+1} starting with initial value u^p.

In order to calculate successive approximations for X, Y, Z we need the following data:

1. Initial values for X, Y, Z.
2. A percentage N. This specifies the maximum percentage difference between two successive approximations before we conclude that a final value has been found (the approximations are said to be 'convergent').
3. A value n. This is used to specify the maximum number of successive approximations made before we conclude that no final value will be found however many approximations are made (the approximations are said to be 'divergent').
4. Three constants k_1, k_2, k_3. These are used as 'damping factors' when making approximations to X, Y, Z respectively.
5. Other data used by the subroutines F_1, F_2, F_3 which does not concern us.

This is all supplied to the program as initial data. Now let k denote the damping factor and F denote the function which correspond to u. Then given u_r^p the next approximation to u^{p+1} is calculated by keeping the other two variables constant and applying the formula:

$$u_{r+1}^p = u_r^p + k[F(u_r^p) - u_r^p]$$

If u_{r+1}^p is within $N\%$ of u_r^p, then we set

$$u^{p+1} = u_{r+1}^p$$

but otherwise we continue by making a further approximation:

$$u_{r+2}^p = u_{r+1}^p + k[F(u_{r+1}^p) - u_{r+1}^p]$$

After n iterations without convergence, then we arbitrarily set

$$u^{p+1} = u_n^p$$

and conclude that the approximations will not converge; our version of the program then stops, but a variation would be to try again with different initial data.

4.5.2. Expressing the algorithm as a structure

We can now summarize the approximation technique. We start with initial values for X, Y, Z and proceed in the following steps:

1. Calculate a new value X^1 for X using the approximation method described above. The successive iterations may be represented as a loop which can end in two different ways; there is a maximum number of iterations (n), but the loop may terminate earlier after say p iterations (where $p \leq n$) if the approximations converge. This is described in Figure 4.5.1, in which the

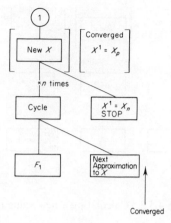

Figure 4.5.1   Calculating a new value for X

connector refers to another diagram produced in step 2 below. Note that during this step Y and Z remain constant.

2. Using X^1, make a first approximation Y_1 to Y. Using Y_1, recalculate X using X^1 and Y_1 as initial values for X, Y respectively. This gives X^2. Using X^2, make a second approximation Y_2 to Y. Repeat until a final value Y^1 is found. Again, there is a maximum number of iterations (n), but the loop may terminate earlier, after say q iterations (where $q \leq n$), as illustrated in Figure 4.5.2. At this stage X will take the value X^q. During the whole of this step Z remains constant.

3. Using Y^1 and X^q, calculate a first approximation Z_1 to Z. Using Z_1, recalculate Y (and hence necessarily recalculate X) using Y^1 and X^q as initial values. Repeat until a final value Z^1 is found, as illustrated in Figure 4.5.3. At this stage Y will take a new value Y^r, say, and X a new value X^s, say.

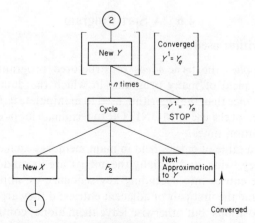

Figure 4.5.2   Calculating a new value for Y

126

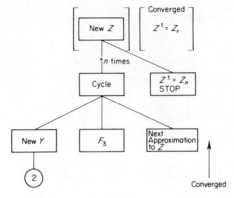

Figure 4.5.3   Calculating a new value for Z

At this stage it would be usual to recalculate F_1, F_2, F_3 using the final values X^s, Y^r, Z^1 (to safeguard against any 'discontinuity' in F_1, F_2, F_3):

$$X = F_1(X^s, Y^r, Z^1)$$
$$Y = F_2(X^s, Y^r, Z^1)$$
$$Z = F_3(X^s, Y^r, Z^1)$$

Provided the results (X, Y, Z) are within the tolerance limits defined, then X^s, Y^r, Z^1 solve the three equations simultaneously:

$$X^s = F_1(X^s, Y^r, Z^1)$$
$$Y^r = F_2(X^s, Y^r, Z^1)$$
$$Z^1 = F_3(X^s, Y^r, Z^1)$$

It remains only to read in the initial data and the design is complete.

4.6   A Sort Program

4.6.1 The algorithm used

This example applies the basic ideas of structured programming to a sort program. It is typical of many programs in which the data used is of less structural significance than the algorithm used to manipulate it. It also provides a further illustration of the use of MONITOR to terminate loops early, in this case to optimize execution times.

You are given a table of entries held in main memory; each entry is uniquely identified by a key value, and initially the entries are in random sequence. In order to sort the entries into ascending key sequence we apply the following algorithm: examine the first pair of adjacent entries; if they are out of sequence exchange their positions, but otherwise leave them alone; continue by stepping along the table one entry at a time to examine in turn each pair of adjacent entries, until the end of the table is reached (this completes a 'pass'); now execute passes until eventually the complete table is in sequence.

For example, suppose that the table contains just five entries and that their key values are 1, 2, 3, 4, 5, and that initially the table is set up in the following order:

4 3 5 2 1

After successive passes the entries occur in the following order:

3 4 2 1 5   (pass 1)
3 2 1 4 5   (pass 2)
2 1 3 4 5   (pass 3)
1 2 3 4 5   (pass 4)

As specified the algorithm given will always work because:

1. After the first pass the highest entry finds its correct position.
2. After the second pass the second highest entry finds its correct position.
3. It follows that if there are N entries, at most $N-1$ passes are required.

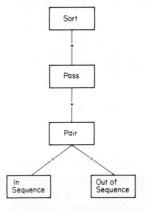

Figure 4.6.1   The basic structure for a sort program

This technique is often known as a 'bubble' or 'exchange' sort and is expressed as a structure diagram in Figure 4.6.1; note that the structure is based on the algorithm used and not on the data manipulated. In fact, the structure diagram simply describes the order in which passes and swaps are executed in order to complete the sort.

Each loop may be controlled by a simple count or index:

1. For the inner loop, we use J to subscript the entries (from 1 to N)
2. For the outer loop we use I to count the number of passes (maximum $N-1$).

128

Using the standard method for loop control, the schematic logic follows:

```
         Move 1 to I
SORT   LOOP until I = N
         Move 1 to J
         PASS   LOOP until J = N
                 PAIR   IF Entry (J) > Entry (J + 1)
                         Swap Entry (J), Entry (J + 1)
                 PAIR   ELSE
                 PAIR   ENDS
                 Add 1 to J
         PASS   ENDS
         Add 1 to I
SORT   ENDS
```

This completes the basic program. We shall now attempt to optimize the sort, still using structured principles, in the following stages:

1. Reduce the length of successive passes.
2. Stop after a pass on which there were no swaps.
3. Start a pass at the first entry which could be out of sequence.

As an illustration, suppose the table consists of 10 entries initially in the following order:

$$1 \quad 2 \quad 3 \quad 4 \quad 6 \quad 5 \quad 7 \quad 8 \quad 9 \quad 10$$

If J represents an index to the table, then corresponding to the three stages of optimization, we have:

1. The second pass can terminate with $J = 5$.
2. The sort can terminate after two passes.
3. The second pass can start with $J = 4$.

The possibility of further optimization is ignored.

Each stage is intended to reduce sort execution times. However, in order to optimize we have to introduce extra code and there will always be occasions on which this penalty paid outweighs any benefits achieved. I shall describe only the logic principles involved without trying to quantify the penalties and benefits; the reader must guard against assuming that the 'optimized' version will *necessarily* execute faster—it all depends on factors such as the size of table and the position and number of entries out of sequence.

In order to implement the first stage we need two variables, P (to remember the position of the last swap on this pass) and Q (to remember the position of the last swap on the previous pass). The schematic logic follows:

```
         Move 1 to I
         Move N to Q
SORT   LOOP until I = N
         Move 1 to J, P
```

```
        PASS   LOOP until J = Q
                PAIR   IF Entry (J) > Entry (J + 1)
                       Swap Entry (J), Entry (J + 1)
                       Move J to P
                PAIR   ELSE
                PAIR   ENDS
                Add 1 to J
        PASS   ENDS
        Add 1 to I
        Move P to Q
SORT   ENDS
```

The amendments made leave the structure unaltered. The penalty paid is the introduction of a small algorithm to calculate the limit of the next pass.

The second stage of optimization can be implemented by counting the number of swaps on a pass, and amending the condition which terminates the outer loop. Let us define a field CT to hold a count of the number of swaps on the current pass. The schematic logic follows:

```
        Move 1 to I, CT
        Move N to Q
SORT   LOOP until I = N or CT = 0
        Move 1 to J, P
        Move 0 to CT
        PASS   LOOP until J = Q
                PAIR   IF Entry (J) > Entry (J + 1)
                       Swap Entry (J), Entry (J + 1)
                       Move J to P
                       Add 1 to CT
                PAIR   ELSE
                PAIR   ENDS
                Add 1 to J
        PASS   ENDS
        Add 1 to I
        Move P to Q
SORT   ENDS
```

In this solution CT is introduced to force early termination of the outer loop. The advantage of this technique is that the structure is largely left unaltered and still makes use of nested logic only; disadvantages are the use of CT as both a count and a two-valued switch (to indicate whether or not there were swaps on a particular pass), the need to initialize CT to some arbitrary non-zero value, and the compound condition used to terminate the outer loop. For many purposes, however, the design is good enough. The interesting point is that the need for CT can be avoided by the use of a logic monitor, and that the third stage of optimization then becomes trivial.

4.6.2 MONITOR as an optimization tool

We have made the point on many occasions that the logic monitor can be used to provide a second exit from a loop. In this example we want to impose a maximum number of iterations ($N - 1$) on the outer loop, but in practice stop after the first pass on which there were no swaps. We need then to apply MONITOR to the outer loop:

```
         Move 1 to I
         Move N to Q
M        MONITOR Early-termination-of-sort
SORT     LOOP until I = N
           ⋮
         QUIT M IF No-swaps-on-current-pass
           ⋮
         Add 1 to I
         Move P to Q
SORT     ENDS
M        ADMIT
           ⋮
M        ENDS
```

The next question is how to identify a pass on which there were no swaps; this can be done by splitting the inner loop into two: up to the first swap and from the first swap through to the end. And since there is no need to distinguish the two ways in which the outer loop ends we can use the default version of MONITOR (Section 3.4) as follows:

```
         Move 1 to I
         Move N to Q
SORT     LOOP until I = N
         Move 1 to J, P
         PASS1   LOOP until Entry (J) > Entry (J + 1)
                 QUIT SORT IF J = Q - 1
                 Add 1 to J
         PASS1   ENDS
         PASS2   LOOP until J = Q
                 PAIR  IF Entry (J) > Entry (J + 1)
                       Swap Entry (J), Entry (J + 1)
                       Move J to P
                 PAIR  ELSE
                 PAIR  ENDS
                 Add 1 to J
         PASS2   ENDS
         Add 1 to I
         Move P to Q
SORT     ENDS
```

Although this looks more complicated than the use of a count, it is in fact quite simple and avoids any suspicion of the use of switches. The equivalent structure diagram is given in Figure 4.6.2.

Implementation of the third stage of optimization depends on the technique used for the second level. If a count was used, then you must now:

1. Introduce a switch (or re-use the same count) to remember whether or not a swap has been made this pass.
2. Each time the need for a swap is detected, test the switch to see whether or not this is the first swap made on this pass.
3. If it is the first swap, remember J; otherwise do nothing.
4. For the next pass, use the value remembered in step 3 above to determine an initial value for J.

The disadvantage of this technique (and the corresponding inefficiency introduced) is the need to test the switch every time a swap is made. The details are left to the reader.

However, if the monitor technique was used instead, then all you need now do is remember J at the start of the second half of a pass, and use this remembered value to determine an initial value for J on the next pass. Let K denote the value of J remembered at the start of the second half of a pass. The complete logic is then:

```
        Move 1 to I, K
        Move N to Q
SORT    LOOP until I = N
        Move 1 to P
        Move K to J
        PASS1   LOOP until Entry (J) > Entry (J + 1)
                QUIT SORT IF J = Q − 1
                Add 1 to J
        PASS1   ENDS
        If J > 1 Move J − 1 to K
        PASS2   LOOP until J = Q
                PAIR    IF Entry (J) > Entry (J + 1)
                        Swap Entry (J), Entry (J + 1)
                        Move J to P
                PAIR    ELSE
                PAIR    ENDS
                Add 1 to J
        PASS2   ENDS
        Add 1 to I
        Move P to Q
SORT    ENDS
```

Unlike the alternative method using a count, there is no penalty to pay here to achieve this third stage of optimization. Since a great many programs (not only

132

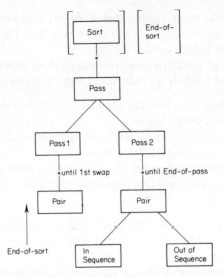

Figure 4.6.2   Optimized structure for a sort program

sorts) contain loops which have to be optimized, the structural principles are of wide application; the differences between one such program and another concern the interpretation of the algorithm used, the methods used to control the various loops, and the source of loop-terminating conditions. Although the use of MONITOR can have the effect of making the logic appear more complex than it really is, it does avoid the need for switches; in my opinion this often gives a better and clearer design even if its implementation may require the use of an explicit GOTO.

Chapter 5
On-line Systems

In this chapter we show how to analyse the control logic for 'on-line' systems. The term 'on-line' is used to denote any system where the user is provided with one or more terminals (each consisting of keyboard and VDU screen) which can be used to interrogate or manipulate the contents of files and records, usually held in the form of a data base. We shall assume (although this is not essential) that the unit of communication between user and system is the screen, and that the transfer of data is controlled by a conventional transaction processing monitor (or, as it is usually called, a tp monitor) which itself runs under the control of the machine operating system, or executive. The system is expected to respond to user demands within tolerance limits satisfactory to the user (often not more than a second or two), but there are usually no limits to the time spent by the user at a terminal; in this sense the user is held 'on-line' to his data without interruption, and the terminal is dedicated to this task. This continuity also goes some way to explain why the term 'system' is conventionally used (instead of 'program') to describe the software written to control and execute user demands. The reader must not confuse the use of 'monitor' as in 'tp monitor' with MONITOR as defined in Chapter 3.

The central feature of on-line systems is the constant communication which takes place between user and system; the system communicates with the user by displaying a screen of information; the user, in turn, communicates with the system by providing or completing information requested on the screen, and then pressing one of a range of 'function keys'. It is usual to speak of the screen and function key as being 'entered' into the system. The screen content may range from a 'menu' of facilities available to a display of file or record contents, and sometimes provides prompts from the system, describing the options available to the user. The function keys used may be special-purpose keys, or make use of existing standard keys such as Carriage Return; when depressed they act as a signal to the system that the user has finished with the current screen, and define the action requested including the next screen type to be displayed. In some systems equivalent facilities are provided using a single function key which is interpreted in conjunction with a field (often called an 'action code') reserved on the screen for that purpose. The two methods are equivalent; in what follows we assume the presence of a range of function keys.

The interplay between the system and user responses is usually subject to certain rules depending on the facilities made available to the user, and is called a conversation. An example is given in the next section. We are concerned to analyse the rules which govern the order in which screens can be requested and processed, and to use them to derive corresponding control logic.

5.1 A Simple Conversation

An on-line file maintenance system has been designed to allow a user to enter record amendments from a terminal. In this system, there is just one terminal; two screen types can be displayed, and a number of possible function keys entered. The two screen types are:

1. Record identification screen. This allows the user to identify the next record to be maintained.
2. Record display screen. This allows the system to display the current state of the record identified, and the user to enter amendments.

On start-up, the record identification screen is displayed.

The function keys are given descriptive names as summarized in general terms below:

Key	Function
ACCEPT	This requests the system to update a record for which amendments have just been entered, and then bring up the record identification screen ready to identify the next record to be maintained
AMEND	This requests the system to retrieve a record identified on a record identification screen and to bring up the record display screen ready for record maintenance
CLEAR	This requests the system to restart work on the record currently identified by ignoring amendments entered (if any) and displaying the record in its initial state
KILL	This requests the system to abandon work on the record currently identified, and to allow the user to start again by identifying a new record for amendment
TERMINATE	This terminates all activity at the terminal. It can only be entered after completing all amendments for the current record

Some other keys are interpreted by the tp monitor as function keys but are always treated as errors by the system. We shall think of function keys ACCEPT and AMEND as the 'normal keys', and function keys CLEAR, KILL, and TERMINATE as providing 'escapes' from a 'normal' sequence of events in which only function keys ACCEPT and AMEND are used.

This description of the system required contains implications about the order in which screens should be displayed, and consequently about the order in which function keys (which act as requests for the next screen type to be displayed) can be entered. The 'context', or 'sequencing', rules implied are not absolutely precise as defined, and some interpretation will be necessary later. Nevertheless, it is evident that an error will arise if an incorrect, or out-of-sequence, function key is entered; the system simply reports the error and asks for an in-sequence function key. Even if the function key entered is in sequence, the data entered on the screen may itself be invalid; in this case also a report is given on the screen and the system requests that the error be corrected. In both cases, no other changes are made to the screen content.

For simplicity we assume that any record can be fully displayed on one screen. We shall also assume that, for our purposes, we can ignore all details of screen formatting, including field protection, as well as any interpretation of the data entered other than as noted. No validation is carried out before a function key has been entered, and the data base is not updated until a valid set of amendments has been entered together with an in-sequence ACCEPT function key.

This completes the system description. Of course, the system only works provided the data base is constructed to allow the accesses required. In this example they are simply:

Read record
Write record

Both operations assume that the file is indexed. In this sense, the definition and construction of a conversation has consequences for the demands made on the data base used.

When accessing the data base it is always possible that errors will arise. We distinguish:

1. Normal error-free processing.
2. Data base access errors from which the system recovers and continues.
3. Other error conditions under which the conversation is undefined and user-controlled processing is abandoned.

Errors of type 3 are usually handled by the data base access and/or tp monitor software and are not considered further here. Any other data base error is reported on the screen to the user and treated on a par with other validation errors (the details of which are omitted).

The following notes show how to analyse the control logic using structured programming concepts.

5.2 The Basic Control Logic

Each time the system receives input from the user, the information entered consists of:

1. The current screen type (record identification, or record display screen).
2. Screen data (other data on the screen, but excluding the function key).
3. A function key (ACCEPT, AMEND, CLEAR, KILL, TERMINATE, or other) indicating what the user wants to do next.

We can think of these items as jointly constituting a 'record' passed from the user to the system; the 'record key', or identifier, is the current screen type, and the 'record details' are any other data associated with the screen. One such detail is the function key.

Think now of the succession of records (i.e. screen type, plus screen data, plus function key) input to the system as constituting a serial file; each record on the serial file consists of an identifier (the screen type) and data (whatever other information is on the screen, plus the function key). We can now apply the structure diagram notation to describe the order in which these records are input to the on-line system. We shall build our picture of this serial file in stages.

The first stage considers the normal sequence of events, in which only function keys ACCEPT and AMEND are used, and in which the possibility of escapes or errors of any kind is ignored. The system starts by displaying a record identification screen; the records input to the system then occur in the following order:

1. Record identification screen, plus screen data, plus function key AMEND.
2. Record display screen, plus screen data, plus function key ACCEPT.
3. 1 and 2 in that order, repeated indefinitely (since we are, at present, ignoring the TERMINATE function key).

This order is described in Figure 5.1, where the name 'Terminal' is used for the topmost box to emphasize that we are considering the sequence of functions entered at a terminal over a period of time, and the name 'Cycle' is used as an application-independent name for a loop or iteration.

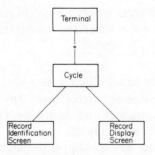

Figure 5.1 The normal sequence of screens displayed

The most significant processing functions are:

1. Read. This means that the system reads the next record—namely, the screen type, screen contents and function key—from the terminal.
2. Write. This means that\the system writes a record—namely, ₁a screen to be displayed—to the terminal. The screen written may be a record identification screen or a record display screen.

In this type of system we may think of the instructions:

Write screen, followed by
Read screen

as a unit. For, from the system's point of view, the effect of 'Write screen' is to announce completion of processing the previous screen, to display a new screen for completion by the user, and to suspend work until the new screen is entered together with a function key; the effect of 'Read screen' is simply to restart the system immediately following the previous 'Write screen'. We shall, therefore, redefine these processing functions slightly:

1. Read. This now covers the complete transfer of a screen to and from the user. We denote this using the (R) symbol.
2. Write. This is now confined to the creation of any data to be displayed. We denote this using the (w) symbol, but defer its formal allocation in the logic until Section 5.4.

The next question is how to allocate the Read, as defined, on the structure diagram. We reason as follows. Each Read reads a screen type plus screen data plus function key. The screen type read is known in advance, in the sense that it is the same as the screen type last written. Whenever a screen is read, therefore, the screen type is known and there is no need to evaluate it. In particular, since the loop proceeds indefinitely, and since the screen type is not evaluated in order to terminate the loop, the Read can be treated as part of the loop content.

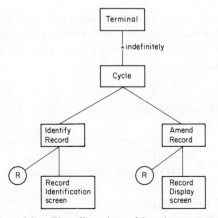

Figure 5.2. The allocation of Read statements

The Read can now be allocated on the structure diagram as shown in Figure 5.2. We emphasize the following points:

1. Since we are at present ignoring the possibility of errors or escapes, we are guaranteed to Read an in-sequence and valid screen.
2. On start-up the system prompts the user by creating a record identification screen; thereafter the system writes record display and identification screens alternately. The allocation of a processing function to create these screens is covered later.
3. The Read instruction displayed means 'Read a screen'. Any data base access is assumed to form part of the detailed screen processing, and is omitted from the diagram.

A consequence of the design given is that when later we add in logic to evaluate other function keys entered, we shall be forced to use a MONITOR to escape from the loop, or to modify the loop termination, or both. This will be covered in Section 5.4; before that we want to re-evaluate the concept of read-ahead.

5.3   Read-ahead in On-line Systems

Omitting unnecessary sequence groups, the schematic logic corresponding to Figure 5.2 would be:

```
TERMINAL   LOOP indefinitely
           CYCLE   SEQ
                   Read (Identification screen)
                   DO Record-identification-screen
                   Read (Display screen)
                   DO Record-display-screen
           CYCLE   ENDS
TERMINAL   ENDS
```

Experience shows that this logic can cause confusion because it apparently breaks the rules embodied in the read-ahead principle as formulated in Chapter 1. A more literal interpretation of the read-ahead principle might have produced the following:

```
           Read
TERMINAL   LOOP indefinitely
           CYCLE   SEQ
                   DO Record-identification-screen
                   Read
                   DO Record-display-screen
                   Read
           CYCLE   ENDS
TERMINAL   ENDS
```

The following additional notes are included (at the risk of repetition) to expand on and justify our approach.

The read-ahead principle followed from:

1. The use of nested logic building blocks, and particularly the desire to standardize loop construction by placing the test for the end of a loop at the start of the loop.
2. A consideration of systems in which there was no way to anticipate the result of a Read; consequently the logic must always evaluate the result of each Read in order to find out what to do next.
3. The exploitation of a relationship between an order of events, and the design of control logic to analyse that order.

As a consequence, particularly of 2, the processing required to detect and analyse an event was, typically:

Read record; then
evaluate the record type; then
select correct record processing routine (depending on the evaluation).

The evaluation effectively routed the logic to that point in the program concerned with processing the record found. In the present context the record read is the screen, but this is now identified by a screen type which can be anticipated from the previous screen written. Hence point 2 above no longer applies. In the logic given this means that there is no need to evaluate the result of a Read and the loop can proceed indefinitely; so the Read can be taken into the loop and be followed immediately by the correct event type. This justifies the approach taken. However, although the screen type can be anticipated, the function key used cannot be anticipated. Some function keys entered act as a request to the system to ignore the screen type, and take alternative action. So the processing required to detect and analyse an event is now:

Read record; then
evaluate function key (and not the screen type); then
process the screen type read (unless the function key indicates otherwise).

Evaluation of the function key then routes the logic to that point in the system at which the processing requested by the user can be safely carried out. The additional logic required will be covered in the next section.

In on-line systems the logic always finds its way to that part of the system concerned with the display and processing of a new screen *before* that screen is read; in contrast, batch systems find their way to that part of the program concerned with processing a particular record type *after* a record is read. This is the fundamental difference between on-line and batch-mode systems which most affects the design of control logic. It results in an extension to the read-ahead principle, because some of the assumptions made earlier no longer apply. It also reinforces the conclusion drawn in Section 1.9, that interpretation of the read-ahead principle may sometimes be necessary. This is not surprising; in any subject, the principles used must be allowed to evolve, as experience throws new light on old problems. We acknowledge that it is always possible to take a different view; one such possibility might be to think of the screen type and function key as together identifying a screen. In my opinion this is simply a mistaken view of the role of the function key but we shall, nonetheless, explore it a little further in Section 5.5.

We now go on to consider the additional logic to detect and recover from escapes and errors, and to consider the provision of user prompts.

5.4   Escapes, Errors, and Prompts

The next design stage is to drop the assumption made in Section 5.2 that function keys would be depressed only in the correct sequence:

AMEND
ACCEPT
AMEND
ACCEPT
AMEND
etc.

This will, after all, be the case only under the most favourable circumstances.

The additional facilities available in this system were summarized in the table of function keys given in Section 5.1; we shall interpret these rules to mean:

1. Where the system is expecting AMEND, the following escapes could be entered and be in sequence:
   (a) KILL. This is allowed, although not strictly necessary. Its effect is only to start again with a fresh record identification screen.
   (b) TERMINATE. This terminates all processing.

   Any other function key entered is out of sequence, and an error; the system asks for an in-sequence function key, leaving the record identification screen in its current state. The user could, in theory, make several 'attempts' to enter an in-sequence function key (AMEND, KILL, or TERMINATE). The additional logic to cover the conditions noted is given in Figure 5.3; in accordance with Section 5.3, the loop is marked as proceeding 'indefinitely'.
2. Where the logic is expecting ACCEPT, one of the following could be entered and be in sequence:
   (a) KILL. This terminates processing of the current amendment, and effects a return to the record identification screen.
   (b) CLEAR. This clears any amendments entered, but leaves the record display screen showing the record identified in its initial state.

   Any other function key entered is out of sequence, and an error; the system asks for an in-sequence function key, leaving the record display screen in its current state. Again, the user could make several 'attempts' to enter an in-sequence function key (ACCEPT, KILL, or CLEAR). Indeed, we could even

141

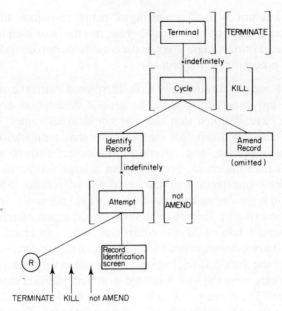

Figure 5.3   The logic to detect and control escapes

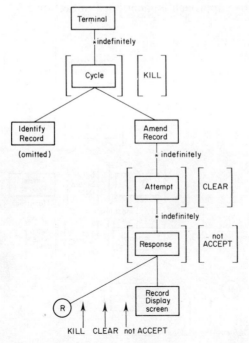

Figure 5.4   Further logic to detect and control escapes

142

talk of an attempt as itself consisting of many 'responses' until CLEAR is entered. Even though this is a bit elaborate, it is the basis used in Figure 5.4 to describe the additional logic to cover the conditions noted; again, each loop is marked as proceeding 'indefinitely'.

In reaching Figures 5.3 and 5.4, we have interpreted a little the meaning of each function key, but consistently with the general description given earlier. In particular, we have assumed that the user could validly enter TERMINATE immediately following display of the initial record identification screen. The solution given is precise, and covers all the cases; if there are alternative interpretations then the choice between them is largely a matter of style.

This completes our picture of the serial file of screens input, started in Section 5.2, and is the design level at which we would normally stop; but for this example we want to go a little further since the detection of errors during the validation of screen data could also contribute to the conversation. Thus, each time the logic finds an in-sequence function key, the system validates the screen data entered; if the data is valid, the system continues with the next screen type requested, but otherwise the user is invited to amend the data entered and make another attempt. The corresponding loop control must now be altered; we shall allow the loop to continue 'indefinitely', and treat detection of valid screen data as a further escape. This is consistent with our general view of the nature of these loops. Adopting this approach, Figures 5.5 and 5.6 extend Figures 5.3 and 5.4 respectively to show the additional logic to detect and recover from invalid screen data. An alternative approach is mentioned in Section 5.5.

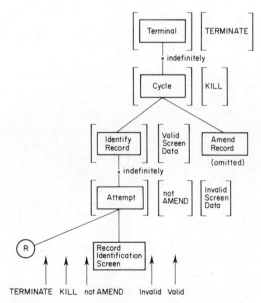

Figure 5.5   Detecting validation errors

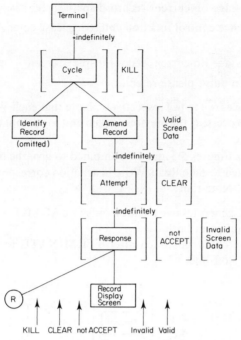

Figure 5.6   Detecting more validation errors

We now introduce a method to annotate the diagram more freely. First, we extend the usual Read symbol by attaching a suffix which acts as a cross-reference to a table or list specifying the Read required in greater detail. In this system two Reads are required (remember 'Read' means 'display screen and obtain user response'):

1. Read record identification screen. The associated function key entered may be AMEND, KILL, or TERMINATE, anything else being an error.
2. Read record display screen. The associated function key entered may be ACCEPT, KILL, or CLEAR, anything else being an error.

We shall refer to these on the diagram as (R1) and (R2) respectively.

Next, we adopt a similar convention for the Writes (remember 'Write' means 'create data to be displayed'). There are six cases:

1. Write new record identification screen.
2. Write new record display screen.
3. Write error message on current record identification screen:

    'Out-of-sequence control function entered; please enter AMEND, KILL, or TERMINATE'

4. Write error message on current record identification screen:

    'Invalid screen data; please re-enter.'

144

5. Write error message on current record display screen:

   'Out-of-sequence control function entered; please enter ACCEPT, KILL, or CLEAR.'

6. Write error message on current record display screen:

   'Invalid screen data; please re-enter.'

We refer to these as ⓦ1 to ⓦ6 respectively. Note that each Write may be used both to report on processing the previous screen and to prompt the user about the actions he can take.

Figure 5.7 shows Figures 5.5 and 5.6 combined to give the total system logic. The number attached to each Read/Write instruction corresponds to an entry in the lists just given. Note that:

1. Although KILL generates two escapes, only one ADMIT is used, because the same action is taken in both cases.
2. A further Write could be added after TERMINATE to confirm that the system has gone off-line.

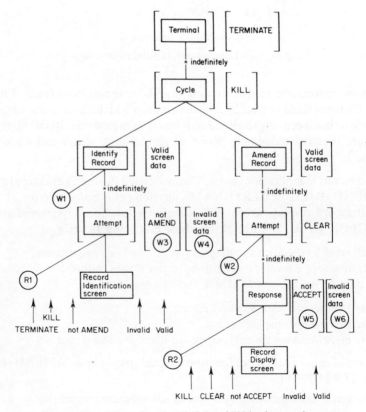

Figure 5.7 Allocating detailed Read/Write instructions

3. The logic could easily be altered to allow more than one error report on one screen (for example, function key out-of-sequence *and* screen data invalid).
4. The logic could also easily be altered to show more detailed errors (for example, to distinguish between account number entered not numeric, and not found on the data base). This level of detail does not affect the basic design presented.

In my experience this level of detail is about right for a structure diagram. It shows all the main logic, and all the reads and writes. It could be turned into formal program structure but this is not really necessary. We shall, therefore, move on.

5.5 Summary of the Design Principles

The following notes summarize the basic approach.

1. In systems of this kind, the problem is to design logic to analyse the order in which screens are processed. This logic is largely concerned with the evaluation of the function key entered since it is this which provides the user with the capacity to influence the next screen type displayed.
2. The function keys provide facilities (*inter alia*) to generate 'escapes' to a higher level to restart processing. These escapes are deliberate, and are intended to be used as such; they are in no sense errors. Nonetheless, 'real' errors can still arise; examples are out-of-sequence, or unrecognizable, function keys, and application-dependent screen data validation errors.
3. We have analysed the logic which controls the order in which screens can be processed. It remains to add the detailed processing of screens themselves; this is unlikely to involve any complex logic. If it does (e.g. to generate a report on a serial file), then that logic can be designed using the principles described in earlier chapters, but is probably best covered in a separate diagram.
4. Each time a screen is written, it may contain:

    (a) a report on the result of processing the previous screen (including function key); and/or
    (b) a prompt advising the user of the facilities now available to him.

    The reports and prompts necessary can be deduced from the structure diagram; in this sense the diagram represents one result of system design, but is also source material for user operating instructions.

The parallel between batch and on-line processing will be evident. In both cases we are concerned with designing the high-level logic; this logic is complex, requires special techniques, and is largely the result of system design decisions; it remains to complete the design of boxes at the lower levels; the low-level boxes may themselves contain extra logic, but generally this will be confined to a description of the business rules and be rather simpler than the high-level control logic.

As in batch systems, the design produced is fully modular, and consists of high-level control logic, plus detailed application-dependent processing routines. Thus 'DO Record-Identification-screen' means 'call a subroutine to process the contents of a record identification screen, knowing that the function key depressed was in sequence'. There is, in our design, one such subroutine to process each screen type. The structure diagram represents a piece of high-level control logic which describes when, and under what conditions, to invoke the low-level subroutines. Subject to the points to be noted in Section 5.6 below, the high-level logic may itself be built using in-line or out-of-line code (as described in Section 1.2).

The differences between batch and on-line processing will be equally evident. In batch systems the next record type read cannot, in general, be predicted from the previous record type read; in contrast, the next screen type read in an on-line system is anticipated by the function key entered with the previous screen. Further, in batch systems any departure from a 'normal' or 'correct' sequence of events will be an error; since there is no way to request correction of the error, other rules must be framed to interpret errors found and recover from them. Examples were given in Chapters 3 and 4. In on-line systems, the user-controlled escapes from the normal sequence of events are deliberate; these cannot be thought of as errors, although that is not to say that 'genuine' errors cannot arise. Unlike a batch system, on detecting an error, an on-line system always has the ability to stop and prompt the operator to get a correct response. It is particularly the user's ability to direct the system through the use of function keys which has led to the different styles for constructing the high-level logic.

Next, a few comments on the design produced. We have constructed each loop as if it proceeded indefinitely; consequently the only exit is via a QUIT. It would be possible to redesign the loops; using a subset of Figure 5.5, for example, we could write instead:

IDENTIFY LOOP until valid screen data entered
        DO Attempt
IDENTIFY ENDS

This has the disadvantage that we must use a valid/invalid flag or switch, and this must be set to 'invalid' before entering the loop. Equally, the outermost loop could be written:

TERMINAL LOOP until TERMINATE entered
        DO Cycle
TERMINAL ENDS

as if the function key were part of the screen type identifier.

However, there is no great or obvious advantage to this approach, and it will usually make implementation harder. The central question is: does the system go on for ever, with TERMINATE used to bring it to a premature halt, or does the system terminate naturally and inevitably when TERMINATE is entered? In my experience, most programmers find it most natural (and certainly easier to implement) to think of TERMINATE (and likewise CLEAR and KILL) as deliberate escapes. It makes sense, therefore, to code them as such, accepting the need for a substantial number of MONITOR/QUIT statements.

At all levels, MONITOR and QUIT proliferate and this can make the diagrams large and apparently complex. We have to accept that this is just part of the nature of on-line systems, dominated as they are by the need for escapes. In Figure 5.7 seven MONITORs are required in all; assuming they are numbered appropriately, then the logic at the lowest level (when looking for function key AMEND) might read:

```
ATTEMPT   SEQ
          Read (RI)
          QUIT M1 IF TERMINATE
          QUIT M2 IF KILL
          QUIT M4 IF not AMEND
          DO Record-identification-screen
          QUIT M4 IF screen data invalid
          QUIT M3 (unconditionally)
ATTEMPT   ENDS
```

The use of multiple QUITs and multiple MONITORs in this way falls within the rules presented in Chapter 3 (see particularly Sections 3.4 and 3.5).

Finally, note that we have so far ignored any complication arising from multiple terminals, or from constraints imposed by the tp monitor itself. The first point will be covered in Section 7.5, the second in the next section.

5.6   The Interface with a TP Monitor

Figure 5.7 provides a good description of the system control logic; it is, for example, easy to read off the effects of any function key entered at any point, and to determine the context in which all processing is carried out. From this point, the normal procedure would be to follow an installation-dependent set of 'mapping' rules to produce compilable code. However, the presence of the tp monitor may mean that this is not necessarily quite as easy as it sounds. Consider the meaning of each Read:

'I (the system) have finished processing the current screen, and have reported the results (if any) of such processing; before I can carry on I must get the next screen-plus-function-key; since it is the tp monitor's job to communicate with the terminal I am effectively idle until the tp monitor tells me to restart; when it tells me to restart I want to resume from the point following the Read.'

From now on it all depends on the interface provided by the tp monitor. In the first place we distinguish the following cases:

1. The tp monitor thinks of itself as a subroutine of the system code. In this case there is no problem—effectively, 'Read' means 'make a subroutine call to the tp monitor', and the system restarts from the instruction following the subroutine call when the subroutine returns control in the normal way.
2. The tp monitor thinks of itself as a calling program and the system code is a subroutine called by the tp monitor. In this case there is a problem—there are two Read instructions in the logic designed, both buried deep inside a nested structure. It is not easy to arrange for the tp monitor to return control to the instruction following the Read (for reasons to be explained in detail in Chapter 6).

In case 1 the transition from structure diagram to application code is straightforward; the logic simply thinks of the terminal as a serial file from which records (i.e. screens) can be read, as from any other serial device (such as a magnetic tape). Such an implementation is often said to be 'conversational'. Case 2 is the same in principle, but the implementation is much more complex. In fact, a transition from structure diagram to application code which preserves the structure can only be made if logic inversion is used. This technique is covered in Chapter 6, and so we reserve our comments. For the time being, here is an alternative. It takes advantage of the following idea, intended to be representative of the facilities provided by any tp monitor which thinks of the user's code as a subroutine of itself. The result is often said to be 'pseudo-conversational'.

We think of the application software as a set of transactions, each transaction being implemented as a subroutine which can be invoked by the tp monitor. We do not need to define the concept of a transaction precisely, but roughly, we would expect to find some transactions provided to interpret function keys entered together with at least one transaction to process each screen type. Each transaction returns to the tp monitor after completing its execution, and may specify the identity of the next transaction to be invoked. It may also specify whether or not further input is required from the user terminal before executing the transaction specified. Whether this input is required or not, and if it is, then independently of the function key entered by the user, control will eventually be passed by the tp monitor to the transaction specified.

Using these ideas, we can take the structure diagram, identify the transactions required, and define their interfaces with the tp monitor. Suitable transactions would be:

1. One transaction for each Read. We call these Read transactions; they evaluate the function key entered.
2. One transaction for each screen type. We call these application transactions; they process the screen data entered.

For our system we have two Reads and hence two corresponding Read transactions. Since there are two screen types we need two application transactions (to process record identification and record display screen data respectively). Let us define, therefore, four transactions as summarized below:

Transaction	Function
T1	Analyse results of (R1)
T2	Analyse results of (R2)
T3	Process record identification screen
T4	Process record display screen

On completion, each transaction may specify:

1. The identity of the next transaction to be processed. We shall express this using the statement:

$$\text{Next-id} = \text{xxx}$$

where 'xxx' identifies a transaction which is known to, and which can be executed by, the tp monitor. The special identity 'End-of-program' signifies to the tp monitor that activity at the terminal is now complete.
2. Whether further user input is expected from the terminal before control is passed to the transaction specified in Next-id. The statement used is:

$$\text{Read} = \text{Yes}$$

or

$$\text{Read} = \text{No}$$

Both statements 1 and 2 are mandatory. By implication, each time further user input is expected, the system first displays the results of processing the previous screen.

Finally, we define 'Return' as an instruction which returns control from a transaction to the tp monitor.

5.7 Evaluation of a Pseudo-Conversation

We can now use the structure diagram to specify each transaction. For transactions T1 and T2 we simply follow the logic specified beginning at the appropriate read instruction, and list the processing functions required, until the logic is ready to process a screen or request further input:

Transaction T1

This evaluates the result of (R1).

Function Key Entered	Actions Taken
TERMINATE	Next-id = End-of-program Read = No Return
KILL	Write record identification screen (W1) Next-id = T1 Read = Yes Return
AMEND	Next-id = T3 Read = No Return
Other	Write error message (W3) Next-id = T1 Read = Yes Return

Transaction T2

This evaluates the result of (R2).

Function Key Entered	Actions Taken
KILL	Write record identification screen (W1) Next-id = T1 Read = Yes Return
CLEAR	Write record display screen (W2) Next-id = T2 Read = Yes Return
ACCEPT	Next-id = T4 Read = No Return
Other	Write error message (W5) Next-id = T2 Read = Yes Return

Transactions T3 and T4 are simpler and may be specified using informal pseudo-code. Again we simply follow the logic specified in the structure diagram beginning at the point where the logic has detected the appropriate screen type.

Transaction T3

This processes data entered with a record identification screen:

```
Validate record identification screen data
IF      Invalid
            Write error message (w4)
            Next-id = T1
ELSE
            Write record display screen (w2)
            Next-id = T2
ENDS
Read = Yes
Return
```

'Validate' includes 'retrieve record (if there is one) from the data base'.

Transaction T4

This processes data entered with a record display screen:

```
Validate record display screen data
IF      Invalid
            Write error message (w6)
            Next-id = T2
ELSE
            Write record identification screen (w1)
            Next-id = T1
ENDS
Read = Yes
Return
```

This completes the pseudo-conversation. The end result is four transactions and apparently no high-level logic; in addition, each transaction is GOTO-less. All this is superficially attractive. However, although each transaction is now exceptionally simple, the high-level picture offered by the structure diagram is no longer present in the code. This is not necessarily serious; the point is to recognize the benefits of the picture as a design tool and the loss suffered if it is not preserved as part of the code. We now try to quantify this loss.

The following shows that part of the schematic logic corresponding to

152

Figure 5.7 concerned with the identification screen:

```
M1              MONITOR TERMINATE
TERMINAL   LOOP indefinitely
           M2         MONITOR KILL
           CYCLE   SEQ
                      M3              MONITOR valid screen data
                                      Write Ⓦ
                      IDENTIFY   LOOP indefinitely
                                 M4              MONITOR errors
                                 ATTEMPT   SEQ
                                 Read Ⓡ
                                 QUIT M1 IF TER -
                                 MINATE
                                 QUIT M2 IF KILL
                                 QUIT M4 IF not
                                 AMEND
                                 DO Record-identifica-
                                 tion-screen etc.


           CYCLE   ENDS
           M2         ADMIT KILL
           M2         ENDS
TERMINAL   ENDS
M1              ADMIT TERMINATE
M1              ENDS
```

Suppose now that the result of Ⓡ were KILL; then the following schematic instructions would be executed:

1. QUIT M2 IF KILL (escape to M2 ADMIT)
2. TERMINAL ENDS (branch back to the start of the loop)
3. TERMINAL LOOP indefinitely (null test for End-of-loop)
4. Write record identification screen Ⓦ
5. IDENTIFY LOOP indefinitely (null test for End-of-loop)

before again reaching the schematic Read Ⓡ.

Compare this with the use of pseudo-conversational techniques as described. Suppose we are executing T1 and have detected function key KILL. The statements:

```
Write record identification screen Ⓦ
Next-id = T1
Read = Yes
Return
```

have the same effect as the succession of instructions listed above—namely, to create the new screen and then to direct the logic to that part of the system which evaluates the next result of (RI). Any other processing functions allocated within the schematic logic would become part of T1, while the branch instructions implied by the structure diagram (and equivalent schematic logic) are now implemented by:

1. A return to the tp monitor; and later
2. A return to the system code, but not at the point immediately following the return.

Thus the design picture offered by the structure diagram becomes distorted. Consequently there is now no convenient way to read the code and understand the conversation implied. Experience shows that the consequences of amendments made may now not be fully appreciated, possibly resulting in system maintenance headaches later.

Pseudo-conversational techniques are used most frequently when the system code has to be implemented as a subroutine of the tp monitor. I have even seen them used when the tp monitor is a subroutine of the application code. The motivation is only partly to produce GOTO-less transactions; it may also be necessary in order to produce acceptably efficient code. Whenever they are used, the structure diagram can help to identify the transactions, but there is no way to retain the structure in the finished code. But to go further, logic inversion is necessary; these problems will, therefore, come up again in the next chapter. We shall then substantiate the view that the needs of design (that is, to preserve the structure) and the facilities provided for implementation do not match. In the circumstances given, pseudo-conversational techniques represent a possible compromise.

5.8   A More Complex System

The previous sections contain all the technical material required to design many conversations. In the remainder of this chapter we apply the principles to a more complex example, taken from an insurance broking system (though the application is really immaterial), intended to be typical of a wide range of 'menu-driven' systems.

We again restrict ourselves to one terminal, assume that communication between user and system is controlled by a tp monitor, and that the records used are held on some form of data base. In this case the data base refers to an accounts system, and the subset of the system with which we are concerned provides facilities to browse through ledger detail records for selected customer accounts. We assume, therefore, that the data base provides access facilities to:

1. Locate start of account, and reply account present or absent
2. Read forwards or backwards, one ledger detail at a time, and reply found or not found.

In the complete system there are many possible screen types; of these only four concern us. Likewise there are many function keys used, of which only six concern us. The screen types are:

1. First-level menu. This invites selection of one of several possible subsystems, of which we are interested only in ledger processing.
2. Second-level menu. This invites selection of one facility within the ledger processing subsystem, of which we are interested only in ledger display.
3. Detail display. This displays the content of ledger details using 'Mode 1': one screen line per detail, twenty details per screen.
4. Detail display. This displays the content of ledger details using 'Mode 2': four screen lines per detail, five details per screen.

Some of the function keys used are given descriptive names, others use codes:

ENTER   This indicates that menu selection has been completed
CLEAR   This escapes to the second-level menu
PF1   This scrolls forward one detail at a time
PF2   This scrolls backward one detail at a time
PF3   This escapes to the first-level menu
PF4   This changes the display mode from Mode 1 to Mode 2 or vice versa

An extra key (TERMINATE, say) is required to terminate processing and escape to the topmost level; we shall simplify the system by ignoring this.

The system starts by displaying a first-level menu inviting selection of one of the following options:

1. Ledger processing
2. Account maintenance
3. Others (omitted)

We consider option 1 only. Assuming then that no errors are detected on the completed screen, and that the operator presses ENTER, the system responds by displaying a second-level menu; this invites identification of the account and the selection of further options:

1. Ledger display
2. Cash split
3. Others (omitted)

Again, we consider option 1 only. The operator presses ENTER and the system responds by validating the account number and trying to locate the account. Assuming no errors are found, the system displays a screen of details using Mode 1, one detail per screen line.

The operator now thinks of the screen as providing a window on the account selected. The window may be moved along the account using one of the following function keys:

PF1   This scrolls forward one detail at a time
PF2   This scrolls backward one detail at a time

The system must ensure that PF1 does not try to read beyond the end of the account, and likewise that PF2 does not try to read before the start of the account.

At any stage the mode can be changed using function key PF4, and an escape can be made to a higher level using one of the following keys:

PF3   This escapes to the first-level menu
CLEAR   This escapes to the second-level menu

The following notes show how to design the logic required to analyse the operator responses including detection of, and recovery from, escapes and errors. It is assumed that suitable input/output instructions are available to locate the account, read records from it, and report errors detected; as before we ignore those 'system' errors which are detected by the data base and/or tp monitor software, and which terminate all user activity.

5.9   The Conversation Design

Building on the experience gained, we start straight away with the logic required under normal conditions, including escapes but ignoring the possibility of errors. The results are given in Figures 5.8 and 5.9. Figure 5.8 describes the logic of menu processing, while Figure 5.9 describes the logic to control user browsing facilities. In both diagrams the Read symbol ⓡ retains its meaning as defined in Section 5.2; the symbol ① acts as a connector between the two diagrams. Any data base access is assumed to form part of screen processing.

Figure 5.10 provides an alternative design for that part of Figure 5.9 which deals with Mode 1 (the remainder is omitted only to keep the diagram to a manageable size). The revised diagram looks more complex, but the detailed style shows the scrolling clearly and can be a help when trying to analyse the error conditions which can arise.

These diagrams show how the context is controlled using the function key, while ignoring the possibility of errors. The additional logic to detect and recover from errors can now be determined by inspecting each Read to ensure that all the possible results are accounted for. The four Read instructions used in Figures 5.8 and 5.9 are:

1. Read first-level menu screen
2. Read second-level menu screen
3. Read detail display screen (Mode 1)
4. Read detail display screen (Mode 2)

We refer to these as ⓡ₁ to ⓡ₄ respectively.

For each Read we need to take account of the following possibilities:

1. An out-of-sequence or unrecognizable function key may be entered
2. Screen data entered with an in-sequence function key may be invalid
3. Scroll forward may try to read beyond the end of account
4. Scroll backward may try to read before the start of account

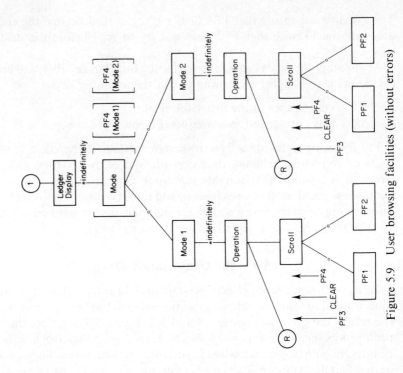

Figure 5.9 User browsing facilities (without errors)

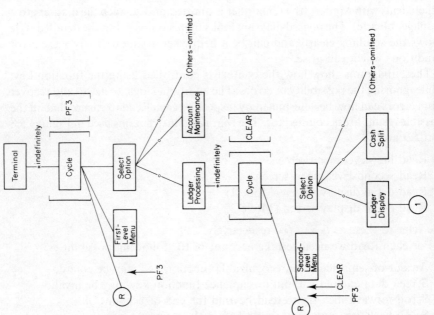

Figure 5.8 Menu-level processing (without errors)

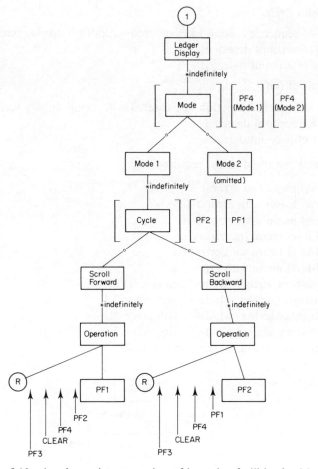

Figure 5.10   An alternative expression of browsing facilities for Mode 1

A complete list of the errors follows; each is cross-referenced to the Read from which it can arise:

1. As a result of (R1):
    1.1 Out-of-sequence function key entered with first-level menu
    1.2 Invalid screen data (if any) on first-level menu

2. As a result of (R2):
    2.1 Out-of-sequence function key entered with second-level menu
    2.2 Invalid screen data (account number) on second-level menu

    Error 2.2 covers the two cases:

        2.2.1 Account number invalid
        2.2.2 Account not found on file

    though we shall not distinguish these in the finished design.

3. As a result of (R3):

   3.1 Out-of-sequence function key entered with detail display screen

   3.2 End-of-account detected

   3.3 Start-of-account detected

4. As a result of (R4):

   4.1 Out-of-sequence function key entered with detail display screen

   4.2 End-of-account detected

   4.3 Start-of-account detected

We can now list the displays required:

1. First-level menu (no errors)
2. First-level menu with error 1.1
3. First-level menu with error 1.2
4. Second-level menu (no errors)
5. Second-level menu with error 2.1
6. Second-level menu with error 2.2
7. Detail display screen, Mode 1 (no errors)
8. Detail display screen, Mode 1, with error 3.1
9. Detail display screen, Mode 1, with error 3.2
10. Detail display screen, Mode 1, with error 3.3
11. Detail display screen, Mode 2 (no errors)

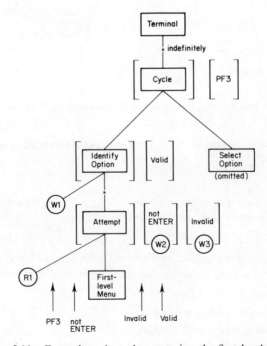

Figure 5.11   Error detection when entering the first-level menu

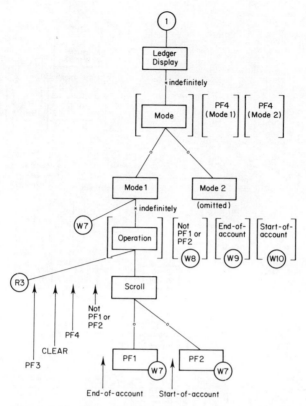

Figure 5.12   Error detection when working in Mode 1

12. Detail display screen, Mode 2, with error 4.1
13. Detail display screen, Mode 2, with error 4.2
14. Detail display screen, Mode 2, with error 4.3

These are referred to as ⓦ–ⓦ⃝ respectively.

While communicating each error to the user, we could include a prompt to correct it. Each Read is now amended to provide a loop to allow many 'attempts' to correct errors; the loop terminates as soon as valid data is entered together with an in-sequence function key. The addition of all error conditions tends to make the diagrams grow fast; for this reason Figures 5.11 and 5.12 amend only part of Figures 5.8 and 5.9 respectively. The Reads and Writes are numbered in accordance with the lists above. Figure 5.13 amends the alternative logic of Figure 5.10. Any logic omitted follows the patterns given.

5.10   The Equivalent Pseudo-Conversation

In this section we utilize the ideas and notation developed in Sections 5.6 and 5.7. For this system there are four Read instructions and four screen types. We can,

160

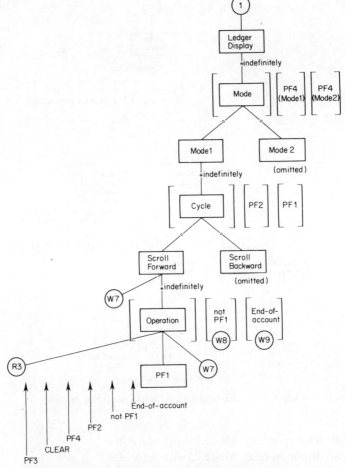

Figure 5.13   Alternative error detection for Mode 1

therefore, define eight transactions:

Transaction	Function
T1	Analyse results of (R1)
T2	Analyse results of (R2)
T3	Analyse results of (R3)
T4	Analyse results of (R4)
T5	Process first-level menu
T6	Process second-level menu
T7	Process detail display screen (Mode 1)
T8	Process detail display screen (Mode 2)

The following notes detail each transaction. The reader is encouraged to check these against the structure diagrams (Figures 5.11 and 5.12), while recalling that these are incomplete extensions of Figures 5.8 and 5.9.

Transaction T1

This evaluates the result of (R1).

Function Key Entered	Actions Taken
PF3	Write first-level menu (w1) Next-id = T1 Read = Yes Return
ENTER	Next-id = T5 Read = No Return
Other	Write error message (w2) Next-id = T1 Read = Yes Return

Transaction T2

This evaluates the result of (R2).

Function Key Entered	Actions Taken
PF3	Write first-level menu (w1) Next-id = T1 Read = Yes Return
CLEAR	Write second-level menu (w4) Next-id = T2 Read = Yes Return
ENTER	Next-id = T6 Read = No Return
Other	Write error message (w5) Next-id = T2 Read = Yes Return

Transaction T3

This evaluates the result of R3.

Function Key Entered	Actions Taken
PF3	Write first-level menu W1 Next-id = T1 Read = Yes Return
CLEAR	Write second-level menu W4 Next-id = T2 Read = Yes Return
PF4	Change display to Mode 2 W11 Next-id = T4 Read = Yes Return
PF1	Next-id = T7 Read = No Return
PF2	Next-id = T7 Read = No Return
Other	Write error message W8 Next-id = T3 Read = Yes Return

Transaction T4

This evaluates the result of R4.

Function Key Entered	Actions Taken
PF3	Write first-level menu W1 Next-id = T1 Read = Yes Return
CLEAR	Write second-level menu W4 Next-id = T2 Read = Yes Return

Transaction T4—contd.

Function Key Entered	Actions Taken
PF4	Change display to Mode 1 ⓦ₇ Next-id = T3 Read = Yes Return
PF1	Next-id = T8 Read = No Return
PF2	Next-id = T8 Read = No Return
Other	Write error message ⓦ₁₂ Next-id = T4 Read = Yes Return

Transaction T5

This processes data entered with a first-level menu screen.

Validate first-level menu screen data
IF Invalid
      Write error message ⓦ₃
      Next-id = T1
ELSE
      Write second-level menu ⓦ₄
      Next-id = T2
ENDS
Read = Yes
Return

For this transaction, the selection of Next-id might also depend on the screen data entered; selection of the ledger processing option is the only possibility considered.

Transaction T6

This processes data entered with a second-level menu screen.

Validate second-level menu screen data
IF Invalid
      Write error message ⓦ₆
      Next-id = T2

ELSE
> Display screen of details (Mode 1) (w7)
> Next-id = T3

ENDS
Read = Yes
Return

For this transaction, the selection of Next-id would normally depend on the screen data entered; selection of the ledger display option is the only possibility considered.

Transaction T7

This displays a screen using Mode 1.

IF PF1
> Read forward next detail
> IF End-of-account reached
>> Write error message (w9)
>> Next-id = T3

> ELSE
>> Scroll forward 1 detail (Mode 1) (w7)
>> Next-id = T3

> ENDS

ELSE
> Read backward next detail
> IF Start-of-account reached
>> Write error message (w10)
>> Next-id = T3

> ELSE
>> Scroll backward 1 detail (Mode 1) (w7)
>> Next-id = T3

> ENDS

ENDS
Read = Yes
Return

Transaction T8

This displays a screen using Mode 2.

IF   PF1
> Read forward next detail
> IF End-of-account reached
>> Write error message (w13)
>> Next-id = T4

> ELSE
>> Scroll forward 1 detail (Mode 2) (w11)
>> Next-id = T4

> ENDS

ELSE
>   Read backward next detail
>   IF Start-of-account reached
>> Write error message (W14)
>> Next-id = T4
>   ELSE
>> Scroll backward 1 detail (Mode 2) (W11)
>> Next-id = T4
>   ENDS
ENDS
Read = Yes
Return

Transactions T7 and T8 could be combined, or each split into two, without seriously compromising the design principles.

Chapter 6
Logic Inversion and Multitasking

We have now completed our discussion of the logic monitor for which we have given a reasonably wide range of illustrations. It is now time to move on to a new technique; this is called 'logic inversion' and is similar to the so-called multitasking feature of many programming languages and operating systems. Before we explain the design problems which inversion sets out to solve, here are a few preliminaries:

1. Of the three loose ends identified at the start of Chapter 3, we have cleared up one (namely, the logic to detect and recover from record sequence errors); the other two (page overflow, and pseudo-direct access techniques in file matching programs) remain outstanding and will be covered shortly.
2. There is no way to implement the logic monitor in commonly used programming languages without the use of an explicit GOTO. On balance, we choose to use the technique, and consequently accept the need for explicit GOTO's, because the concept is helpful and expressive. Much the same is true of inversion; I am confident that you will find it a powerful design concept, but we note now that there are implementation problems. The strategies open to us are covered in Section 6.9. We shall think of both techniques as GOTO-less at the design level.
3. We can think of MONITOR as weakening one of the assumptions of nested logic. (To remind you: the basic building blocks of nested logic are useful when describing complete structures, where there is an implicit guarantee that events will happen in the order described by the diagram. The logic monitor permits us to design logic even if no such guarantee is available). Inversion weakens a second assumption implied, but not expressed: namely, that there will always be one diagram which completely describes a given structure. After removing this restriction we shall be able to allow two (or more) diagrams to coexist in the same program.

6.1 A Suitable Case for Treatment

We start with an example to illustrate the motivation. This is taken from basic commercial programming; although it is very simple it contains all the essential features we require, and the results are relevant to batch-mode, on-line, and real-time systems.

A program reads a serial input file together with a parameter card, and creates a printed report, as summarized in Figure 6.1. It may be helpful to think of the

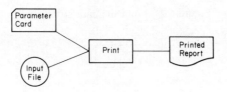

Figure 6.1   A print program

input file as some kind of master file, and the printed report as a 'hard' (printed) copy of the records held. From time to time records may be amended with the result that master file and hard copy get out of step; this program is provided to bring the hard copy up-to-date.

The three files used exhibit the following features:

1. Serial input file. The first record has the nature of a file header, and contains special values which are always printed. The second and all subsequent records may be marked as 'changed' or 'unchanged'; together with the parameter card value described below, this property is used to determine whether to print the record. The structure of this file is given in Figure 6.2.
2. Parameter card. There is just one parameter card which can take the value A, C, or D. These values tell the program how to process the input file:

   Value A. This means that the program should print all records, including the first.
   Value C. This means that the program should print the first record, and then print those following records which are marked 'changed'.
   Value D. This means that the program should print only the first record from the input file.

   The structure of this file is given in Figure 6.3; it would, of course, be perfectly acceptable to put in an extra level to show 'File consists of one parameter card, which is then of type A, C, or D'.
3. Printed report. Whatever value the parameter card shows, the printed report always has the same basic layout:

   All pages have the normal page headings and page number.
   The first input record, which is always printed, is printed on its own on the first page.

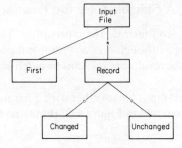

Figure 6.2 Input file data structure

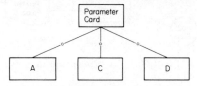

Figure 6.3 Parameter card structure

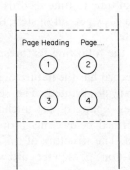

Figure 6.4 Report layout

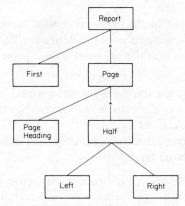

Figure 6.5 Report structure

The second and subsequent records (if any) are printed 'two up, four to a page', in the order shown in Figure 6.4, where each record occupies approximately one quarter of a page of print.

We note that the last page may not be complete.

Figure 6.5 describes the structure of the printed report assuming all pages are complete. This could be drawn differently (for example to show the four reports on a page as a sequence), but such changes would have no major impact on the design. In any event, the interest is in what happens next, and not in the details of each diagram, so let us move on. We shall add in the special considerations at End-of-file in the next section.

This completes the program description and some initial design. The question now is: how should the design be completed using structured programming principles? We could (following the lines of earlier examples) find a way to combine the three data structure diagrams given into a single program structure; this can be done (and we shall see the results later), but first there are some other considerations relevant here.

6.2   A Modular Design

We have, on many occasions, asserted that the programs designed were fully modular, and that the special contribution of structured programming was to the design of the complex control logic which frequently characterizes the topmost module(s); at the same time we have noted that the principles described can also be applied to the design of logic internal to the lower-level modules, although here the logic tends to be less complex. It is worth examining for a moment how the concept of modularity applies to the present example.

Modular programming invites the use of subroutines; the subroutines should be chosen so that:

1. Each module performs a logical subset of the total processing.
2. Each module is functionally independent of each other module.

Ideally, each module should also be so designed that it is single entry, single exit, simple, testable, maintainable, and so on.

Now, in this program we can identify two quite distinct functions:

1. Select those records on the input file which need to be printed.
2. For those records selected, format and print the report.

These are functionally independent in the following sense:

1. When deciding which record to print next, the factors involved are:

    parameter value (A, C, or D)
    record type (first record, changed, or unchanged record)

    In particular, no account is taken of where the last record was printed.

170

2. When deciding where to print the next record selected, the factors involved are:

first page or subsequent page
page layout (two-up, four to a page)
some special considerations about the last page

In particular, no account is taken of how the record was selected.

These considerations are sufficient to suggest that the program should be built from two quite distinct modules—one to implement each of the functions identified. This has all the advantages normally associated with modularity, including for example the ability to change the rules for selection without altering that part of the program which does the printing, and vice versa. If the point is taken, then it makes no kind of sense to build one program structure from the three separate data structures, since this would only give a single monolithic program (as noted already, we shall try this out later, just to see what happens). The best that can be done is to combine the two input data structures to give one diagram which describes the input as a whole, and find some new way to combine this with the output data structure, such that input and output structures remain visibly separate and committed to their independent roles.

There are various ways to combine the two input file data structures; one such way is shown in Figure 6.6, which also displays the loop-terminating conditions. Effectively, this suggests that we have one physical input file, and that the role of the parameter card is to give that physical file three separate logical structures depending on the parameter value. If you prefer to think of the parameter card differently (as for example, to tell the program what to do with an individual input record), then the diagram would be redrawn with the parameter card appearing below record level—the detailed alterations required are omitted. In

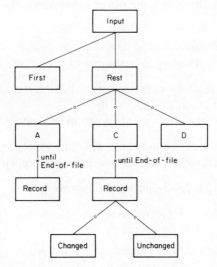

Figure 6.6   Combining the two input data structures

the absence of further information, the choice must be considered largely a matter of style. Next, Figure 6.7 extends Figure 6.5 to show the loop-terminating conditions and one of several possible methods to handle End-of-file; it is implied that End-of-file after completing one half is not End-of-page; it is just End-of-file in the middle of a page.

We now have two diagrams—one describes how to analyse the input to identify those records which need to be printed (Figure 6.6), and the other describes how to construct the output to print those records selected (Figure 6.7).

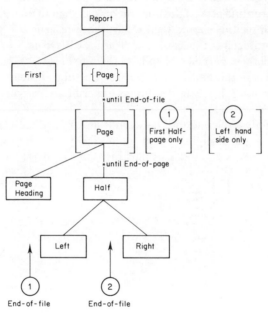

Figure 6.7   The extra logic to detect End-of-file

For brevity we shall refer to these diagrams as X and Y respectively, and in order to achieve the functional independence required, we decline to combine X and Y to give one diagram suitable for the program as a whole. And since we are used to thinking of a structure diagram as equivalent to a piece of logic, I shall also take the schematic logic as given. A glance at the two diagrams confirms that they are functionally independent in the sense described above, and indeed in any other way that an advocate of modularity could wish; it seems common sense, therefore, to allow X and Y to coexist; we have only to decide now how to link them together to form a program.

As in all the examples presented in this book, the special contribution of structured programming is to the design of high-level control logic. This logic is now split between the two functionally independent modules X and Y. We shall, therefore, apply structured programming principles separately to the design

172

of logic internal to X and Y; the motivation (which leads ultimately to the inversion concept) is to retain the functional independence achieved, while designing the internal control logic of each module using (so far as is possible) structured concepts. Since we have never before allowed two diagrams to coexist in the same program in this way, we had better proceed slowly.

6.3   Intermediate Files

The normal way to link two modules together to form one program, is for one module to be a subroutine of the other. In our example, the natural thing to do is to have Y a subroutine of X. The function of X is then to analyse the input and determine which records should be printed; those records selected for printing are passed as parameters of successive subroutine calls from X to Y; the function of Y is to receive these parameters and use them to construct the printed report. Note that there is nothing to stop us having X a subroutine of Y (and we shall check this in Section 6.10). This decision is not critical; the critical decision is to to keep X and Y separate.

In order to analyse the interface between X and Y further, it is helpful now to redesign the program slightly, and temporarily, by introducing a serial intermediate file between X and Y as illustrated in Figure 6.8; in this new design

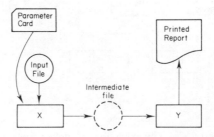

Figure 6.8   Introducing an intermediate file

the function of X is to write records on to the intermediate file, while the function of Y is to read records off it. If such a file existed then X and Y would be two free-standing programs. Figures 6.6 and 6.7 could then be updated with suitable processing functions (such as Read, Print) allocated. Since Y would then read the intermediate file, the Read statement in Y would mean 'Read intermediate file' and be allocated according to the read-ahead principle, while the condition 'until End-of-file' in Y would be taken to mean 'until End-of-intermediate-file'.

But in the real world there is only one program, and no such intermediate file; we can, however, now reason as follows:

1. *If* X and Y were implemented as free-standing programs communicating via an intermediate file, then we would be able to allocate a Read statement in Y.
2. But there is no such intermediate file.

3. Instead, we know that the records that Y would have read now appear as the parameters of successive subroutine calls from X to Y. These are the same records, and occur in the same order.

Thus the output from X is the input to Y, and we may infer that 'Read intermediate file' in Y means 'receive the parameter of the next subroutine call from X'. In detail:

1. Each call from X says, effectively: 'I, X, have found the next record that Y requires; all I need to do is pass it to Y confident that Y will deal with all questions concerned with page layout; when Y has finished, control will return to me and I shall continue executing with the instruction following the call.'
2. The processing function 'Read intermediate file' in Y means: 'I, Y, have finished with the previous record from X and want the next record from X; since X knows all about record selection, all I need to do is return to X and await the next call; when the next call comes I shall continue executing with the instruction following the Read.'

In this way, everything that Y finds out by reading the intermediate file is communicated to Y as the parameter of a call from X. In particular, since Y

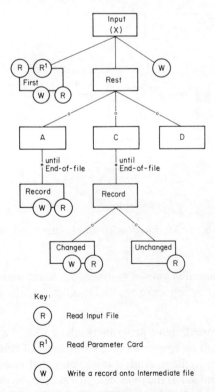

Figure 6.9   Module X with input/output instructions

detects End-of-intermediate-file, X must be sure to call Y after detecting End-of-file. All this is included in Figures 6.9 and 6.10, which now replace Figures 6.6 and 6.7 respectively.

In order to link X and Y together we have now to find a way to tie up the calls from X with the corresponding Reads in Y. And since we have gone to considerable trouble and expense to get this far, the linkage should ideally not disturb the structures identified for X and Y (after all, the linkage in question is the *only* new feature of this example).

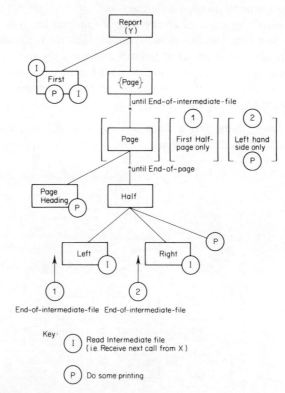

Figure 6.10   Module Y with input/output instructions

The technique required is known as inversion. Since many programmers find the term 'inversion' puzzling, here are two thoughts which may go some way to rationalize it:

1. To use inversion you design a program (such as Y) in the normal way, as if its input were collected on to a serial file; but instead of being implemented as a program with its own file to read, it is implemented as a subroutine to which the same input is passed as the parameters of successive subroutine calls. Thus the program is 'inverted' from a 'main' program which is responsible for

reading its input, to a subroutine (or 'inverted' program) to which its input is passed.

2. Main programs analyse files into records; inverted programs construct files from records. However, all programs are designed the same way (as if they were analysing a serial input file); it is only the detailed implementation of the Read instruction which distinguishes the two.

Neither of these points is entirely convincing. Nonetheless, the name 'inversion' now seems to be established to describe the general technique and so we shall continue to use it. In the next section we see how inversion provides a kind of multitasking, in which one task is a calling program and the other a called subroutine. We then go on to consider structure diagram and schematic logic conventions and some detailed implementation problems.

6.4 Multitasking

Inversion is a special case of the multitasking feature frequently found in real-time systems. Since these form the main subject matter of Chapter 8, we shall restrict ourselves at this stage to a brief summary, sufficient only to establish the concepts required, and point the way to a suitable notation.

The term 'multitasking' is usually used to describe any system built from two or more interdependent 'tasks', where the tasks can be thought of as programs running in parallel under the overall control of an operating system. In real-time systems, such as process control, the tasks are frequently given the special name 'process'; the use of the same word 'process' is just an unfortunate coincidence; sometimes 'activity' is used instead. Communication between, and synchronization of, processes is achieved using high-level instructions which we shall later (in Chapter 8) call 'Send' and 'Receive'. The unit of information passed (from sender to receiver) is called a message; since there may be several processes running in parallel, it is usual to allow that a second message may be sent to a process before it has finished processing the first; accordingly there can be several messages awaiting receipt by any process, and these are said to constitute a 'queue'. The Send instruction adds a new message to the queue; the Receive instruction takes a message off the queue. In languages designed with this multitasking feature in mind, there may also be variations on the basic Send and Receive instructions described, while the detailed implementation ensures that it does not matter which process starts execution first. There are also usually no restrictions on the number of occasions that Send and Receive instructions can be used in any given piece of code. All this is described in greater detail in Chapter 8.

We have identified a special case in which there are just two tasks, which we shall continue to call X and Y. Instead of being implemented as processes, communicating via messages held on a queue, one task (X) is implemented as a main program and the other (Y) as a subroutine, the queue size is restricted to just one message, and the content of the queue called a record. Correspondingly, we replace Send and Receive by two new instructions, called Restart and Suspend respectively, to communicate between X and Y. These are used as follows:

1. Restart Y. This instruction (for use in X) says:

remember where X is up to
stop execution of X, start execution of Y
continue execution of X with the next instruction when Y next says Suspend

2. Suspend. This instruction (for use in Y) says:

remember where Y is up to
stop execution of Y, start execution of X
continue execution of Y with the next instruction when X next says Restart Y

We shall assume that the instruction Restart Y is implemented as a conventional subroutine call. The unit of information passed would then be called a parameter, and there would only be one call outstanding at any time. In contrast, the Suspend instruction is inevitably quite different from the conventional return from a subroutine call, for Suspend not only terminates the current execution of Y but ensures that next time Y is called (using Restart) it restarts from the point where it last said Suspend.

We can then think of Suspend as a two-part instruction:

1. Return to X

and later

2. Continue with the next instruction.

We need to distinguish two special cases of Suspend in Y:

first time through, Y must start from the beginning (without having previously said Return)
last time through, Y returns to X (and is never called again to continue with the next instruction).

It is as if one Suspend instruction is split—part 2 above is executed at the beginning of Y, and part 1 at the end of Y. All other Suspends in Y consist of both parts 1 and 2.

It is not essential to implement Restart as a conventional subroutine call. But a more sophisticated implementation, which makes Restart more like the Send instruction found in real-time systems, is outside the scope of this book. This possibility, together with the fact that the use of Restart acts as a reminder that there is a corresponding task, implemented as a subroutine, which contains Suspend, is sufficient justification for using the new instruction. We note now that we shall later use Restart and Suspend to allow more than just two tasks to communicate; Suspend then returns to whichever calling program last said Restart Y, while Y may later be restarted by any other task. As with Send and Receive, there are no restrictions on the number of occurrences of Restart or Suspend instructions in one task.

We can now distinguish three possible implementations of a Read instruction:

1. Make a subroutine call. The instruction is usually written:

   Read (file)

   or

   Call (subroutine name)

   and may be replaced by in-line code. All the Reads in Chapters 1 to 5 (except as noted in Sections 1.9 and 5.6) were of this kind. If a subroutine call is used the record read is returned as a reply. We shall denote the return from a subroutine call with the instruction 'Exit'. This implementation of Read is widely used and generally accepted.
2. Receive the next call made to this subroutine. The instruction is written:

   Suspend

   The subroutine which contains Suspend is called using the Restart instruction defined above. Although most high-level languages provide no direct implementation of Suspend, we shall take the view that it is a new and desirable concept. Accordingly, the remainder of this chapter is largely devoted to refining its definition; further examples of its use are given in Chapters 7 and 8. Unlike 1 above, this implementation of Read is less widely appreciated.
3. Receive the next message passed to this process. Further consideration of this case and the associated instructions Send and Receive is deferred until Chapter 8. We note, however, that Send and Receive instructions are widely implemented in high-level languages designed for multitasking between processes; as described in Chapter 8, communication between them becomes the responsibility of the operating system. This implementation of Read is a commonplace in real-time systems.

Read instructions are always allocated according to the Read-ahead principle. Corresponding to the cases listed above we have:

1. The records read are the contents of a serial input file. One Read executed results in one record read.
2. The records read appear on a notional serial intermediate file, created by one or more calling programs. One record read corresponds to one call made; only one call is outstanding at any time.
3. The records read form a message queue, created by one or more other processes. One message received corresponds to one message sent, but there may be several messages on the queue at any one time.

We shall maintain that any program written using nested logic, with or without MONITOR, which contains one or more read instructions as defined above, is GOTO-less, at least at the design level. This is an attractive property, making designs easy to read and understand. Regrettably, as noted earlier, we shall find it impossible to implement the design without the use of explicit GOTO's, at least in existing languages. We shall then have to contrast (in Section 6.9) the needs of design with the constraints imposed by the implementation tools available.

We return now to complete the structure diagram and schematic logic notation for inversion. Some further observations on multitasking are in Section 6.10 and Chapter 8.

6.5   Structure Diagram and Schematic Logic Conventions

The various implementations of Read are distinguished on the structure diagram by attaching a suffix to the standard (R) symbol:

Read Instruction	Symbol
Call	(R_c)
Suspend	(R_s)
Receive	(R_r)

Corresponding to each Read instruction we shall think of a Write instruction whose job it is to make the result of each Read available. Accordingly, we adapt the Write symbol (w) used in Chapter 5 and Section 6.3, and again distinguish the various implementations by attaching a suffix:

Write Instruction	Symbol
Exit	(w_e)
Restart	(w_r)
Send	(w_s)

The symbols (R_r) and (w_s) will not be used until Chapter 8. As noted above, the final Suspend in a subroutine only effects a return to the calling program, and may usually be omitted without loss of meaning; no special notation is used to highlight the initial Suspend. Since any subroutine must have an exit, it is only rarely necessary to use the (w_e) symbol in practice.

The same $\bigcirc$ symbol may also contain:

the letter R or W (without a suffix). This still means Read or Write respectively, but the implementation is either irrelevant or clear from the context

a different letter (such as (x), (P)). This can be used to represent either Read or Write; the file referenced should be clear from the context. If there is any risk of ambiguity a key is provided

a number (such as (1), (2)). This always represents a connector as described in Chapter 1.

Given two structure diagrams, such as the X and Y of our example, all we need to do is show:

1. Those points at which X calls Y.
2. Those points at which Y reads a call from X.

We recall that this was done in Figures 6.9 and 6.10. As noted in Figure 6.9, the symbol (w) was used to mean 'Write a record' and is now equivalent to (w,), or Restart Y. The parameter of each call is a printable record, except for the very last call which communicates End-of-file. Likewise, in Figure 6.10 the symbol (I) means 'Read intermediate file', and is now equivalent to (R,), or Suspend. The result of each Read is a printable record, except for the very last one which detects End-of-intermediate-file. Figures 6.11 and 6.12 update Figures 6.9 and 6.10 respectively to display the new instructions. So long as it is understood that there are now two diagrams, and that there is a one-to-one correspondence between the parameters of calls made in one diagram and the results of reads made in the other, there is no need for any further diagrammatic convention, and we move on to consider the equivalent schematic logic.

Because of their importance we shall now think of Call, Exit, Restart, Suspend, Send, and Receive instructions as part of the schematic logic; we shall continue to use Read and Write as generic terms which may be interpreted in any of the ways listed above depending on the context. There being no new points of principle, we can write down the schematic logic corresponding to Figure 6.11 in the normal way. This gives:

```
INPUT   SEQ
        Read input file
        Read Parameter card
        Restart Y
        Read Input file
        REST    IF A-run
                A       LOOP until End-of-file
                        Restart Y
                        Read Input file
                A       ENDS
        REST    ELSE    C-run
                C       LOOP until End-of-file
                        RECORD  IF Changed
                                Restart Y
                                Read Input file
                        RECORD  ELSE
                                Read Input file
                        RECORD  ENDS
                C       ENDS
        REST    ELSE    D-run
                (Null)
        REST    ENDS
        Restart Y
INPUT   ENDS
```

180

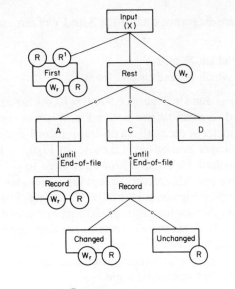

Key: (R) Read Input file

(R¹) Read Parameter card

Figure 6.11   Module X showing calls to Y

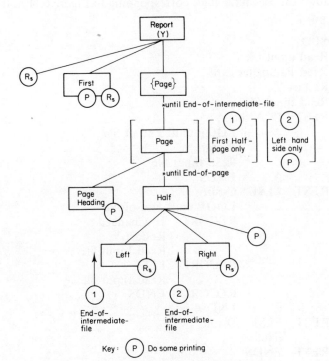

Key: (P) Do some printing

Figure 6.12   Module Y showing returns to X

The logic of Y is described by the structure diagram of Figure 6.12, where the Suspend instruction means 'Receive parameter of next subroutine call from X'. We can again write down the schematic logic in the normal way. This gives:

```
REPORT  SEQ
        Suspend
        Print First page
        Suspend
        {PAGE}  LOOP until End-of-intermediate-file
                M       MONITOR End-of-intermediate-file
                PAGE  SEQ
                      Print Page-heading
                      {HALF}  LOOP until End-of-page
                              HALF  SEQ
                                    QUIT M IF End-of-
                                        intermediate-file
                                    DO Left
                                    Suspend
                                    QUIT M IF End-of-
                                        intermediate-file
                                    DO Right
                                    Suspend
                              HALF  ENDS
                              Print Half-a-page
                      {HALF}  ENDS
                PAGE  ENDS
                M       ADMIT First-half-page-only
                        (Null)
                M       ADMIT Left-hand-side-only
                        Print Last Half-page
                M       ENDS
        {PAGE}  ENDS
REPORT  ENDS
```

The schematic instructions Restart and Suspend are jointly read as follows. Whenever a piece of logic (X, say) is found which contains an instruction Restart Y, there will be a corresponding subroutine (Y) which contains one or more Suspend instructions. Either X or Y, or both, may contain a monitor. Each Suspend instruction inside Y is equivalent to a Read. But do not be fooled by this Read; this Read does not mean 'Read next record from a serial input file'; instead it means: 'If there were a serial input file then this is where Y would read it; but there is no such file; instead Y must suspend, return to the calling program X, and restart at the instruction following this Read when the calling program next says Restart Y'. In all respects the logic of Y is constructed according to the best principles of structured programming and functions exactly as it would have done had there been a serial file to read. In particular, the schematic logic is

GOTO-less. We shall speak of the called subroutine as being 'inverted with respect to the intermediate file' passed from the calling program.

The logic is now complete except for some processing functions (such as open and close, and loop counts and controls), and, of course, any detailed language-dependent implementation considerations. These are covered in the next section.

6.6 The Implementation of Inversion

Whereas the implementation of nested logic and the logic monitor is comparatively straightforward (and so deferred to the Appendix), the implementation of inversion is relatively troublesome. For this reason we shall go into some detail here, and take time later to assess the consequences (in Sections 6.7 and 6.9). To focus our attention, we postpone completion of our print program and introduce a new but simpler structure. This artificial case will be sufficient to establish a general coding technique. In Section 6.7 we shall identify all the problems associated with it. We shall then return to the print program in Section 6.8 and, in Section 6.9, consider the design compromises which might be made in practice.

Consider the following. You are given a simple file whose structure is described in Figure 6.13; the logic to process this file (including the Reads) creates no problem and is given in flowchart form as Figure 6.14. Suppose now that when

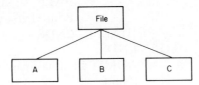

Figure 6.13   A simple data structure

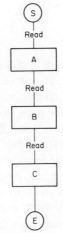

Figure 6.14   Flowchart of the logic to read and process the file

the program was initially specified, it was assumed that the records A, B, C would be available on a serial input file. It now turns out that the source of the records to be processed is not yet decided; in order to protect the design work already completed, a new program will be written whose sole responsibility is to locate the records A, B, C, and pass them to you in the correct order as the parameters of separate subroutine calls. Your program has the same job to do, but is now a subroutine (call it Y) of a calling program (call it X) whose detailed construction is not known to you; all you know is that each time you are called, a record is passed as parameter, and that the records passed will be A, B, C, in that order.

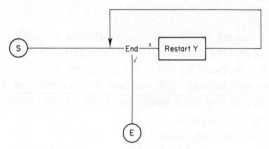

Figure 6.15 A calling program

The logic of the calling program could be as simple as that in Figure 6.15, but could equally be much more complex. In schematic form the logic of Y can be described quite simply:

```
FILE   SEQ
       Suspend
       DO A
       Suspend
       DO B
       Suspend
       DO C
FILE   ENDS
```

We assume that the host language does not provide the equivalent of Suspend. If we still want to retain the structure, and still want this structure to be present in the finished program, we have to resort to the following. The first time Y is called, it must start from the beginning and continue until next ready to say Suspend; the second and subsequent times Y is ready to say Suspend, it must instead:

remember where Y is up to

return to the calling program

restart from the instruction following Suspend next time it is called.

Each Suspend in Y is now effectively an entry point from the calling program. But it makes no sense to implement Y as a subroutine with three entry points, not because of any objection to multiple entry points in principle, but because the calling program would then have to decide which entry point to use, and to do this it would have to know in what order to use the entry points, and this in turn means it would have to know all about the internal structure of Y. This would be self-defeating because the calling and called programs would then not be functionally independent in the manner required.

The only alternative is to use a single entry point. This necessitates the introduction of a switch for use inside Y; since we tend to dislike the use of switches (as in Section 3.2.2), we shall call this switch a 'state variable' (more on this in Sections 6.7 and 6.9). Using the state variable we can summarize the alterations now required to Y as follows:

1. Delete each Suspend instruction, and introduce a state variable preset to some initial value. (We shall call this state variable 'SV').
2. Replace the first Suspend by a 'Go to ... depending on ...' or its equivalent (depending on the language used, and how the state variable is implemented).
3. Replace the second and subsequent Suspends by instructions to:

   (a) Update the state variable
   (b) Go to a common exit point

   and add a label to identify the restart point.
4. Add a common exit point at the end, and an initial label at the start.

In flowchart form, the new logic is given in Figure 6.16. In informal code this is equivalent to:

```
        Go to L1, L2, L3 depending on SV.
L1.
FILE    SEQ
        DO A
        Move 2 to SV.
        Go to END.
L2.
        DO B
        Move 3 to SV.
        Go to END.
L3.
        DO C
FILE    ENDS
END.    Exit.
```

The mixture of schematic logic and 'lower-case COBOL' is deliberate. We note that the state variable, which conceptually belongs to the subroutine, must be initialized correctly before the subroutine is called for the first time. In practice this can only be done at compile-time, or by the calling program. Resetting the state variable back to its initial value after executing the subroutine for the last time would make the subroutine 'serially reusable'.

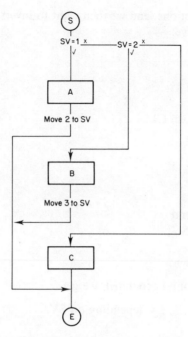

Figure 6.16 The implementation of inversion

The initial label (L1) and common exit point (END) implement the two special cases of Suspend (first time through and last time through respectively) noted in Section 6.4.

6.7 Some Language Problems

Before evaluating this logic we should note that the method used may give rise to implementation problems in high-level languages. Consider the more complex structure of Figure 6.17. If the boxes A, C, D represent records, and C1, C2

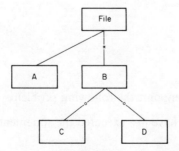

Figure 6.17 A more complex data structure

represent suitable conditions, and we then want to invert this with respect to a calling program, we have:

```
FILE   SEQ
       Suspend
       DO A
       Suspend
       {B}   LOOP until C1
             B   IF C2
                 DO C
                 Suspend
             B   ELSE
                 DO D
                 Suspend
             B   ENDS
       {B}   ENDS
FILE   ENDS
```

With the inversion (only) expanded, we get:

```
       Go to L1, L2, L3, L4 depending on SV.
L1.
FILE   SEQ
       DO A
       Move 2 to SV.
       Go to END.
L2.
{B}    LOOP until C1
B      IF C2
       DO C
       Move 3 to SV.
       Go to END.
L3.
B      DO D
       Move 4 to SV.
       Go to END.
L4.
B      ENDS
{B}    ENDS
FILE   ENDS
END.   Exit.
```

This is sufficient to pinpoint the following problems:

1. LOOP. Suppose we have just executed the statement 'Move 3 to SV'. What happens next is:

   1. Branch out of the loop (labelled {B}); and

2. Later, when this subroutine is called again, branch back into the loop (to L3) hoping that the loop will continue to work correctly.

Most, if not all, block-structured languages do not provide an equivalent instruction which would support this. It might work, but you could not complain if it did not.

2. IF...ELSE.... The label L3 represents a label between 'IF' and 'ELSE' and the label L4 represents a label between 'ELSE' and 'ENDS'. Some high-level languages do not provide an equivalent instruction for which this is permitted.

Further, suppose the logic had been written using a mixture of in-line and out-of-line code:

```
FILE    SEQ
        Suspend
        DO A
        Suspend
        DO {B}
FILE    ENDS
{B}     LOOP until C1
        B   IF C2
            DO C
            Suspend
        B   ELSE
            DO D
            Suspend
        B   ENDS
{B}     ENDS
```

Then, as before, any Suspend instruction executed in subroutine {B} has the effect of suspending the task (or subroutine) FILE. When the next Restart instruction is executed, the task (or subroutine) FILE must be restarted in the normal way at the instruction following Suspend; in the circumstances specified, this occurs in subroutine {B}. Hence any implementation must ensure that all link addresses, including those represented by the call 'DO {B}', are correctly preserved from one invocation of FILE to the next.

It follows that in order to be safe when using inversion with high-level languages:

1. All loops which contain Suspend should be 'hand-coded' (as defined in the Appendix, Section A.1).
2. All selection groups which contain Suspend should be hand-coded.
3. In-line code should be used for any building block which contains Suspend.

As a consequence, the inverted logic will finally expand to:

Go to L1, L2, L3, L4 depending on SV.

L1.

FILESEQ.

    DO A

    Move 2 to SV.

    Go to END.

L2.

{B}LOOP.

    IF C1 Go to {B}END.

BIF.

    IF not C2 Go to BELSE.

    DO C

    Move 3 to SV.

    Go to END.

L3.

    Go to BEND.

BELSE.

    Do D

    Move 4 to SV.

    Go to END.

L4.

BEND.

    Go to {B}LOOP.

{B}END.

FILEEND.

END.

    Exit.

I said that the implementation of inversion was relatively nasty, and now you can see why. But the worst is over; all the coding problems have been exposed. It has to be confessed straight away that the implementation of inversion is not pretty; we have introduced a state variable, and in most languages there will be no way of avoiding explicit GOTO's, not to mention the additional labels. Many programmers, especially those familiar with the benefits of high-level block-structured languages, will quite reasonably protest. Indeed, I have known many who would now choose to abandon the design and try something else; let us, therefore, emphasize that:

1. Although a state variable is necessary, this is not to be taken as an invitation to the free and unrestricted use of switches.

2. The sequence of three instructions:

    .   Move n to SV.

        Go to END.

    Ln.

is precisely equivalent to a Read. (At the start of the sequence given we need the next record; at the end we have got it and can continue processing.) It is just the mechanics of the Read which have changed.

3. Although GOTO's proliferate, they are not spaghetti GOTO's; it is, however, very unfortunate that in most high-level languages they have to be coded explicitly.
4. It is equally unfortunate that the GOTO's are, at present, incompatible with the spirit of block-structured languages.

It really is as if we should like to have available the new high-level instruction Suspend defined earlier, and make this compatible with the code's block structure. Since no such instruction is generally available, we have constructed one; the construction is a good design concept, but raises major implementation headaches. We shall consider the options now open to us in Section 6.9. In the meantime, the reader is invited to consider the following two rhetorical questions. First: what would we think if we had just discovered the need for subroutines, at a time when high-level block-structured languages did not provide a Call statement? Would we then choose to invent a design concept whose function was the same as Call and accept the consequence that we should have to abandon some high-level instructions, undermine the spirit of block-structured code, and accept the need for explicit GOTO's? Second: is the use of multiple Suspend instructions within one task (whether these occur within a subroutine of that task or not), justified by the analogous use of multiple Receive instructions within one process in high-level languages used to implement real-time systems? There is, of course, no point in speculating too much over hypotheticals, though the points raised would certainly be much the same.

6.8 The Logic Completed and Tested

We return now to the example of Section 6.1 and use this to produce final code; in the next section we shall assess the alternative strategies open to us. So far as X (the calling program) is concerned, there is no problem, and the logic may be implemented in the normal way. All the problems occur in Y (the subroutine) for which the schematic logic was presented in Section 6.5; we give below the logic fully expanded to our 'lower-case COBOL'.

        Go to L1, L2, L3, L4 depending on SV.
L1.
REPORTSEQ.
        Print First page.
        Move 2 to SV.
        Go to END.
L2.
{PAGE}LOOP.
        If End-of-intermediate-file Go to {PAGE}END.
MMONITOR.
PAGESEQ.
        Print Page-heading.

```
{HALF}LOOP.
      If End-of-page Go to {HALF}END.
HALFSEQ.
      If End-of-intermediate-file Go to MADMIT1.
      DO Left
      Move 3 to SV.
      Go to END.
L3.
      If End-of-intermediate-file Go to MADMIT2.
      Do Right
      Move 4 to SV.
      Go to END.
L4.
HALFEND.
      Print Half-a-page.
      Go to {HALF}LOOP.
{HALF}END.
PAGEEND.
      Go to MEND.
MADMIT1.
      (Null)
      Go to MEND.
MADMIT2.
      Print Last Half-page.
MEND.
      Go to {PAGE}LOOP.
{PAGE}END.
REPORTEND.
END.
      Exit.
```

If you have any reservations about how this works, try the following test. Assume that the parameter card takes the value C and that the following records appear on the input file:

First
Changed
Unchanged
Unchanged
Changed
Changed
Unchanged
Changed
Changed
Unchanged
Changed
Unchanged

If you follow the logic carefully, you will find that the state variable takes the successive values

$$1, \quad 2, \quad 3, \quad 4, \quad 3, \quad 4, \quad 3, \quad 4$$

It may help to remind you that we have carefully arranged things so that there is a one-to-one correspondence between calls from X and reads in Y. Thus, the intermediate file contains seven printable records (the first record and six Changed records); Y reads this file eight times (once for each record, and once to detect End-of-file) corresponding to the eight calls from X (one to request printing of each of the seven printable records, and one to communicate End-of-file).

Remember also that our design assumes that 'End-of-page' is taken to mean 'after completing both halves of the page'. For the record sequence given, End-of-file occurs after completing only the first half, and is detected by the first of the two QUIT instructions.

6.9 The Design Compromises Available

It has to be repeated that the final logic is probably no-one's idea of 'pretty' code. It is a programming commonplace that excessive GOTO's should be avoided, not to mention labels, switches, and the rest. Yet here we have a piece of code to implement a relatively simple program which uses 19 labels, 12 GOTO's (including one Go to . . . depending on . . .), and a blatant switch. Certainly, some obvious simplifications can be made, such as removing unreferenced labels; but there is nothing to be done about the GOTO's or about the switch, short of changing the design.

The design objectives do not seem open to question. Thus, we started from basic modularity principles; this led us to identify two program components (subsequently labelled X and Y) which were functionally independent in every sense that one could wish. All we then set out to do was to design the control logic internal to each module. We based this on the data structures found (using the ideas now well established); all this seems reasonable enough, but the presence of the subroutine Y forced us to introduce the inversion technique to provide a standard linkage between X and Y which, at the same time, preserved their internal structure. The result, at least so far as Y is concerned, is a piece of not-so-pretty code.

How then are we to assess this code? Here are some possibilities. In the first instance we can:

either 1. Accept the design.
or 2. Reject the design.

In this context 'the design' refers both to the modularity and to the use of standardized logic building blocks. If we accept the design then we must:

either 1. Use a software aid, such as a preprocessor, to extend existing languages to include Restart and Suspend as new logic constructs. The GOTO's and the switch are then not visible to the application programmer.

192

or   2. Use strong coding conventions to minimize any possible confusion caused by the GOTO's and the switch.

Both points of view are acceptable. If, on the other hand, we argue that the coding consequences are so severe that under no circumstances should one retain the design, we are forced to reject it and then we must compromise. Some possibilities are:

1. Write two programs instead of one. In this case X and Y are both written as free-standing programs with a 'real' intermediate file passed between them.
2. Integrate X and Y into one common program structure. Figure 6.18 shows one way to do this (in which the MONITOR required at End-of-file has been omitted). Most designs of this kind will tend to increase the number of QUITs.
3. Partially integrate X and Y by moving some of the functions of Y over to X. This undermines the functional independence, while the state variable can be disguised but not eliminated. The details of such a compromise are discussed in another context in Section 7.3.2.

Again each position is tenable, and the final choice between them must be left to you. No doubt there are other designs, too (such as reducing the number of

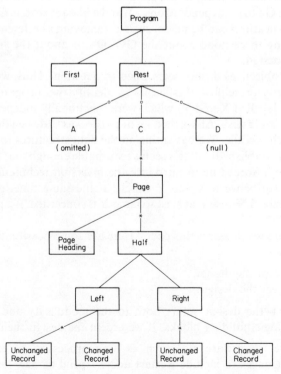

Figure 6.18   A compromise structure diagram

Reads in Y to one). In the last resort it is all a matter of trade-offs. The question to be answered is 'What is important?'. In particular, is it important to preserve structure and/or retain modularity and/or avoid GOTO's?

There is evidently no easy answer. The following seem to me to be the main considerations involved:

1. The need for inversion followed directly from sound design considerations. Since we have set out deliberately to establish good design concepts, we should not be too put off too quickly if sometimes they turn out to be difficult to implement. (Perhaps, after all, it is the implementation tools which are at fault.)
2. Existing high-level block-structured languages tend to think of a program as a single hierarchical structure. This imposes serious constraints on the designs used, and is arguably incorrect (as for the example used in this chapter). In my view it represents a serious weakness in those languages, and this view will be reinforced by the work of Chapters 7 and 8.
3. For practical commercial purposes the number of occasions on which inversion is required is severely limited. Every program needs nested logic; a large proportion need MONITOR; but only a small number need inversion. The need for inversion in on-line work is discussed in Section 7.5, and for real-time systems in Sections 8.6, 8.7, and 8.8.
4. If you abandon the concept of inversion, you are still faced with the problem we set out to solve—namely, how to relate logic design to problem structure using agreed principles, such that the structure is preserved in the finished code.

There is no doubt in my mind that inversion is conceptually right and that Restart and Suspend instructions should be made available exactly like any other instruction (such as a subroutine call). In support of this, we repeat that the designs used are GOTO-less; the problem is that language facilities do not fully reflect the needs of design. In the absence of such a change to the languages we use, one has to compromise somewhere.

Even in the absence of new language facilities, I still think inversion should be used as a design aid, particularly to isolate all the logical conditions to be covered; if practicalities then demand that coding compromises be made, such as changes necessary to preserve the code's block structure, then so be it. I have found this approach to be very successful, and acceptable to those programmers who wish at all costs to take advantage of the facilities offered by high-level languages. Taking a pragmatic view, I urge you to remember that only a small subset of programs require inversion anyway; but when they do, the design problems they present cannot conveniently be solved any other way.

6.10 Multitasking between Modules

In Section 6.3 we chose to think of X as the calling program and Y as the called subroutine. We asserted that this decision was not critical, and that we could equally have chosen to implement Y as the calling program and X as the subroutine. We now want to check that this is the case, and to compare the results with those obtained in a full multitasking environment.

We started with Y as the subroutine; X then thought of Y as a print routine. Now, if X is the subroutine, then Y thinks of X as a read routine, and each time Y calls X it says 'Give me a printable record'. The points at which Y calls X are, therefore, the points at which Y has finished with the previous printable record and wants the next; these are the points at which Y previously said 'Read-intermediate-file'. The parameter of each call from Y to X is a read request. We may think of the succession of read requests as constituting a second serial file read by X; allocation of a suitable Read statement in X follows the read-ahead principle—once at the beginning, and then immediately following completion of processing the previous read request. Apart then from the first, the Reads in X of the intermediate file passed from Y occur at those points at which X has found either a printable record or End-of-file. These are the points at which X previously said Restart Y; however, the final Read in X of the intermediate file passed from Y is never satisfied, since Y makes no further calls to X; it may, therefore, be omitted (as suggested in Section 6.5). These points are illustrated in Figures 6.19 and 6.20; by comparing these with Figures 6.11 and 6.12 we confirm that:

in X, the Restart Y instruction of Figure 6.11 is replaced by Suspend in Figure 6.19, except that the End-of-file Restart is replaced by an initial Suspend

in Y, the Suspend instruction of Figure 6.12 is replaced by Restart X in Figure 6.20

Note that X now reads two serial files, the 'real' input file and the intermediate file passed from Y. The inversion is with respect to the intermediate file only.

The intermediate file is really a two-way file, as illustrated in Figure 6.21. If we arrange for X to call Y, then the intermediate file passed from X to Y contains printable records; with this arrangement Y returns to X with a read request. The instructions used are:

Module	Structure Diagram Symbol	Schematic Logic	Meaning
X	(W,)	Restart Y	Write a printable record onto the intermediate file passed to Y, and read a read request from the intermediate file returned from Y.
Y	(R)	Suspend	Write a read request onto the intermediate file returned to X and read a printable record from the intermediate file passed from X.

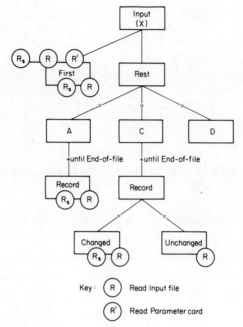

Figure 6.19   Module X as the subroutine

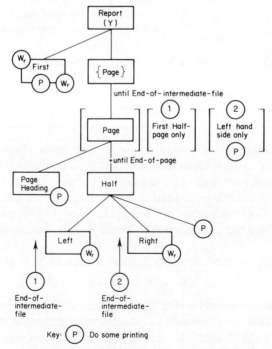

Figure 6.20   Module Y as the calling program

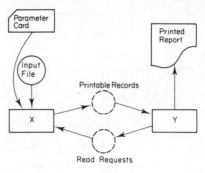

Figure 6.21   The intermediate file as a two-way file

Working in the other direction, that is with Y calling X, the intermediate file passed from Y to X contains read requests and X now returns to Y with a printable record. The instructions used are:

Module	Structure Diagram Symbol	Schematic Logic	Meaning
X	(R,)	Suspend	Write a printable record onto the intermediate file returned to Y, and read a read request from the intermediate file passed from Y.
Y	(w,)	Restart X	Write a read request onto the intermediate file passed to X, and read a printable record from the intermediate file returned from X.

The symmetry suggests that it does not matter technically whether we choose to implement X or Y as the subroutine. Indeed, we should prefer to think of X and Y as tasks; the choice of X or Y as subroutine is then only an implementation consideration. This confirms our earlier assertion that the choice of X or Y as the subroutine was not critical; the critical decision was to retain the modularity, while still designing the logic internal to X and Y using structured programming principles.

More generally we can assert that for any two tasks X, Y of the kind under consideration:

1. If the tasks are implemented as calling program and called subroutine, the called subroutine must itself maintain the state variable and must, in particular, be able to identify the first call. If necessary, either X or Y must be responsible for identifying End-of-file and communicating this to the other.

2. If the tasks are implemented as processes (as in Chapter 8), it becomes the operating system's responsibility to maintain the state variable and to recognize the first time each task is executed. If necessary, either task may recognize End-of-file and communicate this to the other (though there will frequently be no such concept in real-time systems).

In case 1, it is assumed that the calling program executes first. In case 2, the implementation would normally ensure that it does not matter which of X, Y executes first.

Now that we are allowed to construct one program from two diagrams, there is no reason why we should not allow three, four, or more diagrams in the same program, all communicating in the manner described. In particular, we could now allow one subroutine to be called from two or more calling programs. An example of this drawn from process control occurs in Section 8.7. There is no real problem here so long as it is made clear that:

1. Any subroutine expects records on its intermediate file to appear in a certain order
2. All calling programs which contribute to this intermediate file must jointly undertake to create a file in which the intermediate records appear in the order expected.

In extreme cases a more formal diagrammatic technique may be required to show which calls tie up with which Reads. This degree of complexity happens only rarely.

Chapter 7
Applications for Inversion

This chapter explores circumstances in which the need for inversion arises. Section 7.1 describes how inversion might be used in a program in which there is only one nested structure (with or without **MONITOR**) present. Sections 7.2 to 7.5 describe cases where inversion can be used to allow two or more structures to coexist in the same program (the inversion then provides a standardized linkage between them), while Section 7.6 presents a program in which inversion is used to treat multiple orderings independently even where it is not strictly necessary. In each case the finished design is presented as one or more top-down structures; the implementation of inversion means that the program written is no longer strictly a single top-down hierarchy, at least in the sense implied by most high-level block-structured languages.

If you find the consequential coding problems unattractive (as described in Section 6.7), the design compromises suggested in Section 6.9 are always available; since these also have their disadvantages, it is important that you learn to anticipate design or specification changes which might lead to a need for inversion, so that any compromises necessary can be determined early in the project development cycle.

7.1   The Implementation of 'Read'

Technically, the content of this section is mostly recapitulation; it is included to put inversion into the context of our overall approach to program design, and to warn that apparently small specification changes to a program written without inversion may lead to a need for it.

The first step in program design (so far as we are concerned) is to identify the events of significance to a program, and to describe the order in which they occur. As described in Section 1.7 there will necessarily be an associated mechanism for moving on from one event to the next; we refer to this as a Read instruction, and accept that the use of our design techniques will usually lead to the construction of programs in which there are multiple Reads (albeit logical Reads). The Read instructions are allocated within the logic framework defined by the structure diagram according to the read-ahead principle; additional design constraints may lead to the use of a logic monitor. This approach provides a clear and concise expression of logic, which is closely related to corresponding structural features of the program specification, while the designs are also fully modular. No other method for designing program logic brings these benefits.

Following the discussion of Chapter 6, it is important to be clear about the possible implementations of Read; in particular we contrast the following two cases:

1. The Read occurs in a main program and is implemented as a call to a subroutine whose job it is to make available the data required; this may, of course, involve the physical transfer of data from an external device. The called subroutine returns control in the normal way, and the calling program then continues with the instruction following the call.
2. The Read occurs in a called subroutine and is implemented as a return to a calling program whose job it is to make available the data required; as in 1 above this may involve the physical transfer of data from an external device. The calling program then makes a further call to the subroutine which continues with the instruction following the return.

Case 1 is the 'standard' technique and never presents a problem. In particular, most input/output software supplied with high-level languages is written so that it provides for the application program the same interface as a subroutine. Case 2 leads to the use of inversion; but apart from varying the implementation of Read, the rest of the program (and the design principles on which it is based) remain unaltered.

The need for inversion follows, then, whenever an application program contains multiple Reads, and is itself a subroutine of another program which is responsible for effecting the data transfers implied. There are two cases we need to consider:

1. The calling program is manufacturer-written data management software.
2. The calling program is part of the application code.

Sections 7.2 to 7.6 cover case 2. The following are two examples of case 1:

1. On-line systems. The design principles were discussed in Chapter 5, where we identified a Read instruction as meaning 'Get next input from the terminal'. If the tp monitor thinks of the application program as a subroutine of itself (and we noted that not all tp monitors work this way), then the control logic designed can be implemented simply by inverting it with respect to the invocations from the tp monitor. This could avoid the need for the pseudo-conversational techniques described in Section 5.6, but itself has the disadvantages associated with inversion.

2. Data base systems. As noted in Chapter 2, the use of data bases makes no fundamental difference to the design approach advocated; software to access the data base is usually supplied as a subroutine called by the application program. However, suppose that in such a program checkpoints may be taken whenever the data base is accessed, while the associated restart facility demands the existence of a single restart point (effectively the first instruction in the program). Then, in order to restart from the instruction following the Read which generated the checkpoint, the logic must be inverted, at least if the structure is to be preserved. (The associated state variable would be saved as part of the checkpoint.)

Not surprisingly, then, the interface provided by the manufacturer's data management software is of the utmost significance. In the worst case, one facility can be used without inversion, while the addition of another may necessitate it. It is difficult always to anticipate the effect of such changes, which are largely outside the programmer's control.

We shall continue to take the view that the need for inversion (with its associated state variable and GOTO's) could be avoided by the provision of instructions similar to Suspend and Restart (as described in Chapter 6). Their absence is taken as symptomatic of a faulty interface between calling program and called subroutine; as a consequence, we have no alternative but to create them as design aids, and adopt one of the implementation compromises described in Section 6.9 (or indeed any other *ad hoc* solution).

For the rest of this chapter we consider the use of inversion to solve problems wholly within the programmer's control.

7.2 Structure Clashes

A structure clash exists whenever:

there are two or more nested structures present in one program (each of which may contain MONITOR); and

there is no way to combine these into one common structure without violation of the rules presented.

Under these circumstances we choose to allow the separate structures to coexist in the same program; the two diagrams are said to be 'decoupled', and may be referred to as 'component structures'. The inversion technique described in Chapter 6 is used to link the diagrams together, always communicating via some form of intermediate file or files, so 'synchronizing' activity in the component structures and 'resolving' the clash.

We start by classifying the various types of structure clash and the form of intermediate file used. Later sections give practical examples.

Let A, B represent records of interest to a program. Suppose further that groups of records can be identified according to rules summarized in structure diagrams such as those illustrated in Figure 7.1. We can think of X, Y as files. The

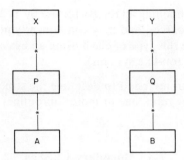

Figure 7.1   Data structures used to illustrate structure clashes

exact number of intermediate levels present (such as P, Q) is not material, nor does it matter if the records themselves have an internal structure or if other records (such as headers and trailers) are introduced. In practice the 'records' may be transactions, events, or some other meaningful unit of information with corresponding changes to the interpretation of the groups P, Q, X, Y. The notes below refer to A's and B's; any other subsets of X, Y could be used so long as the properties noted are maintained.

1. *Boundary Clashes.* A boundary clash occurs when the A's and B's are the same records and occur in the same order, but one P does not necessarily contain an integral number of Q's, nor does one Q necessarily contain an integral number of P's. X may or may not be identical to Y. If X is identical to Y, the two structures are both present on the same file; if X is not identical to Y, then the same units A, B are integrated according to different rules to form distinct files. The decoupled structures X, Y communicate via an intermediate file which consists of all the A's (and hence all the B's) in the same order as they occur on X and on Y. We illustrate this type of clash in Section 7.3 using the printed reports of the example of Section 2.4 together with an extension of the example of Section 4.2 (syntax analysis).
2. *Ordering Clashes.* An ordering clash occurs when the A's are again the same as the B's, but this time are ordered differently. The two structures communicate via an intermediate file which consists of all the A's (and hence all the B's), but this file must now be sorted into different orders for use by X and by Y. On occasions it may be possible to reorder the A's and B's one subset at a time (for example, if the groups identified by P are the same, and in the same order, as those identified by Q, but the records within these groups are ordered differently). We illustrate this type of clash in Section 7.4 using a variation of the example introduced in Section 6.1.
3. *Interleaving Clashes.* An interleaving clash occurs when the A's and B's are distinct records interleaved to form a single stream, such as:

$$A, \quad B, \quad A, \quad B, \quad B, \quad A, \quad B, \quad A, \quad A, \ldots$$

In this case two intermediate files are created, one containing all the A's for use by X and another containing all the B's for use by Y. The A's and B's usually arise from distinct sources, and may consequently not be the same type of record. We illustrate this type of clash using an extension of the systems of Sections 5.1 and 5.8 (on-line systems).

In each case the use of inversion to decouple the structures will result in the creation of one main program, one or more subroutines, and one intermediate file for each subroutine.

7.3 Boundary Clashes

7.3.1 Decoupling logical and physical structures on printed reports

A boundary clash usually occurs between some 'logical' requirements of the program and some 'physical' constraints of a storage device. Printed reports provide a good first illustration; another is given in Section 7.3.4. In fact, we detected such a clash in Section 2.4 where we were concerned, if you remember, to analyse a serial input file (whose name we abbreviated to CPTF) to produce two printed reports. One of the printed reports was called the 'Group Purchase Analysis Report' (GPAR for short) and for this report we had one detail line printed for each record, and one total, or summary, line for each charge account. A new page was started each time the group number changed; thereafter a new page was started whenever the previous page was full, as illustrated in the report layout reproduced in Figure 7.2.

When designing this program we soon discovered that no one structure diagram could be produced which reconciled satisfactorily the need to take account of both charge account and page boundaries on the same report. At the time we concluded simply that there was a 'structure clash' between logical and physical structures, that is between charge accounts and pages. We overcame the problem by ignoring 'page' as a structural feature, and treating the logic of page overflow as an 'exception' not subject to the normal rules, for which some non-standard logic would have to suffice. The main program logic then analysed only the 'logical' structure as represented by charge accounts; as a result we derived the program structure originally given as Figure 2.20, of which a subset is reproduced as Figure 7.3.

The overlapping of logical and physical boundaries is a symptom typical of boundary clashes. Fortunately, inversion expands the concepts and techniques available to us, and helps resolve the clash by providing the ability to think now of one program as built from two (or more) structures.

Let us then refer to the structure presented in Figure 7.3 as X, and feel free to introduce new structures as and when the need arises. Following the ideas of Chapter 6, we imagine that each time the main program (that is, X) detects a need to print a line, it writes a record on to an intermediate file; imagine, further, that another program (we shall call it Y) now exists whose job it is to read this intermediate file, print the reports, and insert page headings.

The relationship between the two programs is illustrated in Figure 7.4. The

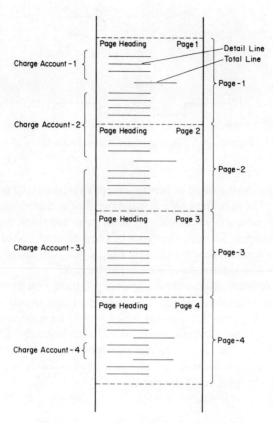

Figure 7.2   Layout of a printed report

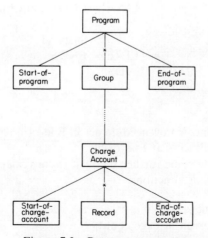

Figure 7.3   Program structure

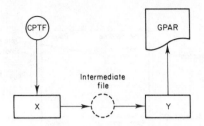

Figure 7.4   The use of an intermediate file

function of X remains the same as before, except that its output is now the serial intermediate file. The function of Y is to read the intermediate file and to print the report. Since Y is now concerned only to insert page headings, and not to make any further distinction between the types of lines printed, the structure of the report can be represented quite simply as in Figure 7.5. This also shows the points at which Y reads the intermediate file passed from X.

Instead of implementing Y as a free-standing program with its own serial file to read, we want Y to be a subroutine of X. Instead of writing records on to the serial intermediate file, X passes the records which would have been written, as the parameters of successive subroutine calls to Y. In the language of Section 6.5 we must now invert Y with respect to the intermediate file passed from X; the inversion turns Y into the subroutine required. Each call in X is now replaced by 'Restart Y', and the logic for Y becomes:

```
REPORT   SEQ
         Suspend
         {PAGE}   LOOP until End-of-intermediate-file
                  PAGE   SEQ
                         Print Page-heading
                         {LINE}   LOOP until End-of-page
                                  Print Line
                                  Suspend
                         {LINE}   ENDS
                  PAGE   ENDS
         {PAGE}   ENDS
REPORT   ENDS
```

We note also that since Y now needs to detect End-of-intermediate-file, X must introduce a special call to Y at End-of-file.

In order to illustrate some further points it is convenient to introduce some more detailed processing functions:

1. Open and Close the report
2. Initialize and increment a page count
3. Initialize and increment a line count.

We can now update the schematic logic as follows:

```
REPORT  SEQ
        Open Report
        Suspend
        Initialize Page-count
        {PAGE}  LOOP until End-of-intermediate-file
                PAGE  SEQ
                      Print Page-heading
                      Initialize Line-count
                      {LINE}  LOOP until End-of-page
                              Print Line
                              Increment Line-count
                              Suspend
                      {LINE}  ENDS
                PAGE  ENDS
                Increment Page-count
        {PAGE}  ENDS
        Close Report
REPORT  ENDS
```

This is the 'structured' account of page overflow referred to in Section 2.4.3. With the inversion (only) expanded it becomes:

```
        Go to L1, L2 depending on SV.
L1.
REPORT  SEQ
        Open Report
        Initialize Page-count
        {PAGE}  LOOP until End-of-intermediate-file
                PAGE  SEQ
                      Print Page-heading
                      Initialize Line-count
                      {LINE}  LOOP until End-of-page
                              Print Line
                              Increment Line-count
                              Move 2 to SV.
                              Go to END.
                      L2.
                      {LINE}  ENDS
                PAGE  ENDS
                Increment Page-count
        {PAGE}  ENDS
        Close Report
REPORT  ENDS
END.    Exit.
```

206

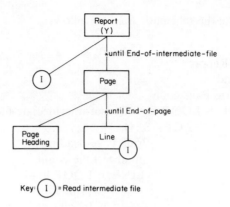

Key: (I) = Read intermediate file

Figure 7.5   Report structure

We note that the state variable creates two entry points:

1. Entry point L1. First time through, we start at the beginning, open the report, initialize the page count, print the page headings, initialize the line count, print the line and increment the line count.
2. Entry point L2. Second, and all subsequent times through, we restart in the middle of the loop called {LINE}; the effect is to branch immediately back to the beginning of the loop to test for End-of-page. If it is not End-of-page we just print the line, and increment the line count. If it is End-of-page but not End-of-intermediate-file we increment the page count, print the page headings, initialize the line count, print the line, and increment the line count, but otherwise just increment the page count and close the report.

In effect, the state variable is just a 'first-time switch'.

7.3.2 Design principles versus coding practicalities

This is *not* the logic which most programmers would normally use to handle page overflow. Indeed, when we first considered this example in Section 2.4 we compromised with a comparatively simple piece of logic; the following notes show how a desire to avoid inversion (if I may put it that way—most of us were probably unaware of all this when we first coded page overflow) may lead to the compromise logic normally found.

A major objective of inversion is to maintain full independence between X and Y: in this program the subroutine Y should be able to take all its own decisions about the construction of the report, even to the extent that X does not need to know there is a report. As a result, instructions to open and close the report (assuming these operations are necessary) were allocated in Y. In order to try and avoid the need for inversion, we could now move these instructions from Y to X (to be executed at Start-of-program and End-of-program respectively). We could also make the following changes:

1. Initialize Page-count at compile time (to zero).
2. Initialize Line-count at compile time (to a value which will force End-of-page first time through).

This strategy undermines some of the independence between X and Y, but as a consequence:

1. The state variable is unnecessary: we can safely restart from L2 every time (including the first).
2. There is no need for Y to test for End-of-intermediate-file (and no need for the corresponding call from X).

The logic of Y now reduces to the following:

```
                Go to L2.
{PAGE}   LOOP indefinitely
         PAGE   SEQ
                    Print Page-heading
                    Initialize Line-count
                    {LINE}   LOOP until End-of-page
                             Print Line
                             Increment Line-count
                             Go to END.
                    L2.
                    {LINE}   ENDS
         PAGE   ENDS
                Increment Page-count
{PAGE}   ENDS
END.     Exit.
```

By removing unconditional GOTO's and null tests, this is equivalent to:

```
IF       End-of-page
         Increment Page-count
         Print Page-heading
         Initialize Line-count
ELSE
ENDS
Print Line
Increment Line-count
```

And this is the logic first given in Section 2.4.3.

We can draw the following conclusions:

1. Inversion can be used to express the logic of page overflow.
2. Because of the implementation difficulties associated with inversion, this is unlikely to appeal to many programmers as a 'sensible' way to proceed (at least without some form of software aid to disguise the GOTO's).
3. By making the compromises given, we can apparently simplify the logic (to that just given).

The simplified logic is GOTO-less and avoids the inversion linkage, but the independence between X and Y has been lost, while Y no longer truly reflects the structure of the report. The purist will, however, probably prefer the inversion technique, on the grounds that the line count and page count can both be initialized to more natural values and that the use of inversion gives a design which can be amended more easily. Consider, for example, the effect of introducing the need for page footings.

Using inversion the logic is easy to amend since it already provides an End-of-page slot:

```
REPORT   SEQ
             Open Report
             Suspend
             Initialize Page-count
             {PAGE}   LOOP until End-of-intermediate-file
                         PAGE   SEQ
                                    Print Page-heading
                                    Initialize Line-count
                                    {LINE}   LOOP until End-of-page
                                                Print Line
                                                Increment Line-count
                                                Suspend
                                    {LINE}   ENDS
                         PAGE   ENDS
                         Print Page-footing
                         Increment Page-count
             {PAGE}   ENDS
             Close Report
REPORT   ENDS
```

In contrast, if inversion is not being used, we must make all the compromises noted (except that the page count can now be initialized to 1), and in addition introduce a new First-time-through switch:

```
IF      End-of-page
        IF      First-time-through
                Set Not-first-time-through
        ELSE
                Print Page-footing
                Increment Page-count
        ENDS
        Print Page-heading
        Initialize Line-count
ELSE
ENDS
Print Line
Increment Line-count
```

Although the details are different, this is the type of compromise which we hinted at in Section 6.9. A little more complication of this kind, and the benefits of the purist solution (using inversion) become more evident. We can go so far as to say that the logic of page overflow *necessarily* involves inversion; but by making the rules of page overflow simple the inversion can be disguised.

Here is another thought. As every programmer using a block-structured high-level language knows, the loop through the lines on the page cannot be written using an instruction equivalent to:

LOOP until End-of-page
Print Line
ENDS

The reason is that after printing one line, an entry must be later be made effectively into the middle of the loop to print the next line; and as noted in Section 6.7 this is, generally speaking, not supported. So the loop has to be hand-coded. By forcing End-of-page first time through, even this loop can be turned into a simple condition statement.

Many programmers, then, disguise the need for inversion; a common symptom is that loops disappear and condition statements proliferate. In this example, not too much harm is done; my point is only that if we are looking for generality then we must recognize and accept the need for inversion; the alternative is to lose sight of the structure even if the results are sometimes GOTO-less.

7.3.3 Interactions between logical and physical structures

Inversion provides a method to separate out logical from physical con-siderations; thus, in the example just given X takes all its own decisions about what to print, while Y takes all its own decisions about where and when to print it. The interface between X and Y assumes only that X will pass to Y the records that Y requires, and in the order Y requires them. However, X and Y are not quite so independent as this suggests. Apart from the inversion linkage (represented by the Restart and Suspend instructions), other interactions may exist between X and Y. We have already seen (Section 2.4.3) one such interaction; at Start-of-group:

1. X must change the page headings to be printed by Y on subsequent pages; and
2. X must ensure that Y continues printing on a new page.

Here are three further examples of similar interactions between X and Y.

7.3.3.1 Line spacing

Suppose the report is printed in single spacing, except that double spacing is used after page headings, and before and after the charge account total line. Let Line-space contain a value which determines the line spacing used before the next line is printed. Then the spacing requested can easily be achieved as follows:

1. Every time Y is executed it leaves the line spacing (for the next line) set to single space:

REPORT   SEQ
          ⋮
REPORT   ENDS
END.
                Move 1 to Line-space.
                Exit.

We think of this as a 'default' setting.

2. After printing the page headings, Y must override the default:

Print Page-heading
Move 2 to Line-space

3. At End-of-charge-account the calling sequence to print the charge account total line is altered to:

Move 2 to Line-space
Restart Y
Move 2 to Line-space

Neither 1 nor 2 affects the independence of X and Y. But to achieve the spacing requested in 3, the calling program (X) deliberately manipulates Y's Line-space, on the grounds that X knows better.

7.3.3.2 Page content

The observant reader will note that we have done nothing to stop a charge account total line being the first line (apart from page headings) printed on a page. If this is unsatisfactory then the calling sequence in X is, for total lines only:

IF   End-of-page
             Subtract 2 from Line-count
ELSE
ENDS
Move 2 to Line-space
Restart Y
Move 2 to Line-space.

We have thus identified another forced interaction between X and Y; in this case it is Y's Line-count which may be manipulated by X.

Other examples concern the manipulation of page headings; for example, if Start-of-charge-account coincides with Start-of-page, print one set of page headings, but otherwise print another set. The possibilities multiply if page subheadings are also used, but further details are omitted.

7.3.3.3 *Page format*

Finally, suppose that it is a requirement to print the charge account number on the same line as the first detail in the charge account but on no other line. Then:

1. At Start-of-charge-account set up a logical Start-of-charge-account print line containing the charge account number only (but do not call Y to print it).
2. Then, merge this with the Detail print line, while ensuring that *after* the first Detail line is printed, the charge account number is replaced by spaces.

If the charge account total were to be printed against the last line in the charge account (and not on a line on its own), a First-time switch would be required to distinguish the first line printed in a charge account. The calling sequence of Detail lines is now:

```
IF          First-time (in this Charge Account)
            Set up Detail line
            Set Not-first-time
ELSE
            Restart Y
            Set up next Detail line
ENDS
```

and at End-of-charge-account:

```
Set up total line
Restart Y
```

In this case there is a logical End-of-charge-account line; the problem (such as it is) is that when printing a detail line we do not yet know whether this is the last line. The technique given ensures that within a charge account we are always printing one line in arrears.

Page overflow is a good example, then, of the interactions which can occur between otherwise independent logical and physical data structures. These interactions occur surprisingly frequently.

7.3.4 Blocking and deblocking

Page overflow is just one example of a widespread phenomenon known as blocking. A second, more general, illustration is given now based around the system described in Section 4.2 which, if you remember, was concerned with the analysis of a simplified job control language. We recall the design given in Figure 4.2.3 and reproduced as Figure 7.6, and extend the syntax used as follows. The job control is input in fixed-length blocks (such as cards); in addition, each job specification is to be free-form—that is, a specification can begin in one block and finish in the same block, but equally it may continue over two (or more) blocks; furthermore, the next specification may begin in the same block as a previous specification finished. (This may be unusual in the context of job

212

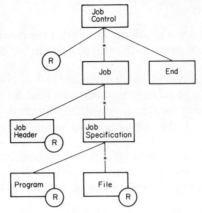

Figure 7.6   Structure of a job control stream

control, but is common enough elsewhere.) Suppose next that each statement (Job Header, Program, etc.) in a specification consists of a simple character string, that character strings are delineated by separators, and that no statement goes across a block boundary. The separators used are space and comma subject to the following rules:

1. Job Header and Program statements are both terminated by a space.
2. Each File statement is terminated by a comma.
3. The End statement consists of a unique character string (say 'End'), and is itself terminated by a space.

Job Header statements begin with a special character (/, say) while Program statements begin with a letter. The statements are now interpreted by their relative position, their terminator, and their internal construction. Any number of additional space characters may be inserted between statements; these act as 'noise' and may be ignored.

It should be clear from the discussion given in Section 7.2 that there is now a boundary clash between 'Job Specification' and 'Block'. There being no prospect of finding one diagram which combines both specification and block, we have to allow two diagrams.

Let us then imagine that a program is required to analyse the job control stream, and to identify the individual job specifications present. The program is built from two components (called X and Y) communicating in the now standard way via an intermediate file, as illustrated in Figure 7.7; we have not yet decided which is to become the main program and which the subroutine. The records on the intermediate file are:

1. Statements (passed from X to Y), including their terminator.
2. Read requests (returned from Y to X).

We should now be able to identify one set of rules showing how to analyse blocks

213

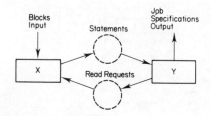

Figure 7.7   The use of an intermediate file

into statements and another set of rules showing how to construct job specifications from the same statements.

In this program it is probably most natural to think of X as a read subroutine called by Y (but as noted in Chapter 6 we could equally choose to have Y as a subroutine of X). The design for Y is based on the logic of Figure 7.6, on which we note:

the Read instruction is now implemented as 'make a subroutine call to X' (that is, Restart X)

'End-of-job-specification' is detected by finding the first statement which is not a File statement (that is, the first statement not terminated by a comma)

'End-of-job' is detected by finding a new Job Header

'End-of-file' is detected by software (on detecting the End statement) in Y. An extra call is required from Y to X if X is responsible for closing any input file.

These points, together with the loop-terminating conditions, are presented in Figure 7.8; as before, the detection of statement sequence errors is omitted. The parameter passed from Y to X will be a read request, except at End-of-file when it

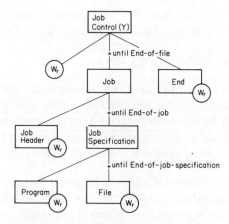

Figure 7.8   Analysing the job control stream

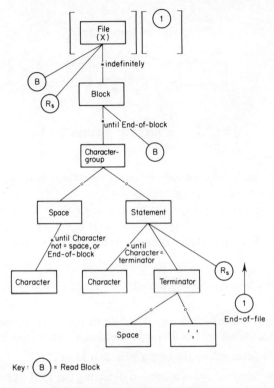

Figure 7.9   Deblocking the input

is a close request. The subroutine X might then be based on the logic of Figure 7.9, in which we note the following:

1. The software End-of-file may occur before completion of the processing of the current block; this accounts for the monitor shown.
2. The possibility of detecting a hardware End-of-file (in X) has been ignored.

The central features of the design given are:

1. Both X and Y are written as 'top-down' hierarchical structures.
2. Even though it was assumed in the discussion given that Y would call X, the design can equally be implemented with Y as a subroutine of X.
3. It follows that, at least at the design level, there is no need to decide which of X, Y will act as the main program and which as the called subroutine.

Suppose now (again following the lines of Section 4.2) that each statement in a specification may have an internal structure, as illustrated in Figure 4.2.4 and reproduced (without the logic of error recovery) as Figure 7.10. We refer to this diagram as Z and the components of a statement as fields.

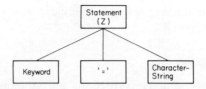

Figure 7.10   Internal structure of a statement

The functions of X, Y, Z are now respectively:

1. Locate fields (and not statements) within blocks.
2. Analyse sequence of statements within job specifications.
3. Analyse sequence of fields within statements.

Subject to any points noted below, X, Y, Z communicate as shown in Figure 7.11, which now replaces Figure 7.7.
   Suppose that the rules for field recognition are:

1. A keyword is a character string 'JOB', 'PROGRAM', 'FILE', or 'END' terminated by a space.
2. '=' is the first non-space character following the keyword, and is terminated by a space.
3. A string begins with the first non-space character after '=' and terminates at the next space.

Then we need to make the following alterations to the designs given:

1. In Figure 7.9, replace 'Statement' by 'Field', and terminate a field with a space.
2. In Figure 7.8, all statements are recognized by the keyword found.

In addition, Figure 7.10 must be enhanced (possibly using one of the techniques suggested at the end of Section 4.2) to detect and recover from errors within a statement. Revised diagrams are omitted.
   X is now inverted with respect to the calls from Z, but there is no need to invert Z with respect to the calls from Y because each call restarts Z at its single entry point. It is important to recognize that a subroutine (like Z) may have an internal structure, but that it is inverted only if a second invocation can restart the subroutine at the point following the return from the previous invocation. Of course, we could easily introduce more structures (such as printed reports) into this example, so that more than one component is inverted. But in the present

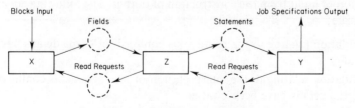

Figure 7.11   A complex calling sequence

context we should learn nothing new. An example in which two components are inverted is given in Section 8.7.

7.3.5 Data transmission

Suppose that a microcomputer is used to aid communication between a mainframe and terminal. The mainframe sends 'packets' of information to the terminal; each packet corresponds to the content of a screen and is transmitted in fixed-length blocks of, say, 256 bytes. Each block transmitted consists of 'protocol' and text, and is formatted as follows:

Byte	Content
1	STX (Start of text character)
2–254	Message text (maximum 253 bytes)
255	ETX (End of text character)
256	BCC (Block check character)

When constructing the message text, the mainframe treats the content of a screen as a character string (24 lines of 80 characters), and packs the data as follows. If two or more spaces occur consecutively they are replaced by a special 'escape' character followed by a one-byte count of the number of consecutive space characters found. The escape character and count may then be transmitted in different blocks. The final block transmitted in a packet may be padded with 'null' characters to complete the block. We shall consider the design of a program to run in the microcomputer to strip off the protocol, and unpack the message text into fixed-length lines ready to be displayed on the screen. In practice such a program might be designed to run in 'real-time'; since the real-time aspects form the subject matter of the next chapter, we shall confine ourselves to a brief description of how inversion might be used to help implement the software required.

We think first of the software required as consisting of two components (called X and Y). The function of X is to receive blocks, strip off the protocol, and pass the remaining characters found to Y; this is described in Figure 7.12. The function of Y is to receive a character stream from X and reconstitute screens; this is described in Figure 7.13, in which the unpacked characters (except nulls) are used to build up screen lines. The use of inversion helps divorce the recognition of input from the construction of output. The following advantages might ensue:

all validation relating to the protocol is confined to X; the details have been omitted

all validation relating to the interpretation of message text is confined to Y; again, the details have been omitted

any changes to the protocol need affect only X; likewise any changes to the unpacking rules are confined to Y.

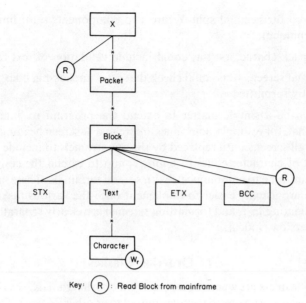

Key: (R) : Read Block from mainframe

Figure 7.12   Data transmitted with protocol

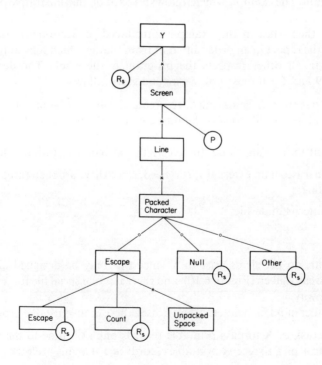

Key: (P) : Display a screen

Figure 7.13   Data unpacked for screen display

We could go further and split Y into two components (also linked via the inversion technique):

one to unpack characters; this could include validation of text received

one to format screens; this could check that after unpacking, lines and screens are correctly formatted

It would then be a simple matter to extend the program to 'interpret' lines received (so that, for example, some lines are treated as screen headings to be kept constant for all screens until replaced by the mainframe); to include conversion from one set of character codes to another; and to extend the conventions to allow the mainframe to communicate with several terminals. These, and similar, amendments are usually easier to implement once the various tasks (checking protocol, validating text, and formatting screens) are clearly separated. For this purpose, inversion is ideal.

7.4 Ordering Clashes

An ordering clash occurs when the output from one diagram (X, say) is the same, but not in the same order, as the input required to another (Y, say). The inversion technique can be used to retain the two diagrams X and Y as components of the same program. The example which follows is based on the illustrative program of Chapter 6.

Suppose then, that in the example introduced in Section 6.1, records are printed on the report in an order different from that in which they appear on the input file. In all other respects the program is the same. The design given (Figures 6.9 and 6.10) must now be amended as follows:

1. The output from X is amended, to create a real intermediate file.
2. A sort is introduced, to sort the intermediate file into an order suitable for printing.
3. The input to Y is amended, to receive the sorted intermediate file.

No problem arises if an external sort is used, since there are then three programs instead of one:

1. Create intermediate file.
2. Sort it.
3. Print it.

In particular, no problems arise in Y since this may be designed around the structure already given (Figure 6.10), and there is a real serial file for Y to read in the normal way.

On the other hand, if an internal sort is used there is now just one program and:

1. It is the task of X to pass printable records one at a time to the sort.
2. It is the task of Y to receive printable records one at a time after they have been sorted.

We recall the logic for Y as presented in Figure 6.10 and concentrate on examining the new interpretation and implementation of the instruction inside Y called 'Read intermediate file'. This instruction now means:

'I, Y, have finished with the previous sorted record and want the next sorted record. On completion of the Read, I shall continue with the next instruction'.

There are then two cases to consider:

1. The Read is implemented as a call to a subroutine whose function it is to retrieve the next sorted record; when the next sorted record is available, processing continues with the instruction following the call.
2. The Read is implemented as a return to a calling program whose function it is to retrieve the next sorted record; when the next sorted record is available, processing continues with the instruction following the return.

In other words: is the sort a subroutine of Y, or Y a subroutine of the sort? The answer is context-dependent; sometimes it is done one way, sometimes the other.

In any event, the logic of Y can always be based on that given in Figure 6.10 since at the design level it simply does not matter whether Y is implemented as a main program or as a subroutine. If it turns out that Y is the subroutine, then the only change required is to invert Y with respect to the invocations from the sort. In this way inversion can sometimes be used as a defensive tool by deferring some implementation decisions until an interface is defined or clarified.

7.5   Interleaving Clashes

There are two cases; each may be illustrated using examples drawn from the on-line applications studied in Chapter 5. In both cases we think of communication with a terminal as controlled by a tp monitor, which thinks of the application code as a subroutine of itself.

7.5.1 Multiple identical orderings

Suppose that there are n terminals (called T_1 to T_n), and that the activity at each terminal conforms to the conversation rules defined in Section 5.1; the activity at each terminal is nonetheless allowed to proceed independently. There is one tp monitor, whose job it is to poll the various terminals, and to ensure that input from each terminal is processed correctly.

From the tp monitor's point of view, input might now be detected in the following illustrative order:

```
AMEND        (terminal 1)
AMEND        (terminal 2)
ACCEPT       (terminal 1)
AMEND        (terminal 3)
KILL         (terminal 2)
AMEND        (terminal 4)
TERMINATE    (terminal 1)
ACCEPT       (terminal 3)
```
and so on.

Now, all those inputs relating to terminal 1 form a sequence consistent with Figure 5.7. Likewise, all inputs relating to any other terminal form a similar sequence. Thus, the total sequence, as seen by the tp monitor, interleaves the separate sequences as seen by each terminal.

We now refer to the program which processes input from one terminal (based on Figure 5.7) as an application program (or AP). For each AP the Read instruction means 'Get next input for this terminal'. Since there are now n terminals we shall need n versions of this program (called AP_1 to AP_n). Next, suppose that each time the tp monitor detects input for one terminal it writes it on to a special intermediate file associated with that terminal only. Since there are n terminals we shall need n intermediate files (called I_1 to I_n). Each application program (AP_1 to AP_n) can now be based on Figure 5.7 provided it is inverted with respect to its own intermediate file passed from the tp monitor, as illustrated in Figure 7.14.

The inversion associates one state variable with each terminal. Each time we execute a Read in an application program, this now means:

reset and save this terminal's state variable

return to the calling program (i.e. the tp monitor)

restart from the next instruction, but only when the tp monitor detects another transaction input associated with this terminal.

Hence, the tp monitor restarts an application program for a particular terminal by using instructions to:

1. Retrieve the state variable corresponding to this terminal.
2. Restart from the instruction following the last Suspend.

If the logic of Figure 5.7 is re-entrant then only one set of executable code is required; otherwise one copy of the control logic is required for each terminal.

Similar considerations apply to the pseudo-conversational designs used in

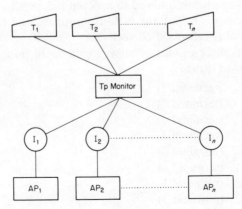

Figure 7.14 Multiple interleaved orderings

Section 5.7 where the 'Next-id' field serves as a state variable for each application program.

7.5.2 Multiple different orderings

On occasions the activity allowed at one terminal will be different from that at a different terminal, but still under the control of the same tp monitor. Suppose then that we have just two terminals; suppose further that the activity allowed at one follows the rules described in Section 5.1, while the activity allowed at the other follows the rules described in Section 5.8. Then the full stream of input detected by the tp monitor might be:

```
AMEND    (terminal 1)
ACCEPT   (terminal 1)
ENTER    (terminal 2)
ENTER    (terminal 2)
AMEND    (terminal 1)
PF1      (terminal 2)
ACCEPT   (terminal 1)
PF1      (terminal 2)
PF4      (terminal 2)
```
and so on.

Evidently the sequence of activities described by Terminal 1 accords with Figure 5.7 while that for Terminal 2 accords with Figures 5.8, 5.11, and 5.12.

As before, we associate one application program, one intermediate file, and one state variable with each terminal. The tp monitor must now write each screen input at a terminal on to the intermediate file for that terminal. The logic required to control activity at each terminal is still based on the designs given but is inverted with respect to the intermediate file passed from the tp monitor. As in Section 7.5.1, pseudo-conversational techniques may still be used, with the 'Next-id' field also serving as the state variable for each application program.

7.6   Synchronizing Structures

The use of Restart and Suspend instructions as described in Section 6.5 effectively synchronizes activity in separate structures. In this section we give just one example where the same technique may be used even though there is no formal structure clash. For this purpose we return to the implementation of pseudo-direct access techniques in file-matching programs first discussed in Section 2.7.

To remind you of the problem: suppose that you are given two files (call them X, Y) whose structures are reproduced in Figure 7.15. Suppose first that X is some kind of transaction file and is accessed sequentially, and that Y is some kind of master file which is accessed directly (that is, via an index). Then the logic for file matching is given in Figure 7.16, where the instruction 'Get Y' represents a direct-access read to file Y, to see if there is on file Y a record whose key is equal to

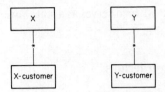

Figure 7.15   Two input files

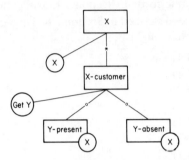

Figure 7.16   File matching using direct access

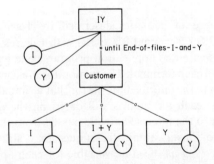

Figure 7.17   Simple collating with the intermediate file

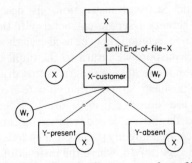

Figure 7.18   Pseudo-direct access from file X

that of the current record on file X. The result of such a direct-access read is a reply which can take the value 'Y-present' (together with the record), or 'Y-absent'.

Now suppose that (for the kinds of reasons presented in Section 2.7) it becomes necessary to access Y sequentially, but you want to retain as a design feature that X should continue to think of Y as a direct-access file. We need to make the following design change: replace 'Get Y' by 'Call Y' where Call Y is a call to a subroutine Y which provides for X the same interface as 'Get Y'. It remains to design and implement the subroutine Y.

The parameter passed from X to Y is the key of the current customer on X. The call from X to Y then asks 'do you, Y, have a record whose key value is equal to the key value passed as a parameter to you?; reply Y-present or Y-absent'.

Think now of the succession of parameters passed from X to Y as constituting a serial intermediate file. The subroutine Y now has two serial files to process (the intermediate file, and file Y itself). The logic of Y can, therefore, be designed using the simple collating technique, as in Figure 7.17 (in which the symbol I represents the serial intermediate file). But since the file I does not really exist, the logic of the subroutine Y is:

```
IY   SEQ
     Suspend
     Read Y
     {CUSTOMER}   LOOP until End-of-files-I-and-Y
                  CUSTOMER   IF I < Y
                             Set Reply = Y-absent
                             Suspend
                  CUSTOMER   ELSE I = Y
                             Set Reply = Y-present
                             Suspend
                             Read Y
                  CUSTOMER   ELSE I > Y
                             Read Y
                  CUSTOMER   ENDS
     {CUSTOMER}   ENDS
IY   ENDS
```

This logic shows the replies returned to X, and assumes a special call from X at End-of-file. The complete logic is given in structure diagram form in Figures 7.18 and 7.19.

Because of the inversion many programmers would find this idea frankly unattractive. The advantages, such as they are, arise from the ability to keep X and Y totally separate; as a consequence:

1. The instruction 'Call Y' (implemented as 'Restart Y') can easily be replaced by any other file access routine deemed suitable (e.g. read record from a data base).

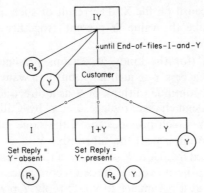

Figure 7.19 The implementation of pseudo-direct access to file Y

2. The two file structures X and Y are kept quite separate; the corresponding modules may then each take their own decisions and be amended, independently of the other.

These are not, of course, overwhelming.

The following would be a possible application. Suppose that X is a sales history master file on which each record represents a summary of business conducted in one month for one customer. The file is sorted into date within customer number sequence. File Y contains the current month's transactions; there is at most one transaction per customer. Using the pseudo-direct access technique a new program is required to update the master file X; this can be done in two ways:

1. X continues as the calling program, and Y as the subroutine; or
2. Y is the calling program, and X the subroutine.

The details are left to the reader.

Chapter 8
Real-time Process Control Systems

Real-time process control systems are used to control processes, usually industrial processes, such as the manufacture of steel, the distribution of gas, or the operation of machine tools. A typical system collects information about the process in order to determine changes required; these may be initiated directly by the computer, or indirectly after human intervention. In either case the feedback from information gathered to responses made results in the control desired. For many processes a fast and accurate response is critical; control systems are, therefore, usually designed to react as quickly as possible, and are said to work in 'real-time'. The term 'real-time' is also applied to similar systems in which the outputs produced are not immediately directed to controlling the activity which generated the inputs. Examples include message switching, data logging, and many kinds of information display.

The software required is more complex than any considered so far; we shall, therefore, need to take more time than usual to establish essential concepts, before working on some practical designs. In spite of the complexity, we shall find that events of interest to the system still happen in a well-defined order; this order can be described and then used to design the control logic in the now normal way. The concepts required are covered in Sections 8.1 to 8.4; Sections 8.5 to 8.9 then go on to apply the techniques to solve some typical design problems. This should be sufficient to establish the principles used, and to help the student with his own examples, but is in no sense intended to be complete or exhaustive.

The results bring together all the structural principles established in earlier chapters. While our principal concern remains with the design of the control logic, we shall also identify, at least in general terms, some of the main processing functions executed. We shall find that these, when considered in isolation, tend to appear relatively simple, but the logic required to link them together soon becomes complex. It is, of course, always open to the designer to reduce the complexity by ignoring or simplifying particular features of the system. Since we are more interested in the general case we shall ignore this possibility.

The discussion is relevant to mini- and microcomputer systems, and is intended to be machine- and language-independent.

8.1 System Concepts

A typical system will have one or more special-purpose hardware devices attached to it. Each device may be used for:

input; this collects data (such as temperature, pressure) about the state of the external world; or

output; the information collected is used (according to some application-dependent algorithms) to determine system responses.

Some devices can be used for both input and output. The term 'telemetry' is used for information collection when the computer system is remote from the process controlled. The term 'scanning' is used when the system itself generates requests for input and may then determine or guarantee the frequency with which inputs are received.

In most systems the computer is dedicated to its task and runs continuously; in some cases the computer is an integral part of a machine or process, and the system is then said to be 'embedded'. Apart from the normal input/output necessary to maintain the control required, most systems will contain:

reference data, which usually remains unchanged during the system's execution, and is used to interpret data input to help calculate data output;

displays, such as VDUs and mimic diagrams, to provide a user with a picture of the computer's view of the the state of the external world; and

built-in facilities for system reporting, interrogation, and performance measurement, including the provision of logs and statistics.

The collection of input, output, and reference data is usually said to constitute a system 'data base'. A system may additionally include features such as:

1. *Dualling.* In order to safeguard against failure of the computer hardware, and to build in provision for hardware maintenance, many systems use two computers. A common technique is to designate one machine to act as a 'duty' machine and the other 'standby', with provision made for the standby to take over automatically should the duty fail, or manually should an operator request it. During normal running (with one machine duty and the other standby), the duty machine might be made responsible for keeping the standby's internal data tables up-to-date; the standby can then be thought of as another special-purpose device attached to the duty machine. An alternative technique is to use special-purpose hardware.
2. *Fault detection and recovery.* Many systems are tolerant to a certain amount of hardware failure. Faults may be detected by further hardware devices (e.g. by monitoring a power supply), or software checks on system integrity and data transfers. In extreme cases, fault conditions will result in changeover

from duty to standby (in a dual system) or system closedown (in a single-machine system). In other cases the system may reconfigure itself (e.g. by directing output to alternative devices), or use alarms (possibly supported by printed reports) to draw attention to fault conditions. If failure of a particular device does not result in system closedown or changeover, some performance degradation would be likely. Recovery of the device may be signalled to the system from a control console; in other cases the system may itself keep testing the device until a satisfactory response is achieved.

3. *Performance measurement.* Since response times are a critical factor, the system may monitor its own performance. (Of course, this is an overhead which itself affects the performance of the main system; the assumption is that the benefits, in terms of problem areas identified, outweigh any disadvantages). Data collected may include any, or all, of:

> the volumes of data input over a period of time
> the number of hardware failures detected and the time taken to correct them
> the state of system data tables
> the percentage of available processor time used.

The results may be made available to a technician via system interrogation requests, dumped onto system logs for off-line analysis, or formatted into printed reports.

4. Simulation and testing aids are also frequently required, but these are outside our domain.

In most 'modern' systems the interface between a hardware device and the computer is so constructed that completion of a data transfer into, or out of, the computer normally results in a signal detected by the computer and known as an 'interrupt'. If and when an interrupt occurs it results in an automatic transfer of software control to code known as an 'interrupt handler', whose job it is to 'service' the interrupt; this code can be designed to protect the remaining software from the immediate effects of the interrupt.

It is a feature of computer hardware design that once a data transfer has been initiated, there is no way to predict when it will complete. Consequently the computer must be prepared to do other work (that is, execute other code) while knowing that an interrupt may take place at any time. Whenever the computer is prepared to break off to service interrupts, it can 'enable' interrupts; otherwise it 'disables' interrupts. A system which is written so that it always responds to interrupts whenever they occur is said to be 'interrupt driven'; a system which is written so that it only allows interrupts at times convenient to the software is said to 'poll' the interrupts. In all cases, the computer must always be executing code; if there is no other work to do, the computer may choose to wait by executing some 'idle' code. In what follows we shall assume an interrupt-driven system, though much of the work can also be applied to systems which use polling.

Since data transfers (into or out of the computer) are relatively slow to complete, it is usually important to overlap one transfer with another so far as this is possible. There may then be several data transfers (into or out of the computer) in progress at any time. There is no way to predict which one will be completed first; accordingly, we think of them as all proceeding 'in parallel' (other terms used are 'asynchronously' and 'concurrently'), and be prepared to service completion interrupts in whatever order they occur. In particular, a second interrupt may be detected before servicing of the first has been completed. The hardware usually determines the order in which to service such interrupts by attaching priorities to them; servicing of one interrupt may then itself be interrupted by detection of another, so long as the second occurs at a higher-priority level. Interrupts at lower levels must await completion of servicing of all interrupts outstanding at higher levels.

The need to respond to interrupts in real-time has led to great concentration on the efficiency of control systems—since, if the system cannot respond quickly enough, there is no point in having it. For the moment we shall take the view that the software must execute certain functions and in a certain order whatever the response times required; so let us concentrate on identifying these first.

8.2 Software Concepts

The hardware used in real-time systems is frequently so special-purpose that it has become customary for the application programmer to design at least some of the interrupt handlers. This applies also to the remaining parts of the system identified below, and contrasts with (say) commercial or scientific systems, where the application programmer is usually substantially protected by operating systems, tp monitors and the like, from the immediate interface with the external world. (Indeed, I have found the term 'real-time' used to refer to the need for the application programmer himself to design code to respond immediately to interrupts received, and not merely, as suggested above, the need for the system to respond quickly.)

In any event, apart from the interrupt handlers, software is also required at least to:

    initiate data transfers and evaluate the results
    process data input to calculate and generate system responses
    maintain a data base
    monitor system performance

This software is usually organized into units which we shall call 'processes'. The term 'process' is a little unfortunate since it can easily be confused with 'process' as in 'process control', or 'process' as in 'processing function'. The term 'task' is frequently used instead. However, at least in this book, the term 'task' is used to refer also to subroutines linked together via Restart and Suspend instructions, as described in Section 6.4.

The processes must collectively carry out all the work required. In particular, since data transfers proceed in parallel, it is usual to devote separate processes to organize the activity required at each device, and to think also of these processes as running in parallel. Further, since the processes jointly contribute to solving a common problem, they are interdependent. Consequently processes must be able to communicate, and one process may be designed to create data required by another; the data passed is known as a 'message', and we shall think of message passing as a form of cooperation between processes synchronizing their separate activities. Just as some data transfers are usually more urgent than others, and so operate on higher interrupt levels, so also some processes are more urgent than others. Accordingly we attach software priorities to processes; in general the computer is always running the highest-priority process for which work (in the form of a message input) is available, and which is not held up waiting for completion of a data transfer. Processes at lower priority levels must then await completion of all work outstanding at higher priority levels, and can be considered as competing for system resources (in this case central processor time).

It is usual to introduce an 'operating system' whose role it is to supervise the competition, and facilitate the cooperation, between processes, and to provide generally for a secure environment in which processes can be safely executed. We then think of a real-time process control system as a set of processes running asynchronously in real-time under the overall control of an operating system. These concepts are interdependent; with some repetition they may be summarized as follows:

1. *Process.* A process is a program; that is, a unit of code executable by the operating system. Processes cooperate by passing messages to each other. The process from which a message originated is known as a 'producer'; the process to which a message is sent is known as a 'consumer'. Any process can be both a producer and a consumer. A message passed acts as a trigger to the consumer process to start execution subject to the resolution by the operating system of any conflicts over priorities and the availability of resources.
2. *Asynchronous.* Processes run asynchronously; that is, there can be several processes all running in the same computer under the overall control of the same operating system. However, only one process has access to the central processing unit at any one time. More accurately, then, only one process is 'running'; other processes are either 'ready' or 'blocked' (other words may also be found describing these states). A ready process is available to run as soon as the operating system makes resources available, while a blocked process cannot be run until it is triggered by a message sent to it.
3. *Real-time.* Interrupts are serviced in real-time; that is, as and when they occur. Each interrupt acts as a signal that a data transfer has been completed. For data input, the producer is the hardware while the consumer is the process which processes it; conversely for data output. After servicing an interrupt, the system may have a choice of work to do (process new data, or carry on with the old work suspended); all conflicts of this kind are resolved by the operating system.

4. *Operating system.* The operating system controls the overall system execution, and provides an orderly environment in which the remaining activities can be executed. In particular, it uses process priorities to help resolve any conflicts over access to system resources; in practice, generalized services such as timing, message passing, and the provision of standard processes, are also regarded as operating system functions. The larger systems may also include memory allocation, data protection, filing, and overlay facilities.

Our principal concern is with the design of software to run under this type of operating system. We note that other operating systems are more concerned to provide utilities to aid:

software development. These cover the conventional edit, compile, link and load, in single- or multi-user development systems.

system construction. These provide greater flexibility by allowing changes to system construction which minimize the need for recompilation or relinking, and build in integrity checks to be used at run-time.

subsystem control. These provide for the execution of run-time operator control commands (start a process, terminate a process, etc.), via a command language interpreter.

system performance analysis. These facilitate debugging at run-time and will usually record the most significant actions, such as start and end of a process, inter-process communication, and execution of other run-time operating system facilities.

The two types of operating system should be clearly distinguished; we are only interested in the run-time facilities described under 4 above, and explained in greater detail below.

8.3   The Operating System

Frequently an operating system is provided along with the hardware used, but on some occasions its implementation still remains part of the application programmer's responsibility. Since an understanding of its role is crucial to the construction of the run-time software, we shall devote this section to a description of the facilities generally attributed to it, noting that in practice the details may vary widely; the remaining processes (that is, apart from the operating system) are referred to as application processes and are described in the following sections.

The operating system exercises its control largely through its function as a process 'scheduler'; thus, whenever a process has completed its execution (for whatever reason) the scheduler decides which process to run next. As noted already, the scheduling algorithm used is usually based upon some form of priority attached to each process, but may also be adjusted at run-time in the light of system load and performance, or at the request of individual processes.

Depending on its implementation, a general rescheduling may also take place whenever any of the operating system services described below are used.

The services provided to application processes can be thought of as additional processes to which messages can be sent, and from which messages can be received, together with a set of high-level macro instructions. Together these effectively extend the language being used, providing facilities for:

1. *Timing*. Application processes can request:
   (a) The time-of-day. This feature would normally only be used for formatting printed reports and system logs
   (b) A timeout. This is a message received after a fixed interval
   (c) A repeat. This is a message received at constant intervals
   (d) A message at a specified time.

   Timer requests can be cancelled at any time.

2. *Message passing*. Because processes run asynchronously and at different priorities, a producer might need to send another message to a consumer before the consumer has finished with the previous message. Consequently, messages passed are held on variable-length 'queues'. The minimum queue size is zero, while the maximum is usually a system parameter; queue overflow is normally considered a system failure condition. The queue is accessible to both producer and consumer via instructions such as the following:
   (a) Send a message to a named process.
   (b) Send a message with priority (that is, the message sent jumps to the head of the consumer process's incoming queue).
   (c) Receive next message from any process.
   (d) Receive next message from a named process.

   These instructions are sometimes called Send and Receive and parameterized to provide variations on the basic theme. The similarity between these instructions and the Restart and Suspend instructions used in Chapter 6 should be noted. When used together, (a) and (d) can implement a 'handshake', where a producer waits until the consumer confirms receipt of a message before proceeding.

3. *Semaphores*. Since processes run asynchronously, conflicts can arise over access to system resources shared between processes (such as hardware devices, queues, or internal data tables). Semaphores provide high-level instructions (often called 'wait' and 'signal') and are used to ensure that, where and when necessary:
   (a) Only one process has access to a shared resource, and excludes all other processes which use it until its own work on that resource is complete.
   (b) One process can be held up until another has achieved certain progress.
   (c) Two processes will not both be held up because each is waiting for resources held by the other.

   Semaphores may also be used to achieve the handshake described under 2 above.

4. *Utility functions.* Many systems exhibit a need for standard device drivers, spooling, performance monitoring, software integrity checks, and error handling. It is frequently possible to generalize the software required and provide it as a facility offered by the operating system, but equally it may be written as further application processes.

The larger systems may also exhibit a need for dynamic memory allocation, and provide run-time overlay facilities. In general there is nothing to stop one part of the operating system calling upon services offered by another part, while the extent of facilities provided depends on the size and complexity of the system under development. We summarize below those facilities we shall require when designing application processes in Sections 8.7 to 8.9.

1. *Communication between processes.* We shall extend the basic Send instruction to name the process with which we want to communicate.

Instruction	Symbol	Meaning
Send (name)	(W_s^{name})	Write message onto the queue into the named process.

No extension is required for Receive; as used in this book, it always announces that a process has completed its execution and is now ready to receive a message from any other process.

2. *Communication between subroutines within a process.* We shall extend the Restart and Suspend instructions to name the subroutine restarted, and to note the value of a suspended subroutine's state variable.

Instruction	Symbol	Meaning
Restart (name)	(W_r^{name})	This restarts the subroutine named at the instruction following the last Suspend executed in that subroutine.
Suspend (value)	(R_v^{value})	This suspends the subroutine which contains the Suspend and returns to the program or subroutine which last called it.

3. *Utility functions.* We provide the following high-level macro-type instructions for use by all other processes:

Instruction	Meaning
Repeat (n)	Request a message once every n seconds
Time (n)	Request one message after n seconds
Cancel	Cancel all timer requests outstanding
Error	A system failure has been detected

In practice, of course, these may be implemented as messages passed to utility processes.

8.4 The Data Management System

Apart from the operating system, the remaining software, which we have called the application processes, can be grouped under the following functional headings:

1. *Data management system.* This supervises the transfer of data into and out of the computer, and maintains the data base. In particular, it takes account of the presence of special-purpose devices each subject to its individual constraints.
2. *Application program.* This interprets data input, and calculates the system's response. The transformation rules implied describe, in a real sense, what the application is all about.
3. *Utilities.* These are more concerned to collect information about, or provide services for, other activities than to contribute directly to them. They will include system monitor, logging, error reporting, interrogation, and integrity checking. Some may be provided as part of the operating system.

The boundaries defined are not rigid and may overlap. The application program is frequently just one process but, especially in large systems, may be built as two or more processes. Either way, it is sometimes desirable to introduce additional 'buffer' processes acting as 'sponges' which prevent system overload by soaking up potential excess demands when communicating with data management or utility processes. Excluding the application program and any buffer processes, the remaining software—that is, operating system, data management system, and utilities—is often called a 'program execution environment'; as its name implies, this provides an orderly environment in which the application program can be executed. For our purpose it will now be sufficient to concentrate on the design of control logic to implement parts of the data management system. The detailed design of the operating system is outside the scope of our discussion, while the application program, buffer processes, and utilities give rise to no points of principle not otherwise covered in this book.

The processes present in a data management system can be classified as follows:

1. *Device drivers.* Together with the interrupt handlers, these include all criteria used to determine whether a transfer of data into or out of the machine has been successfully completed, and so provide an immediate interface with the 'real' world as measured or controlled by an external device. Separate drivers are usually provided for input and output.
2. *Multiplexors.* These receive requests for output at a device, and determine the next transfer to be made once the device driver has successfully completed the

previous transfer. Test messages may also be created if the device is not kept busy, or if it has failed.

3. *Distributors.* These interpret data input from a device and distribute it to those processes which know how to use it. Thus, for input devices, the device driver is concerned only with the physical transfer of data into the machine, while the distributor is able to interpret the data received and ensure that it is actioned correctly.

4. *Data base manager.* This controls access to the system data base and ensures its integrity; the data held might include the application program's current picture of the external world, variable data maintained for internal software purposes, and information retained and logged for system performance analysis. The degree of data protection provided depends on a variety of factors, not least the software complexity that can be tolerated. The need for a data base manager may sometimes be avoided if the system is small, or if semaphores are used to resolve access conflicts.

In a system in which scanning is used, the scan is organized by a process which acts as both multiplexor and distributor.

The approach taken is that, ideally, for each device in any given system:

1. There is one device driver; if the device can perform both input and output functions then two processes are required.
2. There is one multiplexor for each device driver responsible for output. The interface consists of one unit of output.
3. There is one distributor for each device driver responsible for input. The interface consists of one unit of input.

The term 'device' is used here to mean a device which is independently addressable by the computer; it is, therefore, synonymous with the usual meaning attached to 'port'. In the larger systems the computer may send data to, or receive data from, one device in this sense, but additional hardware may be provided outside the computer to make several 'real' devices addressable (such as multiple VDUs attached to one computer on a single port). In our terms there is still one device, and so one device driver, together with one multiplexor or distributor associated with it. If the 'real' devices are driven in parallel, there will be one driver but two or more multiplexors or distributors; to save space these may use 'shared code', and in any case the driver must be re-entrant. The term 'unit' (of input or output) is intended to represent a logical unit; that is, a block, record, or single byte depending on the context and device type. However, some processes may also need to keep internal buffers, and be responsible for blocking output and deblocking input.

The data management processes need to communicate using the Send/Receive instructions defined in Section 8.3 as follows:

1. Each application program communicates only with multiplexors (for output) and distributors (for input).

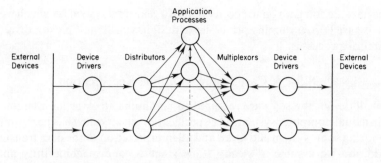

Figure 8.1   A diagrammatic representation of part of a real-time system

2. Each multiplexor communicates with any processes (except drivers) which generate a need for output, and with the driver responsible for effecting the output it requests.
3. Each distributor communicates with the driver responsible for the input it distributes, and with any processes (except drivers) which need to use the input received.

These points are summarized in Figure 8.1; subject to the points given below, this now gives a generalized diagrammatic representation of that part of a real-time system of interest to us. This type of diagram is sometimes referred to as a 'process chart', in which:

1. Each circle represents a process
2. The directional lines represent lines of communication (message passing) between processes

Not all the paths shown need be present in any given system. In general it is also desirable to allow additional communication paths as follows:

1. If data transmitted at a device results in replies received at the same device, then the two device drivers may communicate directly (even if, on occasions, this introduces a need to interpret data received in the receiver process).
2. If data received at a device results in replies transmitted at the same device, then the two device drivers may communicate directly (or via distributor and multiplexor).
3. All processes shown may also communicate directly with the operating system and/or utility processes.

It is also open to the designer to take a different approach and reduce the number of processes present by combining some or all of those shown into one. This might be particularly attractive on smaller systems. It might well reduce some operating system overheads, particularly those associated with scheduling, by reducing the amount of message passing; but it would also increase the size of those processes remaining, and may make maintenance harder later. In any event, the logic required is much the same whatever the number of processes.

236

The next section goes on to specify part of a real-time system for which we shall use structured programming principles to design typical multiplexor, driver, and distributor processes.

8.5 A Case Study—Outline Specification

We shall design the software required to communicate over an intercomputer link in a dual-computer system. The specification given below has been simplified by ignoring some system activities, and all interpretation of the data transmitted; in addition we assume a 'steady state' (that is, one machine duty and one standby), and avoid all problems associated with changes in those states. Nonetheless, the principles are perfectly general, and of wide application. The software could be adapted, for example. to make both machines 'nodes' in a 'distributed' system, and by thinking of one computer as just another device attached to the other, we have prototypes for all kinds of device handling.

A system exists:

1. To maintain a 'mimic diagram' which reports (via visual displays) on the state of a traffic system.
2. To control the system via 'control functions' entered at a terminal (keyboard plus VDU).

The system is implemented using dual minicomputers, with special-purpose telemetry hardware and some microprocessor-based device drivers. The telemetry provides 'indications' which are decoded to interpret the state of the external world (that is, the traffic signals). The telemetry hardware is also used to transmit the control functions entered; these may result in requests for changes to the state of signals, etc. Any changes made will then be detected by the telemetry and communicated to the central computer as further indications. In addition, provision is made to monitor hardware/software performance, with detection of, and recovery from, some error conditions.

During normal running one computer acts as duty, and the other standby. Provision is made for the standby to take over manually under operator control, or automatically under software control, should the duty fail. The standby is therefore kept fully up-to-date with events in the outside world, ready to take over at any time. To this end, key data tables are passed across the intercomputer link from duty to standby. Apart from this, no major processing is carried out within the standby. Operating procedures are designed to minimize the risk of information loss at changeover.

This completes the outline system description. As noted, we are concerned only with the design of software to transmit and receive data across the intercomputer link. In the duty machine this software will:

1. Receive messages from other processes to transmit data to update the standby's data tables (these are called 'work requests').
2. Despatch data across the link and attempt to receive acknowledgements (called 'replies') from the standby.

3. Create and despatch test messages if no requests to transmit other data are received in a specified time interval (say 1 second).

The duty machine will not send a second message across the link until it has received a reply to the first.

In the standby machine the software will:

1. Receive data (work requests and test messages) passed across the link, and use work requests to update appropriate data tables.
2. Despatch acknowledgements of data received across the link, and attempt to receive further data.
3. Create an error message if no data is received across the link in a specified time interval (say 5 seconds).

Each reply sent from the standby to the duty machine will contain a response, designated as ACK or NAK, indicating success or failure respectively of the transfer from duty to standby, as seen by the standby. The criteria used to determine success or failure are described below.

We assume that data is transmitted and received in blocks, and that transmission and reception of data are always terminated by a hardware completion interrupt accompanied by some form of reply word to indicate success or failure of the transfer attempted. For data transmission, this reply must be received within a specified time (referred to as a timeout); otherwise the transfer is deemed a failure. After a successful transmission from duty machine to standby, the duty machine expects to receive a reply from the standby within a specified time; if the reply is not received, the transmission is again assumed to have failed.

All messages received in both duty and standby computers are also subject to formatting and validity checks, the details of which are omitted. In the duty machine a reply received is considered valid if and only if it passes all the formatting and validity checks referred to above, and in addition the reply is ACK or NAK. If the duty receives a valid reply which contains ACK, it prepares to send further work; if the duty receives a valid reply which contains NAK, the transfer is assumed to have failed; if the duty receives an invalid reply it discards it. In the standby machine, data received is considered valid if and only if it passes all the formatting and validity checks referred to above. If, then, the standby receives valid data it replies ACK, otherwise it replies NAK.

If data transmission (from duty to standby, or from standby to duty) fails, a further attempt is made. After three attempts the transfer is aborted. An error (intercomputer link failed) message is raised if:

a data transfer (from duty to standby, or standby to duty) is aborted after three unsuccessful attempts; or

after receiving valid data, further valid data is not received by the standby within the specified time (5 seconds).

Failure of the link always results in a reassessment of the state of the standby

238

machine. Further action is then outside the scope of this exercise. (In practice, the standby might be downgraded to, say, 'out-of-service', so violating the steady-state assumption made, while the duty might continue to test the link until a response is achieved.)

These requirements are reasonable for this type of device, but if any changes were felt to be necessary they should not materially affect the overall design strategy. The details are summarized as they affect each process in the following sections.

8.6   Initial Software Design

Following the guidelines of Section 8.4, for each machine we start off with:

1. One driver for each device
2. One multiplexor for each output device
3. One distributor for each input device.

If, as in this case, the device (that is, the intercomputer link) acts as both input and output, the driver can be split into two:

1. Driver–transmitter (for output)
2. Driver–receiver (for (input).

Since the only data received across the link in the duty machine is replies to messages sent to the standby, the duty machine does not need a distributor; instead, the replies received by the driver–receiver are passed directly to the driver–transmitter. Likewise, since the only data sent in the standby machine is replies to data received, the standby machine does not need a multiplexor.

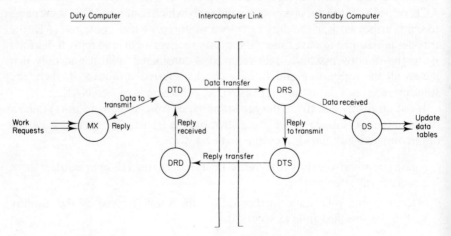

Figure 8.2   Case study—software organization

The processes required are, therefore, as follows:

Machine	Process
Duty	Multiplexor
	Driver–transmitter
	Driver–receiver
Standby	Distributor
	Driver–transmitter
	Driver–receiver

The software organization can now be summarized as in Figure 8.2; this ignores the presence of processes other than those listed above. The processes are named using mnemonics as follows:

Mnemonic	Meaning
MX	*M*ultiple*X*or
DTD	*D*river *T*ransmitter *D*uty
DRD	*D*river *R*eceiver *D*uty
DS	*Di*Stributor
DTS	*D*river *T*ransmitter *S*tandby
DRS	*D*river *R*eceiver *S*tandby

These mnemonics are used in the discussion below.

We repeat that the two drivers (DTD, DRD) in the duty machine could be combined into one process, and likewise in the standby. It would also be possible to combine like processes in the duty and standby machines; the software in each machine would then be identical but operate in duty or standby mode.

We now summarize the lines of communication between these processes. During normal error-free running, each message passed across the link from the duty machine is acknowledged by the standby before another message is transmitted. Using the process names given in Figure 8.2, the normal sequence of events is, therefore:

1. MX in the duty machine sends a message (work request) to DTD and awaits acknowledgement.
2. DTD in the duty machine sends the message across the link.
3. DRS in the standby machine receives the message.
4. DRS in the standby machine sends the message to DS and requests transmission of a reply via DTS.
5. DTS in the standby machine sends the reply across the link.
6. DRD in the duty machine receives the reply.
7. DRD in the duty machine informs DTD that the reply is received.
8. DTD in the duty machine acknowledges receipt to MX.

The sequence is then repeated from the beginning. This describes the system proposed. Checks to ensure that messages are passed between processes in the correct order, as described above, are absorbed into the individual processes. These, together with the additional logic to detect and recover from data transfer failures, are described in the following sections.

Before presenting the results, there are some additional considerations which it is convenient to summarize here:

1. *Error detection.* It is normal practice for all processes in a real-time system to be self-checking. Evidently there must be limits to this, but generally each process should check that messages are received only from those processes from which messages are expected, and when they are expected. If these checks fail the action of the system may be undefined; we must then be careful to distinguish:

> normal error-free processing;
> errors, or escapes, from which the system is expected to recover and continue;
> failure conditions on which the function of the system is undefined.

We note that this reaffirms the identical view expressed in a different context in Section 2.4.4.2. In our design, hardware interrupts and some timing messages received when not expected are simply discarded, and the system continues. This decision has no great significance; it could easily be replaced by, for example, an algorithm to detect a system failure after a sufficient quantity or frequency of unexpected interrupts. All other messages received when not expected are treated as system failures.

2. *Additional system functions.* Although no such functions have been specified in our example, it is normal for each process to make provision now to add in later communication with other processes not yet specified. These may include, in particular, utility processes responsible for monitoring system performance, communicating with a maintenance technician to diagnose run-time faults, controlling state changes in a dual system, and simulating or testing specified functions. This provision must be made even if it is not, at present, used.

These requirements contrast sharply with the assumptions that can be made in other types of systems (such as those covered in Chapters 1 to 7).

We set out in the next section to design logic by inspecting the order in which events of interest to each process occur. In the present context the events are messages received; we shall therefore think of the messages input to a process as constituting a serial file, whose structure can then be described in the normal way. The Read statement will mean 'receive next message'; it will be allocated according to the read-ahead principle and implemented using the Receive instruction. However, we shall also find that the structures present, together with the constraints just noted, necessitate extensive use of inversion. Consequently we shall find ourselves using Restart and Suspend, together with Receive, in the same process.

We shall also identify a need to define application-dependent processing functions, and allocate these within the logic framework defined in the now normal way. The corresponding subroutines are given meaningful names which reflect the function performed. There is no particular reason why these subroutines should not themselves contain Send, Receive, Restart and Suspend instructions.

Whenever inversion is used, the main program takes on the process name (such as MX), while each subroutine is distinguished by a suffix (MX1, MX2, ...). The Restart symbol given in Section 8.3 is then further modified so that, for example, $\widehat{w_r^2}$ is used in place of $\widehat{w_r^{MX2}}$ Each subroutine is given its own internal state variable called respectively SV1, SV2, ... As noted in Section 8.3, the Suspend symbol is modified to contain a note of the value assigned to the state variable. Thus the symbol $\widehat{R_r^2}$ used in subroutine MX2 means Suspend MX2 and set SV2 = 2.

8.7   A Software Multiplexor

The software multiplexor for the duty machine:

1. Receives work requests from other processes.
2. Despatches work to a driver and receives acknowledgement of work done.
3. Creates and despatches a test message to the driver if all other work has been completed, and no new work is received during 1 second. To this end, the multiplexor requests a repeat message once per second from the operating system.

Hence the following messages can be received:

1. Work request.
2. Acknowledgement from driver.
3. Timer repeats once per second.

We think of these as forming a serial file input to the multiplexor. They are best treated as an interleaving clash as described in Chapter 7. In order to resolve the clash, and so fully design the logic, we define four modules:

MX   This retrieves the next message off the incoming queue and decides to which subroutine it is of interest (MX1, MX2, or MX3).

MX1   This handles all work requests received; if a request can be despatched to the driver (DTD) it is passed to MX2, otherwise the work requested is stored until it can be actioned.

MX2   This handles acknowledgements received from the driver (DTD). If further work is waiting, it is sent to DTD, otherwise MX2 suspends itself until such work becomes available.

MX3   This handles timer repeats (as presented, these are received once per second), and decides whether to create a test message. Any test message created is passed to MX2 for despatch.

242

We define the following subroutines to execute application-dependent code:

Subroutine	Function
Storework	Store work request received
Getwork	Get work from store ready to send
Test	Create test message ready for despatch

Figures 8.3 to 8.6 now show the logic required to resolve the clash, ignoring the possibility of errors. In Figure 8.5, if SV2 = 2, the restart should be from MX; if SV2 = 1 or 3, the restart should be from MX1 or MX3. Note how the intermediate file passed to MX2 is created by MX, MX1, and MX3.

We can incorporate the following checks for system failure:

1. A message is received from a process which should not communicate with MX.
2. A message is received from the driver when not expected.

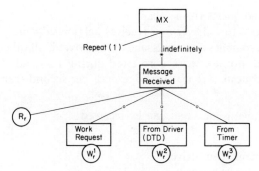

Figure 8.3   Multiplexor: main program

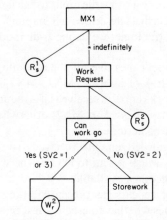

Figure 8.4   Multiplexor: subroutine MX1

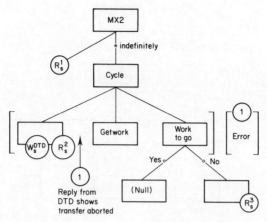

Figure 8.5   Multiplexor: subroutine MX2

Any error so detected has the nature of a 'system failure', as described in Section 8.6, and the action of the multiplexor is undefined; they are best accommodated within MX as shown in Figure 8.7, which now replaces Figure 8.3.

Note that determination of the success or failure of the physical transfer in the duty machine is entirely the responsibility of DTD. This covers all questions relating to repeat transmissions and hardware timeouts, and is covered in Section 8.8. DTD will always eventually reply 'success' or 'failure' to any request for transmission from MX; failure results in an error message created by MX2.

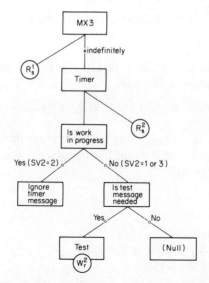

Figure 8.6   Multiplexor: subroutine MX3

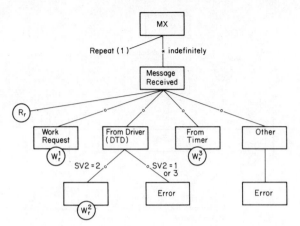

Figure 8.7   Multiplexor: system failure checks

Other features of the design as presented are:

1. Subroutines Storework and Getwork contain algorithms for storing work, and for deciding which work to send next, and are entirely application-dependent. Possibilities include simple queueing (first in, first out) or priority queueing (where queue position depends on the nature of the work stored), while one piece of work stored may or may not overwrite another.
2. There are no restrictions on the content of the subroutines used, except that they must not interfere with the control logic. For instance, Storework may include a handshake with the producer which created the work request but should not use, let alone alter, the value of state variables internal to MX.

8.8   Two Hardware Drivers

8.8.1   A driver–transmitter

Next, we design the hardware driver–transmitter for the duty machine. Under normal error-free conditions this will:

1. Receive, and action, a request from MX to transmit data to the standby computer.
2. Then await receipt of a completion interrupt from the hardware.
3. Then await receipt of a reply from the standby via DRD.
4. Then send a reply to MX.
5. Repeat from 1.

The sequence of events:

transmit data to the standby
receive the hardware completion interrupt
receive a reply from the standby

is termed a 'transfer'.

The transfer is successful if:

the hardware completion interrupt is received within (say) 1.5 seconds
the hardware reply word for this transmission shows no error
a reply is then received from the standby machine via DRD within (say) a
further 1.5 seconds
the reply received is valid and contains ACK.

Under any other circumstances the transfer fails. If a transfer fails it is repeated
with a maximum of three attempts; if after three attempts the transfer is still
unsuccessful, it is aborted. After a successful transfer, or three unsuccessful
attempts, a reply is sent to the multiplexor; no further action is taken until further
instructions are received from the multiplexor.

If we think of hardware completion interrupts as messages received, and allow
for the need to time certain activities, then the process DTD receives the
following messages:

1. Request to transmit data from MX.
2. Hardware completion interrupt.
3. Reply from DRD.
4. Timeout.

There is no structure clash here, although the inversion technique can still be
usefully applied. We define the following subroutine to execute application-
dependent code:

Subroutine	Function
Senddata	Despatch data to link

This subroutine contains all the hardware-dependent instructions necessary to
transmit a block of data.

We build our picture in stages. Figures 8.8 and 8.9 illustrate the case when no

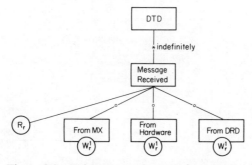

Figure 8.8   Driver–transmitter: main program

246

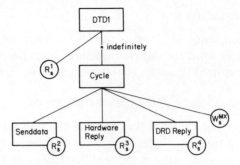

Figure 8.9   Driver–transmitter: subroutine DTD1

errors of any kind are detected and no timeout is detected. Figures 8.10 and 8.11 then update Figures 8.8 and 8.9 respectively to show the additional logic required to detect and recover from transmission failures; error conditions and timeouts are treated as escapes from the normal sequence of events.

Finally, Figure 8.12 updates Figure 8.10; all hardware interrupts and timeouts received when not expected are discarded, while any other message received when not expected is treated as a system failure.

8.8.2 A driver–receiver

Under normal error-free conditions the driver–receiver for the duty machine will:

1. Receive data across the link and validate it.
2. Send a message to the driver transmitter (DTD).
3. Repeat from 1.

Reception of data is successful if:

1. The hardware completion interrupt shows no error.
2. The data is valid (the details are omitted here).
3. The response is ACK or NAK.

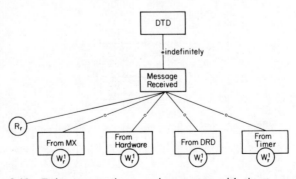

Figure 8.10   Driver–transmitter: main program with timer messages

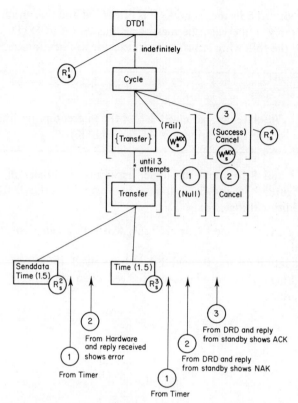

Figure 8.11   Driver–transmitter: subroutine DTD1 with detection of transmission failures

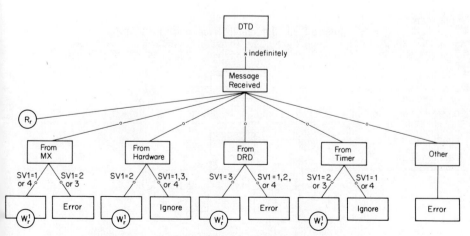

Figure 8.12   Driver–transmitter: system failure checks

If the data received fails these checks it is discarded and the computer continues to expect a reply. Otherwise the message is passed on to DTD.

We define the following subroutine to execute application-dependent code:

Subroutine	Function
Validate	Validate data received across the intercomputer link (including a check that response is ACK or NAK)

Figures 8.13 and 8.14 show the logic, assuming no errors of any kind are detected; Figures 8.15 and 8.16 update Figures 8.13 and 8.14 respectively to show the additional logic for:

1. Hardware errors. If the hardware reply word shows an error, the message is discarded.
2. Data validation errors. If invalid data is received, the message is discarded.
3. Self-checking errors. Any message received when not expected is treated as a system failure.

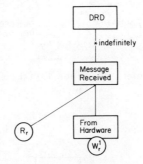

Figure 8.13   Driver–receiver: main program

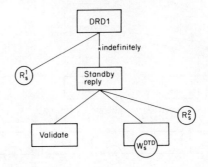

Figure 8.14   Driver–receiver: subroutine DRD1

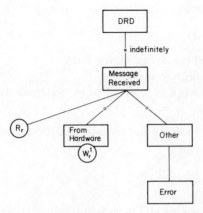

Figure 8.15   Driver–receiver: system failure checks

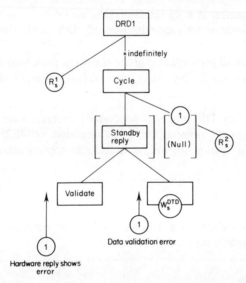

Figure 8.16   Driver–receiver: subroutine DRD1 with detection of errors

Note that this logic cannot be expected to know whether data has been transmitted by DTD; consequently, so far as DRD is concerned, a reply can be received at any time. Additional logic to ensure that a reply is received only when one is expected has, therefore, been made the responsibility of DTD.

8.9   Further Illustrations

This section contains brief notes on the three corresponding processes in the standby machine.

8.9.1 Distributor

The distributor process:

1. Receives work from the device driver DRS.
2. Sends work to application processes.
3. Ensures that some work is received from the driver within a specified time interval (5 seconds).

We shall arrange to receive timer repeats once per second. Then the following messages can be received:

1. Work request.
2. Timer repeat.

We think of these as forming an interleaving clash as described in Chapter 7. In order to resolve the clash we define three modules:

DS   This retrieves the next message off the incoming queue and decides to which subroutine it is of interest (DS1 or DS2)

DS1   This handles all work requests received, and routes them to application processes

DS2   This handles all messages from the timer (as presented these are received once per second); if no work is received for 5 seconds an error message is raised.

Finally, we note that DS1 and DS2 necessarily interact, since each time work is received, DS1 clears the timeout being accumulated by DS2.

We define the following subroutine to execute application-dependent code:

Subroutine	Function
Sendwork	Despatches data received to other processes to update the standby's internal data tables

Figures 8.17 to 8.19 show the logic required to resolve the clash ignoring the possibility of errors.

The logic can also incorporate a check that a message is not received from any process from which it is not expected. The additional logic is included in Figure 8.20.

8.9.2. Driver–transmitter

The driver–transmitter will, under normal error-free conditions:

1. Receive a request from DRS to transmit a reply, and transmit it.
2. Then await the hardware completion interrupt.
3. Repeat from 1.

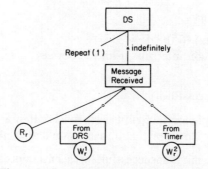

Figure 8.17　Distributor: main program

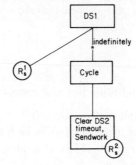

Figure 8.18　Distributor: subroutine DS1

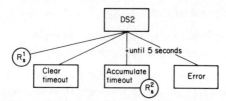

Figure 8.19　Distributor: subroutine DS2

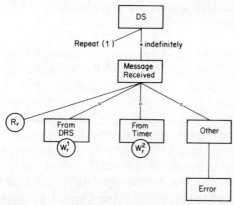

Figure 8.20　Distributor: system failure checks

The sequence of events:

transmit work (data) to the device
obtain the completion interrupt from the device

is termed a transfer.

This transfer is successful if:

the hardware completion interrupt is received within a fixed interval
the hardware reply word for this transmission shows no error.

If one attempt to transmit is unsuccessful, further attempts are made up to a total of three. If transmission of a reply ultimately fails, an error message is raised; otherwise the driver awaits receipt of further work.

The detailed design raises no issues not already covered in Section 8.8, and further details are, therefore, omitted.

8.9.3 Driver–receiver

Under normal error-free conditions this will simply:

1. Receive data across the link and validate it.
2. If it is valid, inform the distributor that work has been received.
3. Request the driver–transmitter (DTS) to send a reply (containing ACK or NAK).
4. Repeat from 1.

Reception of data is successful if:

1. The hardware completion interrupt shows no error.
2. The data is valid (again, the details are omitted here).

If the hardware completion interrupt shows an error, the data received is discarded. If the hardware completion interrupt shows no error, the data received is validated; if valid, it is passed to DS, and DTS is asked to send a reply containing ACK; otherwise DTS is asked to send a reply containing NAK. This process raises no issues not already considered in Section 8.8, and further details are, therefore, omitted.

This completes our discussion of real-time process control systems, for which the software required is the most complex we have considered. Its complexity arises from the need to respond to interrupts, to detect, and recover from, error conditions, and to allow for multiple asynchronous processes. Even so, we have found that processes tend to fall into types, and that the logic internal to each process type can be designed using the principles now well established. Indeed, this chapter brings together all the concepts and techniques established earlier; we have applied them in a new and distinctive context. All the structures defined are dynamic, and none is directly related to static data structures. We reaffirm that we can distinguish the high-level control logic from application-dependent subroutines executed. It is detailed variations in the control logic required, together with possibly more substantial (but wholly application-dependent) variations in the subroutines executed, which distinguish one instance of a process type from another. To this extent the designs presented are models, and make the design of each new instance a degree more predictable. This should result in the production of more reliable software.

The next chapter provides a summary of the results achieved, and a context in which to judge them.

Chapter 9
Retrospect

This chapter provides a context in which to assess the results achieved. It starts with a brief account of a continuing controversy over the use of GOTO, and continues by reaffirming the approach adopted in this book: namely, that we must distinguish the needs of design (for which we can eliminate GOTO's) and the practicalities of implementation (where explicit GOTO's are necessary if we are not to distort the structure). Section 9.3 describes the functional approach to program design and Section 9.4 goes on to draw again the contrast with structured programming; thus, where the functional approach concentrates on techniques suitable for the identification of program functions, structured programming provides techniques suitable for the design of that logic which decides when, and under what conditions, to execute the functions identified. Section 9.5 discusses some related concepts and techniques, and we conclude (in Section 9.6) by reaffirming the case for an integration of structured and functional techniques.

The references quoted refer to the Bibliography at the end of the book.

9.1 The GOTO Controversy

There has been a great deal of discussion in recent years over the desirability or otherwise of the use of GOTO when constructing program logic. The debate proceeds as follows.

Every programming language in everyday use provides an instruction which we refer to as 'GOTO'. For this purpose we may include English and flowcharts, since they both provide a means of expressing program logic. The instruction name may vary from language to language, but the function of GOTO is always the same: to facilitate a direct transfer of control from any one point in a program to any other point in the same program. Usually the only restrictions are that both points fall within the same compilation unit, and that the transfer does not violate any block structure conventions in force.

From this simple observation the traditional case against GOTO is derived. If no restrictions are placed on the use of GOTO, then in the worst case:

1. At no point in a program can you confidently determine how the logic arrived there (because a GOTO could have been coded anywhere else transferring control to this point).
2. At no point in a program can you confidently predict where the logic will go to (because a GOTO could be coded to transfer control to anywhere else).

Admittedly, it is not usually quite as bad as that. But the general effect is that program logic can get into a bit of a tangle. Sometimes an analogy is drawn between the logic of a disorganized program and a bowl of spaghetti; just as the strands of spaghetti tend to fall into no coherent pattern, so too do the GOTO's in such a program.

A consequence is that programs can become difficult to read, difficult to test, and difficult to amend. Not surprisingly, project control can be a problem, programs are frequently delivered late, and system development tends to be expensive. Certainly this is a common experience within the computing industry.

A possible conclusion is that explicit GOTO's are the source of all programming evil. Indeed this is a conclusion frequently drawn; it then follows that elimination of GOTO's should be a principal objective of program design. This idea is known as 'GOTO-less programming', and its proponents often quote the so-called 'structure theorem' in its support. This theorem (which is summarized in the Appendix) states, roughly, that any program, however complex, so long as it has one entry and one exit, can be coded without the use of explicit GOTO's, provided that the language used allows both the construction of high-level loops and CASE-type statements (such as the LOOP and IF... ELSE... statements of our schematic logic). Given this theorem, and the historical tendency for the use of GOTO's to get you into trouble, the opponents of GOTO suggest that the solution to all program design problems must be 'don't use GOTO's' and 'do use LOOP and IF... ELSE... type statements'.

The counter-argument runs as follows. It is certainly true that for many purposes eliminating GOTO's is a desirable objective and will achieve better programs. But it is not universally true, because the price of eliminating GOTO's (at least on complex programs and in existing languages) as described above, can be to complicate the logic by obscuring its structure and necessitating the introduction of switches; this can make things worse, not better. Taking a practical view, we conclude that GOTO-less programming is a desirable objective, can sometimes be achieved and with benefit, but is not always an improvement.

The idea of GOTO-less programming is, therefore, too sweeping. We can certainly agree, from the argument given, that:

1. The GOTO instruction does indeed provide the programmer with too much freedom in constructing program logic.
2. It is desirable to restrict this freedom.

The real question, however, is how the latter should be achieved. In order to provide an answer we have taken the view that programming is a constructional activity, and that, like many constructional activities, it needs to adopt some construction units and some design principles. Since we are concerned with the design of program logic, the construction units are standardized logic building blocks, while the design principles show how to use them. This provides the discipline required. The construction units comprise nested logic, the logic monitor, and a variety of read instructions. The design principles described relate program logic to problem structure, as illustrated in a range of examples. We have found that:

1. The designs produced are GOTO-less in the sense that the GOTO does not appear explicitly; instead it is implied by the syntax of the statements used. (QUIT is the nearest we have come to an explicit GOTO, but even this is a highly restrictive GOTO.)
2. The implementation of the designs produced (in existing programming languages) requires explicit GOTO's; indeed the GOTO's associated with inversion are manifold, and to some extent go against the spirit of traditional block-structured languages.

We have then drawn a contrast between the needs of design and those of implementation; some of the compromises possible were discussed in Section 6.9. Inevitably, it seems, there has, at present, to be a trade-off between design clarity and implementation expediency. It has been my task to provide techniques to achieve design clarity.

A summary of the construction units and design principles developed is given in the next section; the compromises to be taken in practice are for the reader to decide. A summary of other design techniques which concentrate on the identification of different construction units is given in later sections. For further material on the use of GOTO, see [1].

9.2 Structured Programming

In this book we have discussed techniques for the construction of program logic. We have defined some standard logic building blocks (nested logic and logic monitor), and discovered the need for a variety of interpretations of Read (as Call, Suspend, and Receive). We have also shown how to relate the use of these concepts to certain structural features of program specifications. Another concept, recursion, is described briefly in the Appendix. Of these, nested logic and Call can readily be implemented without the explicit use of 'GOTO' in many languages, while the opposite is true of the remainder. If the use of 'GOTO' is felt to be undesirable, then some compromises must be made, as described in Sections 3.1 and 6.9.

A design notation for the logic building blocks has been provided, consisting of:

1. Structure diagrams. These are better than traditional flowcharts for designing program logic.

2. Schematic logic. This is a language-independent expression of program logic; it is up to the reader to provide an equivalent in the programming language he uses.

This notation can provide the basis of new logic design documentation standards. Depending on the context, GOTO's may or may not be used explicitly in the finished program.

The use of structure diagrams helps describe the order in which events of interest to a program happen. We call this order a structure, and the use of structure as a basis for program design we call structured programming. The relationship between structure diagrams and schematic logic ensures that this structure is preserved in the finished program, producing logic which is easier to read, understand, and amend. This is particularly significant and powerful for the design of high-level control logic, but may also be used for low-level application code.

The principles have been illustrated using a variety of examples. The earlier chapters concentrated on commercial applications for which the following were typical:

serial sorted file analysis
validation (including errors and invalidity)
file match
print.

These have been considered operating in batch or on-line mode, and possibly using a tp monitor and/or data base. The later chapters included examples from other application environments such as:

on-line conversations
scientific applications
software utilities
process control.

These more complex examples illustrate the power and versatility of the approach adopted.

The examples used suggest that structure has both a static and a dynamic sense. Data structures, for example, are static in the sense that they exist, in a clear physical sense, independently of the program which analyses them. Program and data structure are then closely related, and in this is the origin of the term 'data structure approach' frequently found in a commercial programming context (see [2]). But other structures, such as algorithms, are dynamic in the sense that they are constructed during a program's execution, and contribute to the processing required, but are less visible in the external world. The identification of suitable dynamic structures is essential to the design of many scientific and real-time programs. The use of structured programming concepts ensures that the structures used are made visible in all cases, and it is this which contributes to the clarity of the designs produced.

The mixture of practice (the design of examples) and theory (the definition of logic building blocks) has been central to our approach. The examples were presented in order of complexity, starting with the simplest. Each new example built on the previous examples, so illustrating and proving (in the sense of 'putting to the test') concepts already agreed, but each example also introduced something new in order to extend the principles developed. This approach is, of course, essentially the standard scientific method and avoids the pitfalls inherent in the simple description of overgeneralized guidelines which are sometimes found.

In this way we continually refined both theory and practice; each new example provided a further check on what had gone before, and an opportunity to learn something new. It is always open to the reader to reject the conclusions drawn, but if you do this, remember that there *is* a problem, and that if you don't like the technique described, some other technique must be devised to solve the same problem. We have to admit, too, that no formal proof is available which demonstrates that the logic building blocks presented are either correct or complete; we can only hope that their relevance and usefulness will be self-evident.

The examples used demonstrate that programs tend to fall into 'types', where each instance of a program type tends to give rise to similar logic design problems. These problems can be solved using the design principles explained in this book to give general solutions which avoid solving the same problems, for each further instance of each class. We can, therefore, think of the designs produced as models; what distinguishes one instance of a program type from another is detailed variations in the control logic required, together with application-dependent algorithms in the subroutines specified.

It is my view that specialized techniques are required for the design of control logic. This logic is responsible for deciding when, and under what conditions, application-dependent processing can be carried out. Each design presented itemizes all such processing, and suggests the content of subroutines required. Of course, these may themselves contain logic, and this may also be designed using the principles described; but once a clear interface is provided (as here) between the control logic and subroutines called, the internal design of those subroutines should be greatly simplified. All this is consistent with the general philosophy advocated throughout this book.

We turn now to a brief description of principles concerned with the identification of program modules.

9.3 The Functional Approach: Modular Concepts

The functional approach to design concentrates on the identification of the 'module' as the primary unit of structure. In any given context the following would be suitable guidelines for the choice of modules:

1. Each module should perform a logical subset of the total processing.
2. Each module should be functionally independent of each other module.
3. Each module should be readable, testable, and maintainable.
4. Each module should be not too big and not too small.

The motivation here is evidently to break a large unit (frequently a program, but possibly a system) down into a number of smaller units (the modules) of a more manageable size. Each smaller unit performs a well-defined function; it can then be designed and implemented and the total solution built from the modules so created.

The relationship between modules identified can be displayed on a 'data flow diagram', or on a 'module hierarchy diagram'. (The term 'structure chart' is often used in place of 'module hierarchy diagram' but is avoided here to avoid risk of confusion with 'structure diagram'). Although the conventions are different, both represent a functional decomposition.

9.3.1 Data flow diagrams

The data flow diagram is designed to show the 'active components' of a system, and the 'data interfaces' between them. The symbols usually used are summarized in Figure 9.1, and an illustration given in Figure 9.2. (Other conventions also exist, but the intention remains the same.) The diagram may be used to show a complete system (which, in a commercial context, may include both clerical and computer-based functions), or a subset. If the diagram assumes a particular implementation it is said to give a physical view, and otherwise a logical view. In the first case we would expect:

a function to be implemented as a clerical procedure, a program, a subroutine, a transaction (as defined in Chapter 5), or a process (as defined in Chapters 6 and 8)

a data store to be implemented as a manual or computer-based file (possibly using a data base)

a source/sink to represent initial/final system data

corresponding to the implementations noted above, a data flow to be implemented as a piece of paper passed between clerical staff, a file created by one program for use by another, data passed between two subroutines called by a common calling program or subroutine, a common communication area accessible by two transactions working under a tp monitor, or a message passed from one process to another.

The notation allows one 'bubble' to be exploded to show its component functions, as illustrated in Figure 9.3. In this diagram A1, A2, A3 are the functional units which go to make up the larger unit A; corresponding changes are implied to the content of data store, source/sink, and data flow symbols. Evidently, the functions A1, A2, A3 may then themselves be exploded, and this type of analysis continued to whatever degree seems appropriate.

Data flow diagrams are the principal tool of 'structured analysis' techniques, supported by related concepts of data analysis, mini-specifications (using 'structured English') and the structured design concepts described in the remainder of this section; for a full description the reader is referred to a specialist text (such as [3] or [4]).

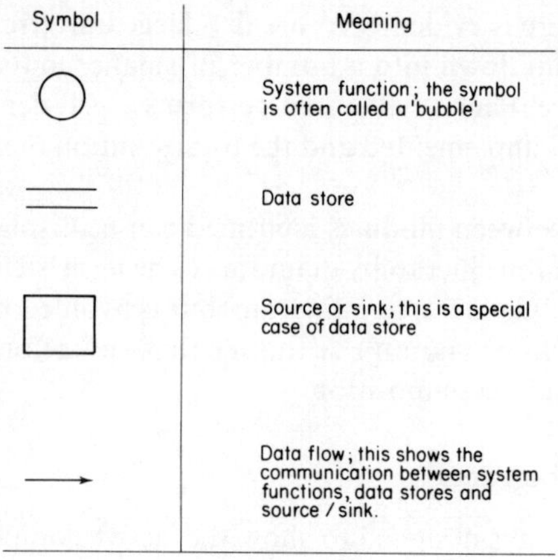

Symbol	Meaning
○	System function; the symbol is often called a 'bubble'
═	Data store
▭	Source or sink; this is a special case of data store
→	Data flow; this shows the communication between system functions, data stores and source/sink.

Figure 9.1 Data flow diagram symbols

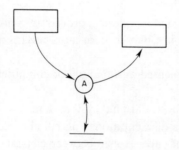

Figure 9.2 A data flow diagram

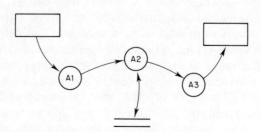

Figure 9.3 Explosion of a data flow diagram

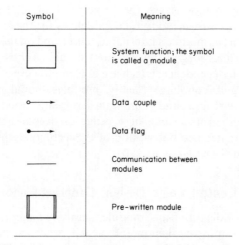

Figure 9.4   Module hierarchy diagram symbols

9.3.2 Module hierarchy diagrams

We may contrast the data flow diagram with the more traditional module hierarchy diagram which exhibits the symbols shown in Figure 9.4. In practice the data couple and data flag symbols are often omitted. The module hierarchy diagram corresponding to Figures 9.2 and 9.3 is given in Figure 9.5; the data couples and data flags shown are illustrative only and are not intended to relate directly to the data flows shown in Figures 9.2 and 9.3. Whereas the bubbles of a data flow diagram may be used to represent clerical procedures, programs, subroutines, transactions, or processes, the dependent modules of a module hierarchy diagram are assumed to be subroutines. Thus A may represent a clerical procedure, program, subroutine, transaction, or process, but A1, A2, and A3 would normally all be subroutines.

The data couple and data flag are then akin to parameters passed and replies returned; the upper level invokes (and so passes a parameter to) the lower level; the lower level returns to the upper level (with a reply). The direction indicator shows which data are parameters passed, and which replies returned. It is a feature of both diagrammatic techniques that this kind of analysis can be done to any level of detail.

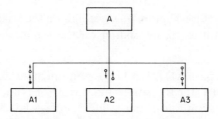

Figure 9.5   A module hierarchy diagram

Module hierarchy diagrams are the principal tool of 'structured design' techniques, which also provide additional guidelines for the choice of modules. These concentrate on the module's internal function, and on the data they jointly reference. The guidelines suggest that modules should be chosen on the basis of their simplicity and independence, which are in turn measured using concepts of module 'strength', and 'coupling'. Ideally, modules should be chosen which exhibit maximum strength and minimum coupling; modules with these properties are identified using one of a range of decomposition techniques. However, for a more detailed description of the technique, the reader is again referred to a specialist text (such as [5]).

9.4 Control Logic Design: Ordering Concepts

While both data flow diagrams and module hierarchy diagrams can be used to show the system functions and their hierarchical dependence, neither is designed to show the order in which these functions are invoked. This role is performed by the structure diagram. Since the diagrammatic conventions have been defined in the main body of the book, familiarity with the notation is assumed here. In order to contrast the different diagrammatic techniques, suppose we know that the functions A1, A2, A3 (of Figure 9.3) are always executed in the order:

A1
then A2 or A3
then A1
then A2 or A3
etc.

Let B denote the selection 'A2 or A3', and C the sequence 'A1 followed by B'. Then the logic internal to A could be described by a structure diagram as in Figure 9.6.

We may, in practice, now differentiate:

1. Those modules which are more concerned with controlling the order in which functions are executed (the boxes labelled A, B, C in Figure 9.6, equivalent to the internal logic of A in Figure 9.2).
2. Those modules which are more concerned with describing the functions themselves (the boxes labelled A1, A2, A3 in Figure 9.6, corresponding to the bubbles shown in Figure 9.3).

The source of the structure diagram now depends on the ordering described. We can distinguish several cases, depending on the significance of the modules portrayed:

1. *Life histories.* Suppose A1, A2, A3 represent functions executed to complete some system activity; the transitions made from one function to the next are often said to constitute an activity 'life history' and can conveniently be described in a data flow diagram: hence the use of data flow diagrams as a tool

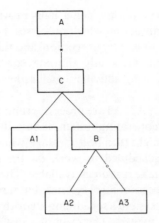

Figure 9.6   A structure diagram

of systems analysis. The corresponding structure diagram would describe the order in which these stages are reached over a period of time (see [6]). We note, however, that computer systems are not traditionally implemented to preserve this particular structure in the control logic; instead it is preserved as the successive values of system variables held on records and files. So far as we are concerned, manipulation of these variables is then considered to form part of the application-dependent code. Consequently, no examples have been included.

2. *Operating instructions.* Next, suppose that A1, A2, A3 represent programs. We can think of the data passed between them as temporary or permanent files. The programs are scheduled by instructions received from an operator through some form of command language. A data flow diagram could then represent what is usually called a system flowchart, showing the programs executed and the files passed from one to another. The structure diagram technique could then be used to describe the order in which the programs are executed; this information is sometimes called the system 'operating instructions'. No such examples have been considered in this book.

3. *Program control logic.* Suppose A1, A2, A3 are subroutines. Then there will always be a set of rules governing the order in which these subroutines are called. This order may be related to the structure of serial files read, or to the nature of the application algorithms being executed. In either case we can take advantage of the rules implied to design the high-level control logic required; the subroutines called become the application-dependent functions executed. Depending on the context, the unit which invokes the subroutines might itself be a clerical procedure, a program, another subroutine, a transaction, or a process. The majority of the examples in this book are of this kind.

4. *Conversations.* Suppose A1, A2, A3 are transactions in a terminal-driven on-line system. Here we can think of each transaction as corresponding to a screen. Each screen input requests the next screen to be displayed. This is

made available via a tp monitor which usually provides facilities to pass data on one screen to the transaction which processes the next. The succession of screens can be thought of as a 'conversation' and this conversation described in a structure diagram. Generally the conversation will control system enquiries, or data processing activities (such as file updates). Examples were included in Chapter 5.

5. *Scheduling*. Suppose A1, A2, A3 are processes running asynchronously under the overall control of an operating system, as described in Chapter 8. The data passed from A1 to A2 might then be a 'message' which acts as a 'trigger' to A2, which is accordingly scheduled to work on the message as soon as the operating system can make resources available. This form of communication is a commonplace in process control systems, but rarely noticed in commercial systems. The operating system's scheduling algorithm determines the order in which processes are activated. The examples in Chapter 8 showed how to design the control logic internal to particular processes; apart from the general concept of process priorities, no examples were given of a scheduling algorithm.

Structured programming and the functional techniques perform different roles: where structured programming describes the order in which events happen (and so functions are executed), the functional techniques help identify those events and functions. Structured analysis also highlights the data flows (in the sense described) while structured design exhibits the hierarchical organization of the subroutines present. Since structured programming and the functional techniques cover different aspects of the same system, an integration of the two is necessary.

9.5 Some Related Terms

While the term 'structured programming' is used in a quite specific sense in this book, it has in practice become something of an umbrella term. We have used it to refer to a particular set of techniques concerned with the design and documentation of high-level control logic. However, it is sometimes used to cover the functional techniques described in Section 9.3 and any, or all, of the related topics listed in this section.

We start with some concepts concerned with the identification of skills required on a software development project, and the organization of those skills into a manageable unit; they are quite specifically *not* concerned with programming techniques, whether those techniques are structured, modular, or anything else. The following notes describe three of the terms sometimes used.

1. *Chief programmer teams*. This is an organizational concept, suggesting that a team should be organized around a chief programmer to improve the manageability and productivity of the project, and to emphasize the need for high-quality design. The team may consist additionally of a back-up programmer, librarian, and other team members. Its objective is to recognize

the different skills required (operating systems, programming languages, data bases, software used, application knowledge, etc.) and to make the best use of the resources available. It refers especially to very large projects, and should be used in conjunction with a design technique (such as structured programming).

2. *Project teams.* At least in a commercial context, there used to be (and sometimes still is) a sharp division between analysts and programmers; indeed, the corporate hierarchy used frequently to be such that analysts and programmers working on the same project were housed in quite separate offices, reporting to different line managers. The consequence was that analysts and programmers never talked to each other (I am exaggerating— but in some cases not by much). To remedy this, analysts and programmers now frequently form a joint project team, also recognizing that different skills are often required on the same project; this organization greatly encourages communication between team members, so reducing errors, ambiguities, and misunderstandings in the project specification.

3. *Structured walkthroughs.* Recognizing the difficulties associated with program development, the structured walkthrough is an attempt to bring each program under more public scrutiny; 'walking through' the program with a third party should uncover unsuspected errors in the program code and/or misunderstandings of the specification used. The catch (and a similar one is true of all organizational solutions) is that one cannot walk through a maze; only if the program (and specification) are reasonably well designed in the first place can a structured walkthrough be successful. In that sense the whole of this book is a contribution to the material required for a successful structured walkthrough.

Some other terms of interest are:

1. *PDL (program design language).* PDL provides an informal language-independent expression of program logic. Its purpose is to enable a programmer to express his thoughts without having to worry about the syntactical detail and constraints of a particular programming language. It can also act as a form of program documentation which, because it avoids excessive detail, is quick to produce and easy to maintain. Ideally it should be easy to convert PDL to compilable or executable code. Other terms used in an equivalent sense are pseudo-code (as defined in Section 1.2) and SDL (system design language). Our use of 'schematic logic' (first introduced in Section 1.2) is similar, although our principal tool is always the structure diagram.

2. *Top-down design.* As the name implies, top-down design suggests that the design process proceeds from the top (most general) level to the bottom (most detailed) level. At any level, we specify what the program does, leaving the next lower level to describe how it works. The programmer's attention is then firmly fixed on the detail relevant to each particular level. As a concept this is fine, but interpretation can vary widely in practice, and detailed consideration of the logic required is avoided. Perhaps top-down design is really motivated

by the need to make programs testable; but even here structured programming provides the solution by making it much easier to get the high-level logic right at an early stage; this can then itself be used to provide a test driver, or harness, for the remaining parts of the program.

3. *Hierarchical input process output (or HIPO for short)*. 'Hierarchical' means 'modular' in the sense defined in Section 9.3. The name 'input process output' reflects the processing executed by those low-level modules which are more concerned with application detail than with control logic. It is supported by a pictorial documentation tool. HIPO is intended to be used as a module documentation technique, and is not suitable, in my view, for logic design, although individual installations may use it both ways. Correctly applied it can provide a useful visual impact.

For further discussion of these subjects, see [7].

9.6   Conclusion

The term 'structured programming' as used in this book is concerned with the design of program logic. It is sometimes used to refer to the functional approach and management procedures listed in the preceding sections, and indeed sometimes covers a mixture of each. Technically it is an important breakthrough, making programs:

> easy to read
> easy to test
> easy to amend.

New documentation tools are also provided, making projects easier to control. The result should be that programs can be produced reliably, on time, and to a price.

It is evident that structured programming is complementary to the functional techniques. We may postulate that the two should be used together:

1. The functional approach should be used to identify program functions, or events.
2. Structured programming principles should be used to design control logic.

Depending on the context, the functions identified might typically be organized into batch programs, on-line conversations, or real-time processes. The control logic will determine the order in which the functions are executed. The functions will then be manifest as:

> subroutines in a program, transaction, or process; or
> transactions in an on-line conversation.

This supports the view that modularity and control logic design are complementary, and not exclusive, activities. Both are required for successful program design. Features of each are:

1. Functional decomposition is easy to grasp and uses familiar concepts of modularity. The tool may be used by non-technical analysts and understood by programming staff.
2. Structured programming concentrates on the design of high-level logic; in practice this logic can be complex and requires specialized techniques. For this reason, perhaps, it is frequently neglected.

I hope that this book will help to correct the imbalance implied, and that the two approaches can now be integrated to form a more unified approach to successful design and implementation.

Appendix

A.1 Language Conventions

The main purpose of this book has been to provide tools to design and document program logic. The notation used was machine- and language-independent, and consisted of structure diagrams, supplemented by schematic logic; since the detailed conventions were fully described in the main text, they are not repeated here. Throughout, it was assumed that schematic logic conventions would, in practice, be replaced by the equivalent logic expressed in a 'real' programming language.

We thought of structure diagrams and schematic logic as a logic framework, inside which we were able to allocate processing functions executed. Of the processing functions identified, we paid special attention to the Read instruction (first introduced in Section 1.7) and its various interpretations; since this instruction formed such a crucial part of the designs produced, it was considered to form part of the structure diagram and schematic logic. Apart then from the tp monitor interface discussed in Section 5.6, all the remaining processing functions identified were expressed using a form of 'lower-case COBOL'; that is, using COBOL-style instructions, but without necessarily following all the strict syntactical conventions of a formal programming language. I trust that the reader will allow that this was done in the interest of making the main text readable. The purpose of this section is to summarize the language conventions used; we build on this in the following section to suggest one way to implement schematic logic in a language like COBOL.

We note that no great significance need be attached to the choice of COBOL as a model for a real programming language. My motivation is simply put. First, it is still (so far as I know) the most widely used programming language; second, its relative informality makes it easy to understand; third (and by no means least), it is familiar to me. To anyone who is more interested in scientific or real-time than commercial applications, or who considers the choice strange when considering non-commercial examples, I can only offer that I thought it best to select one language for use throughout.

When describing logic in the text we used the following instructions in a 'generic' sense:

GOTO
Call
Read
Write

Thus, 'GOTO' is used to describe a branch instruction of the kind provided by most programming languages; the corresponding instruction in COBOL is (as noted below) written 'Go to'. 'Call' is used similarly to describe a subroutine call. 'Read' and 'Write' are used to describe read and write processing functions respectively; the need to interpret these instructions freely, and to consider various implementations, forms one of the main topics of this book (see especially Chapter 6). In particular, we noted that one implementation of Read (as Suspend) would generate a substantial amount of logic in any commonly used programming language, while the detailed implementation of another (Receive) is considered to be outside the scope of this book.

Apart from this, we used our lower-case COBOL to describe processing functions allocated within the logic frameworks designed. These functions are expressed relatively informally, and there is no need to understand more than the intention (after all, the main interest is in designing the logic). Like COBOL, each instruction is written using an English-style format, and can be read and understood by anyone with a minimum knowledge of programming concepts.

The instructions used are:

Accumulate
Add
Change
Check
Clear
Close
Get
Increment
Initialize
Move
Open
Print
Process
Read
Scroll
Set
Swap
Validate
Write

Some of these use recognizable COBOL verbs, others are used with their normal

English meaning; in each case the intention should be clear from the context, and there should accordingly be no risk of confusion.

Each instruction used forms part of a single COBOL-type statement. Any data names referenced:

start with a letter
consist of a string of alphanumeric characters, possibly including space or hyphens
terminate with a space.

Again, strict COBOL conventions are 'stretched' in the interests of readability. It is always assumed that all data names have previously been suitably and correctly declared. If necessary, data names can refer to arrays, and are then suitably subscripted. Statements terminate with a space; examples are:

Accumulate Customer total
Add 1 to I
Open file
Move Entry-value (I, J) to Parameter-reply
Scroll forward
Set switch on

Any conditions, or tests, attached to schematic logic statements are expressed using a mnemonic, such as:

C1
End-of-file

or in full:

$I > N$
$I = 999$

Examples would be:

IF C1
LOOP until $I > N$

We have also, on occasions, found it necessary to define subroutines to execute application-dependent code. The subroutine then becomes another processing function allocated in the frameworks defined. Each such subroutine is given a meaningful name such as:

Batch Header
Start-of-customer

and might be displayed on the structure diagram, or within the schematic logic. An example would be:

DO Start-of-customer.

This was particularly useful in Chapters 2 and 8.

On occasions (especially Sections 6.6 to 6.8) the schematic code is supplemented by its COBOL-type equivalent, usually in order to make the logic more explicit. The rules followed to translate schematic logic into COBOL are covered in Section A.2; we describe below the conventions used in the COBOL generated.

The COBOL instructions used to express logic are:

Go to...
Go to... depending on...(often referred to as a 'computed GOTO' in
                      other languages)
If...

Although they are not used in the main text, we might mention here the COBOL Perform (as a subroutine call), Perform... until... as a high-level loop, and If... Else... as a two-way selection.

Any labels referenced:

start with a letter
consist of an alphanumeric string of characters
terminate with a period followed by a space.

An exception to this occurs when the 'shorthand' conventions described in Section 1.3 are used; this may lead to COBOL-type labels which include { and } symbols. (The alternative shorthand convention described in Section 1.3 would avoid the generation of such labels.) Examples of logic statements are:

Go to END.
Go to L1, L2, L3 depending on SV.
If End-of-intermediate-file Go to MADMIT1.

The use of the special data name 'SV', in connection with inversion, is described in Sections 6.6 and 8.6.

The term 'hand-coded' refers to any COBOL-type statements which either:

1. form a loop (as described in Section 1.2) without the use of Perform... until...

or

2. form a CASE-type statement (as described in Section 1.2) without the use of Else.

Finally, when writing COBOL, the formatting rules are tightened:

labels and instructions always start in fixed columns
statements terminate with a period followed by space.

An example of 'finished' code occurs in Section 6.8.

A.2   Implementation Notes

This section supplements schematic logic with the equivalent code using the lower-case COBOL conventions described in the previous section. For convenience we list below the schematic logic keywords, their meanings, and the main text reference.

Keyword	Meaning	Text Reference (Section)
DO	Subroutine call	1.2
SEQ	Sequence	1.2
IF ... ELSE ...	Selection	1.2
LOOP	Iteration	1.2
MONITOR ... QUIT ... ADMIT ...	Logic monitor	3.3, 3.4
ENDS	End of sequence, selection, iteration or monitor	1.2, 3.3
Call } Exit }	Read/Write	6.4, 6.5
Suspend } Restart }	Read/Write	6.4, 6.5, 8.3, 8.6
Receive } Send }	Read/Write	6.4, 6.5, 8.3, 8.6

Apart from 'DO' and 'QUIT', each keyword is given a label (ideally the same as a label used in the corresponding structure diagram). The labels used:

    start with a letter
    consist of an alphanumeric string of characters
    terminate with a space

The one exception to this is the use of { } to create labels when the diagrammatic shorthand described in Section 1.3 is used.

Some keywords (IF, ELSE, LOOP, MONITOR, QUIT, ADMIT) may have conditions, or tests, associated with them, as described in the text.

The following table suggests one implementation of nested logic in COBOL:

Schematic Logic	COBOL
X SEQ	XSEQ.
DO A	Perform A.
DO B	Perform B.
X ENDS	XEND.
X IF C	XIF.
DO A	If C
X ELSE	Perform A
DO B	Else

X	ENDS	Perform B.
		XEND.
X	LOOP until C	XLOOP.
	DO A	Perform A until C.
X	ENDS	XEND.

The COBOL labels may then be omitted. With these conventions, schematic logic and COBOL are both GOTO-less. We note that:

1. There is no instruction in COBOL equivalent to the 'ENDS' in a Selection; as a result it is advisable to avoid nested If statements in COBOL.
2. There is no general CASE-type statement in COBOL.

Apart from these points, problems can also arise when using inversion (as described in Chapter 6). All problems can be avoided by using the following implementation:

Schematic Logic	COBOL
X SEQ	XSEQ.
DO A	Perform A.
DO B	Perform B.
X ENDS	XEND.
X IF C	XIF.
DO A	If not C Go to XELSE.
X ELSE	Perform A.
DO B	Go to XEND.
X ENDS	XELSE.
	Perform B.
	XEND.
X LOOP until C	XLOOP.
DO A	If C Go to XEND.
X ENDS	Perform A.
	Go to XLOOP.
	XEND.

Recognizing that this implementation would not be attractive to those programmers who wish to avoid using 'Go to', some compromises may be made in practice (as described in Sections 6.9 and 7.3.2).

In my opinion, whichever implementation is used, any building block which is the subject of Perform should be closed (that is, not be subject to MONITOR), and, arguably should not contain a schematic Suspend instruction.

MONITOR can be implemented as follows:

Schematic Logic	COBOL
M MONITOR C	MMONITOR.
A SEQ, IF or LOOP	ASEQ., AIF., or ALOOP.
⋮	⋮
QUIT M IF C	IF C Go to MADMIT.
⋮	⋮
A ENDS	AEND.
	Go to MEND.
M ADMIT	MADMIT.
DO B	Perform B.
M ENDS	MEND.

The implementation of inversion (using Restart and Suspend) is discussed in Chapter 6, and is not reproduced here, while the implementation of Send and Receive is outside the scope of this book (as noted in Section 8.4).

A.3 The Structure Theorem

We have, from time to time (as in Sections 3.1 and 9.1), referred to the 'structure theorem'. Expressed informally, the theorem states that *any* flowchart, however complex (but provided it has one entry and one exit), can be converted to an equivalent flowchart which is nested (that is, can be implemented using the principles of nested logic as defined in Chapter 1). We give below a description of the methods used to prove the theorem, and of its effects.

We start with a flowchart, such as that given as Figure A.1 (not too complex to start with). Then we introduce a switch (we shall call it I) and associate discrete values of I with significant points on the flowchart. In particular, we associate:

1. The value $I = 1$ with the start (entry) point
2. The value $I = 0$ with the end (exit) point
3. A discrete value of I with every test evaluated
4. A discrete value of I at any point where two or more flow lines converge.

Suitable values of I are shown in Figure A.2. A new flowchart can now be built as follows:

1. Construct an outer loop which terminates when $I = 0$; the initial value of I is set to 1. The content of the loop is a CASE-type statement which evaluates all possible values of I (excluding $I = 0$).
2. Inspect the original flowchart to determine the actions required for each value of I distinguished. Terminate each action when the value of I changes and then reset I to its new value. Then continue round the loop.

275

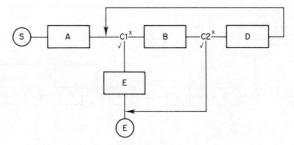

Figure A.1   A sample flowchart

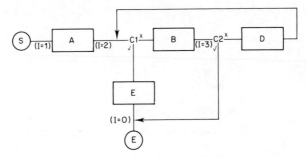

Figure A.2   Associated values of I

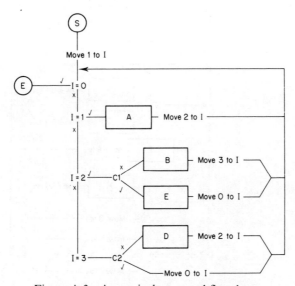

Figure A.3   An equivalent nested flowchart

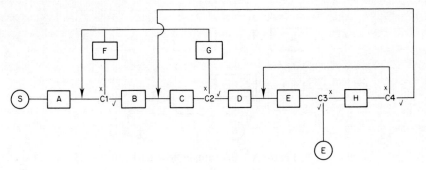

Figure A.4 A more complex case

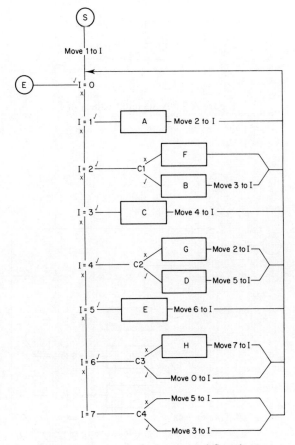

Figure A.5 An equivalent nested flowchart

For the example given, the new flowchart is in Figure A.3. This flowchart is equivalent to the original (in the sense that A, B, E, D, C1, C2 are executed in the same order), and is nested. A more rigorous presentation would prove that the algorithm described works for any flowchart.

It would be possible to make fewer amendments and still produce a nested equivalent; but the method given has the advantage of generality, and could be applied to any flowchart, however complex, such as that in Figure A.4. The reader is invited to check that this is equivalent to the nested flowchart of Figure A.5.

In general the price paid to convert a non-nested flowchart into its nested equivalent is the introduction of a switch; this switch (in my view) makes the logic 'prettier' but can obscure its meaning. We should, however, note that if languages were extended to include the Suspend and Receive instructions defined in Section 6.6, then all our designs would use only nested logic plus MONITOR. (This assertion excludes the problems of recursion described in Section A.4.) From our point of view then, the structure theorem is equivalent to asserting that the use of MONITOR may be avoided by introducing a switch. We prefer the directness of MONITOR. More precisely, we prefer the logic to be based on the structure; the structure theorem should not, in my view, be used to justify the use of nested logic if that means obscuring the structure. The conversion technique described above is, therefore, in my view, mainly of academic interest, and is not recommended as a general practice. Several of the papers reproduced in [1] provide further material.

A.4   Recursion

For completeness, we include here some brief notes on recursion. This topic is not covered in the main text, since relatively few applications need the technique; where it is needed, manufacturers' software is often available to help, and it is also supported by some high-level languages. The following notes are just sufficient to understand the topic in structural terms, and point the way to an implementation in non-recursive languages, but are in no way intended to be complete.

We have hitherto assumed that no component of a building block would have the same structure as the building block of which it was a component. If this assumption is found to be untrue then the structure is said to be recursive. Recursive structures are by no means abundant; two examples are:

1. *The COPY verb.* Languages like COBOL often provide a COPY statement (or its equivalent). The statement is used in source programs and acts as an instruction to the compiler to replace the COPY statement by source statements held on a library file; the file required is referenced by the COPY statement. The structure of the source program is given in Figure A.6. If the statements copied should themselves contain further COPY statements, then this, in turn, results in further statements being copied from another source library, and Figure A.6 may be amended accordingly as Figure A.7. But the

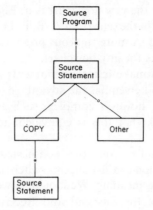

Figure A.6   A source program

new source copied may itself contain COPY statements, and so on. Each COPY statement within the original source program, or within any source code copied, then has a structure identical to that of the original source program. (This, incidentally, is why many implementations of COPY do not allow the statements copied to contain further COPY statements.) Instead of expanding the structure diagram indefinitely, the structure of the original file may be conveniently expressed recursively as in Figure A.8.

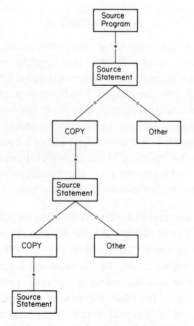

Figure A.7   Expansion of the COPY statement

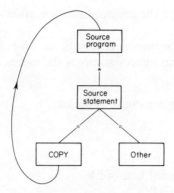

Figure A.8   A recursive structure

2. *Trees*. A (binary) tree is a table in which the entries are linked together in a special way; each entry is called a 'node', and the links are called the 'branches'. One specified node (the 'root') identifies the start of the tree; it contains pointers to two other nodes, and each of these nodes contains pointers to two further nodes, each of which contains pointers to two further nodes, and so on. The following is an illustrative table in which the entries are identified by a key value, and pointers are used to trace paths through the table to locate the entry with the next lower or higher key value (where 'lower' and 'higher' refer to key values in alphabetic order):

Entry-key	High pointer	Low pointer
1 John	2	4
2 Peter	7	3
3 Kenneth	6	0
4 Eric	8	5
5 David	0	0
6 Malcolm	0	0
7 Robert	9	0
8 George	0	0
9 Victor	0	10
10 Tommy	0	0

The organization of the entries in the table is illustrated as a tree in Figure A.9. By definition, each node consists of a low pointer, an entry-key, and a high pointer; each pointer points to a node which is the root of another tree, except that pointers with the value zero mark the end of the tree. Furthermore, all entries located on the tree identified by the low pointer have a key less than the entry associated with the node, while all members of the tree identified by the high pointer have a higher key. The structure diagram, given as Figure A.10, shows the recursivity.

The following would be suitable schematic logic for each of the examples given (the labels are convenient abbreviations of the names attached to boxes in the structure diagram):

1. To construct a complete source program:

```
SP  SEQ
    Open file
    Read
    {SS}  LOOP until End-of-file
          SS  IF COPY
              DO SP (new file)      (Note: recursive call)
          SS  ELSE
              DO Other
          SS  ENDS
          Read
    {SS}  ENDS
    Close file
SP  ENDS
```

Since SP contains a call to itself, it is a subroutine, and its parameter would be the name of the file currently being read.

2. To print out all the entries in ascending key sequence (without sorting the table):

```
NODE  SEQ
      LO  IF Low pointer ≠ 0
          DO NODE (Lo)        (Note: recursive call)
      LO  ELSE
      LO  ENDS
          Print Entry
      HI  If High pointer ≠ 0
          DO NODE (Hi)        (Note: recursive call)
      HI  ELSE
      HI  ENDS
NODE  ENDS
```

Again the schematic logic contains a call to itself; NODE is, therefore, a subroutine, and its parameter is the current pointer value.

The schematic logic shows clearly how recursive structures imply the existence of a subroutine which contains a call to itself, and that this call is made before its own execution has been completed. Not only will this disrupt the normal subroutine linkage mechanism, but the parameter values of one call must be preserved while a recursive call is executed. And since recursive calls (like normal subroutine calls) may be nested to any level (subject only to the normal constraints of

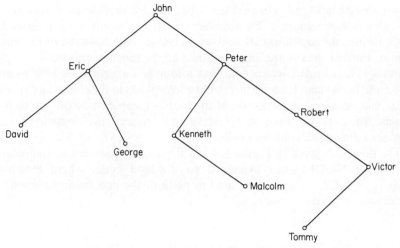

Figure A.9   Representation of a table as a tree

memory size and execution time), so the recursive subroutine linkages and stored parameter values must be nested to any level.

If the language used does not allow recursive calls, then both the subroutine call and exit can be implemented using direct GOTO's. The stored parameter values can be organized through the use of a stack; a stack is an array, each entry of which can hold stored parameter values, together with a stack pointer. Each time a recursive call is made, the old parameters are saved in the stack and the stack pointer updated to point to the next vacant entry. Each time a recursive call is completed, the stack pointer is decremented and the old parameter values restored. It is advisable to include checks to make sure that the stack does not overflow when a recursive call is made; the program terminates when there are no further recursive calls to unwind.

In many programs a recursive call can be made from more than one point. In

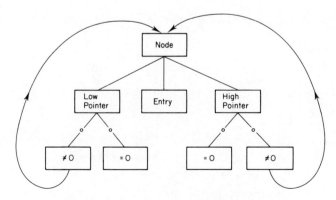

Figure A.10   A recursive tree structure

these cases the linkage mechanism has to be extended to relate each stack entry to the call which generated it. The simplest way to implement this is to extend the stack to include an additional field whose value indicates the call to which it relates. Further details are, however, outside the scope of this book.

Finally, it is instructive to note that a loop is a special case of a recursive structure; in this case the loop increment corresponds to the changing parameter value, but because each iteration of the loop is completed before the next one begins, there is no need to preserve and restore the parameter values corresponding to the different calls.

The flowchart given in Figure A.4 is a flowchart equivalent to the recursive subroutine NODE when expanded to low-level code, where mnemonics A, B, ..., C1, C2, ... have been used in place of the processing functions and conditions implied.

Bibliography

The following is a brief and personal selection; some are cross-referenced in Chapter 9, and others included for general interest.

1. E. Yourdon, *Classics in Software Engineering.* Yourdon Press, 1979. ISBN 0 917 07214 6.
2. M. A. Jackson, *Principles of Program Design.* Academic Press, 1975. ISBN 0 123 79050 6.
3. T. De Marco, *Structured Analysis and System Specification.* Yourdon Press, 1978. ISBN 0 917 07207 3.
4. C. Gane and T. Sarson, *Structured Systems Analysis.* Prentice-Hall, 1979. ISBN 0 138 54547 2.
5. G. J. Myers, *Composite/Structured Design.* Van Nostrand Reinhold Company, 1978. ISBN 0 442 80584 5.
6. M. A. Jackson, *System Development.* Prentice-Hall, 1983. ISBN 0 138 80328 5.
7. E. Yourdon, *Techniques of Program Structure and Design.* Prentice-Hall, 1975. ISBN 0 139 01702 X.
8. O.-J. Dahl, E. W. Dijkstra, and C. A. R. Hoare, *Structured Programming.* Academic Press, 1972. ISBN 0 122 00550 3.
9. N. Wirth, *Systematic Programming: An Introduction.* Prentice-Hall, 1973. ISBN 0 138 80369 2.
10. N. Wirth, *Algorithms + Data Structures = Programs.* Prentice-Hall, 1976. ISBN 0 130 22418 9.
11. A. M. Lister, *Fundamentals of Operating Systems.* Macmillan, 1975. ISBN 0 333 27287 0.
12. C. C. Foster, *Real-time Programming—Neglected Topics.* Addison-Wesley, 1981. ISBN 0 201 01937 X.

Index to Structure Diagram Symbols

Symbol	Meaning	Main Text Reference (Section number)
Space	Sequence	1.1
∘	Selection	1.1
*	Iteration	1.1
[ ]	Monitor/Admit	3.5
↑	Escape	3.5
○	Read/Write	1.8, 5.4, 6.5, 8.6
○	Connector	1.1, 3.5
□	Structure Component	1.1, 6.5

General Index